BILLY GRAHAM
Evangelistic Association

Always Good News.

W9-CDH-925

Dear Friend,

I am pleased to send you this copy of *Choosing the Extraordinary Life* by Dr. Robert Jeffress, senior pastor of First Baptist Church in Dallas, Texas, and an adjunct professor at Dallas Theological Seminary.

Elijah is one of the most remarkable figures in the Bible—from his condemnation of Israel's idol worship to his extraordinary chariot ride into Heaven—and his example has a lot to teach us. In *Choosing the Extraordinary Life*, Dr. Jeffress explores seven powerful lessons from Elijah's life. Dig deeper into Scripture as you discover Biblical principles for handling difficult days, waiting on God's timing, and discovering the Lord's unique calling on your life. It's my prayer that this book will help you *"press on toward the goal for the prize of the upward call of God in Christ Jesus"* (Philippians 3:14, ESV).

For more than 70 years, the Billy Graham Evangelistic Association has worked to take the Good News of Jesus Christ throughout the world by every effective means available, and I'm excited about what God will do in the years ahead. We would appreciate knowing how our ministry has touched your life.

May God richly bless you.

Sincerely,

Franklin Graham
President

If you would like to know more about our ministry, please contact us:

IN THE U.S.:
Billy Graham Evangelistic Association
1 Billy Graham Parkway
Charlotte, NC 28201-0001
BillyGraham.org
info@bgea.org
Toll-free: 1-877-247-2426

IN CANADA:
Billy Graham Evangelistic
  Association of Canada
20 Hopewell Way NE
Calgary, AB T3J 5H5
BillyGraham.ca
Toll-free: 1-888-393-0003

Choosing the
Extraordinary
Life

God's 7 Secrets for
Success and Significance

DR. ROBERT
JEFFRESS

BakerBooks
a division of Baker Publishing Group
Grand Rapids, Michigan

This *Billy Graham Library Selection* special edition is published with
permission from Baker Publishing Group.

©2018 by Dr. Robert Jeffress

Published by Baker Books
a division of Baker Publishing Group
PO Box 6287, Grand Rapids, MI 49516-6287
www.bakerbooks.com

Paperback edition published 2019
ISBN 978-0-8010-9465-1
ISBN 978-1-593-28684-2 (BGEA edition)

Printed in the United States of America

The Library of Congress has cataloged the original edition as follows:
Names: Jeffress, Robert, 1955– author.
Title: Choosing the extraordinary life: God's 7 secrets for success and significance /
   Dr. Robert Jeffress.
Description: Grand Rapids : Baker Publishing Group, 2018. | Includes
   bibliographical references.
Identifiers: LCCN 2018001802 | ISBN 9780801075384 (cloth)
Subjects: LCSH: Christian life. | Success—Religious aspects—Christianity. | Self-
   esteem—Religious aspects—Christianity.
Classification: LCC BV4501.3 .J4349 2018 | DDC 284.4—dc23
LC record available at https://lccn.loc.gov/2018001802

978-0-8010-9417-0 (ITPE)

Unless otherwise indicated, Scripture quotations are from the New American Standard Bible®, copyright © 1960, 1962, 1963, 1968, 1971, 1972, 1973, 1975, 1977, 1995 by The Lockman Foundation. Used by permission. (www.Lockman.org)

Scripture quotations labeled KJV are from the King James Version of the Bible.

Scripture quotations labeled Message are from THE MESSAGE. Copyright © by Eugene H. Peterson 1993, 1994, 1995, 1996, 2000, 2001, 2002. Used by permission of NavPress. All rights reserved. Represented by Tyndale House Publishers, Inc.

Scripture quotations labeled NIV are from the Holy Bible, New International Version®. NIV®. Copyright © 1973, 1978, 1978, 1984, 2011 by Biblica, Inc.™ Used by permission of Zondervan. All rights reserved worldwide. www.zondervan.com

Scripture quotations labeled NLT are from the *Holy Bible*, New Living Translation, copyright © 1996, 2004, 2015 by Tyndale House Foundation. Used by permission of Tyndale House Publishers, Inc., Carol Stream, Illinois 60188. All rights reserved.

Scripture quotations labeled Phillips are from The New Testament in Modern English, revised edition—J. B. Phillips, translator. ©J. B. Phillips 1958, 1960, 1972. Used by permission of Macmillan Publishing Co., Inc.

All italics in direct Scripture quotations are the author's emphasis.

Published in association with Yates & Yates, www.yates2.com.

19 20 21 22 23 24 25   7 6 5 4 3 2 1

green
press
INITIATIVE

To Blair, Barrett, and Blake Sadler—
my triplet grandchildren
born during the writing of this book.
Amy and I pray that each of you would experience
a truly extraordinary life as you serve
the Lord Jesus Christ with all of your heart.

Contents

Acknowledgments

As my schedule becomes more hectic with every passing year, I'm grateful for the wonderful team that surrounds me and assists me in the production of a book like the one you are holding in your hand. Especially do I want to thank . . .

Brian Vos, Mark Rice, Brianna DeWitt, Lindsey Spoolstra, and the entire Baker Books team for being the best publishing partner I've had in the three decades of my writing ministry.

Derrick G. Jeter, our creative director at Pathway to Victory, who immediately caught the vision for this book and was instrumental in helping me craft this book's message about the extraordinary life of Elijah.

Sealy Yates, my literary agent and friend for more than two decades, who always provides encouragement and wise counsel.

Carrilyn Baker, my executive associate for nearly twenty years, for her "above and beyond" efforts in managing the unbelievably complicated work of our office—and always doing so with a smile! And thank you, Mary Shafer, for assisting Carrilyn and me in so many ways—you are a joy to work with!

Ben Lovvorn, the executive pastor of First Baptist Church, Dallas, and Nate Curtis, Patrick Heatherington, Vickie Sterling, Ben Bugg, and the entire Pathway to Victory team, who extend the message of this book to millions of people throughout the world.

And most of all, my wonderful wife, Amy, who has been by my side since we were twelve years old in Mrs. Denny's seventh-grade math class. You have made my life truly "extraordinary!"

An Ordinary Person in Extraordinary Times

My friend Dr. James Dobson has described the ordinary life most men live:

> The straight life for a working man is . . . pulling our tired frame out of bed, five days a week, fifty weeks out of the year. It is earning a two-week vacation in August, and choosing a trip that will please the kids. The straight life is spending your money wisely when you'd rather indulge in a new whatever; it is taking your son bike riding on Saturday when you want so badly to watch the baseball game; it is cleaning out the garage on your day off after working sixty hours the prior week. The straight life is coping with head colds and engine tune-ups and crab grass and income tax forms.[1]

This description, with a few variations, is just as apt for women as well. What Dr. Dobson calls the "straight life" I call the "ordinary life"—the kind of life most people experience from "the womb until the tomb." But I have a sense that the reason you picked up this book is because you want something more than an ordinary life. In fact, I bet you picked up this book because you desire a life that is marked by true significance. Haven't you ever wished that your brief time on earth could have a greater purpose than the daily grind? If you are like most people, your answer to that question is a resounding yes! Guess what? God wants more for you than the humdrum as well.

No matter who you are or what your circumstances might be, God desires to transform your ordinary existence into an extraordinary life.

Now, I know some of you may be thinking, *I am nobody from nowhere. What can I do? No one has ever heard of me and never will.*

I understand your skepticism. It is natural to wonder, *What can I do? I'm just one person.* But never underestimate the difference one person can make in the world. Neither fame nor fortune is a prerequisite for having a significant life. God is in the business of using the ordinary to do the extraordinary.

If you find that hard to believe, consider the life of Edward Kimball.

Ed was a Boston carpet salesman and a Sunday school teacher at Mount Vernon Congregational Church. He taught teenage boys the Bible. One eighteen-year-old boy in his class did not seem interested in spiritual matters, often falling asleep in church and having complete ignorance of the Bible. Ed was concerned about the boy's spiritual destination, so he screwed up his courage one April morning and determined to share the good news of Jesus's death and resurrection with this young man, who worked as a clerk in Holton's Shoe Store in downtown Boston.

Ed was no seasoned evangelist—in fact, he was so nervous that he initially walked right past the store, reconsidering his plan. Maybe talking about Jesus while the young man was at work was not the appropriate time or place. Maybe he should wait. But something inside of Ed said now was the time.

He offered a quick prayer under his breath, turned on his heels, and went through the door. He found the clerk in the back of the store. Placing his foot on a shoebox and a hand on the boy's shoulder, Ed said, "I came to tell you about how much Jesus loves you." They talked for a few minutes, and then the clerk knelt and professed his faith in Christ. Later, the clerk wrote about that moment, "I was in a new world. The birds sang sweeter, the sun shone brighter. I'd never known such peace."[2]

Ed left the shoe store rejoicing that God had used him—a simple carpet salesman—to share the good news of Jesus with this eighteen-year-old shoe clerk. But Ed could not have imagined how his one act of faithfulness would impact millions of lives during the next two centuries.

The young man Ed spoke with that day was Dwight L. Moody, who went on to become one of the greatest evangelists in the nineteenth century. Moody later counseled another young man by the name of J. Wilbur Chapman on the assurance of his salvation. Chapman became a Presbyterian minister and evangelist who greatly influenced an ex-baseball player by the name of Billy Sunday. With his brash and flashy style, Sunday led thousands upon thousands to Christ during his evangelistic crusades.

In 1924, in Charlotte, North Carolina, Billy Sunday held a rally during which many men and women were saved. Out of that campaign came the formation of the Charlotte Businessman's Club (CBMC), which continued to evangelize that region of the state. In 1934, the CBMC organized a series of meetings in Charlotte and invited Mordecai Ham to preach. It was at one of those meetings that another fifteen-year-old young man committed his life to Christ. His name was Billy Graham—a man who preached the gospel to more people around the world than any other evangelist.

In 1953, two years before I was born, in Dallas, Texas, Billy Graham held an evangelistic crusade during which my mother gave her life to Christ. In a very real sense, I am a follower of Christ and serving in ministry today because of an ordinary nineteenth-century carpet salesman in Boston who allowed himself to be used by God in an extraordinary way.

Through his simple choice to follow God's leading into a shoe store, Edward Kimball made an incalculable difference in the lives of millions of people he would never meet. Nothing we know about Kimball suggests his immeasurable impact on the world can be attributed to abundant wealth, unusual giftedness, or phenomenal charisma. Instead, Ed Kimball was an ordinary person who simply made himself available to God . . . much like another man named Elijah who lived nearly three thousand years ago, in a world like our own.

As we will discover, Elijah was a man from humble beginnings who lived in Israel during some of the kingdom's darkest days. He could have settled for an ordinary life, claiming his culture was too depraved and he was just one person. Yet, despite his circumstances, Elijah chose to fulfill God's unique purpose for his life—and, as a result, he made an indelible impact on his world.

A Tale of Two Crumbling Cultures

Let's be honest: the prospect of making an impact on our increasingly anti-Christian culture appears bleak. We look over the horizon of the American landscape and see nothing but desolation and despair. Sometimes we get discouraged, thinking, *Things have* never *been this bad before!* When we read in the Bible about men and women of faith like Abraham, Moses, Sarah, and Elijah, we think, *Being godly was much easier back then without the temptations of the internet, the distractions of technology, and the challenges of parenting in a pagan world.*

It's true that we are eyewitnesses to a culture in decline. Today, we are increasingly pressured to bow to the god of immorality. Secularism is slowly and relentlessly crushing theism as the predominant ideology. And laws, no longer based on godly principles of truth and morality, are being enacted and enforced without regard for individual beliefs.

Yet the very same could have been said of the Israel in which Elijah lived in the ninth century BC. As dark and menacing as our culture is becoming, in reality there is not that much difference between our world and Elijah's. When we travel back in time to the days of Elijah, we discover that the age in which he lived was just as dangerous and decadent as our own. Although Elijah lived in a nation that was sliding further into ungodliness each passing day, he resolved to change the world rather than allow the world to change him. In the pages that follow, we are going to discover how this ordinary person made the choice to have an extraordinary life.

The Dark World of Ancient Israel

Elijah's story, recorded in the book of 1 Kings, opens and closes with death—the deaths of David and Ahab. In between these two funerals is about 150 years of history that tells the story of a nation that rejected God and fell headlong into national ruin.

It all began with Solomon, David's son and heir. "King Solomon loved many foreign women" (1 Kings 11:1). Because of Solomon's voracious sexual appetite—he had seven hundred wives and three hundred concubines—he violated God's command against marrying foreign women (Deut. 7:1–3). The Lord knew that the king's disobedience would cause the people to "turn [their] heart away after [foreign] gods" (1 Kings 11:2). Nevertheless, Solomon ignored God's commands and "held fast to [his wives and concubines] in love" (v. 2). He set up pagan places of worship for his many wives (vv. 4–8), which began a series of destructive events that culminated in civil war and the division of the nation.

The northern kingdom, which retained the name Israel, slid into ruin as it fell deeper and deeper into idolatry. Jeroboam, the northern kingdom's first ruler, instituted bull worship, much like the worship of the golden calf in the wilderness (12:25–33). Building on Jeroboam's wickedness, each successive king persisted in pursuing idols and sexual perversion.

But nothing could have prepared the Israelites for the reign of King Ahab (c. 874–852 BC). Ahab's father, Omri, was a skillful king, moving Israel's capital from Tirzah to Samaria (1 Kings 16:21–28). However, the writer of 1 Kings focuses not on Omri's political achievements but on his idolatry. "Omri did evil in the sight of the Lord, and acted more wickedly than all who were before him" (v. 25), so he was cut off and "Ahab his son became king [of Israel] in his place" (v. 28).

If you were one of Ahab's political insiders or a citizen more concerned about your pocketbook than about your prayer book, then the days under Ahab did not look so bad. In fact, Ahab's reign of twenty-two years appeared stable compared to the previous sixty years that had been filled with bloodshed and assassinations.

Unlike his father's administration, Ahab's reign was marked by peace and prosperity. Ahab and the nation benefited from a trade deal his father had negotiated with Phoenicia, and shipping boomed—along with the royal treasuries of Phoenicia and Israel. Under Ahab it could be truthfully said, "There was a chicken in every pot and a chariot in every garage."

However, God is not impressed by a nation's GDP (gross domestic product) but by its GBP (godly behavior product)— and by that standard Ahab and Israel were running a serious deficit! Ahab was uniquely evil, doing "more to provoke the LORD God of Israel than all the kings of Israel who were before him" (v. 33). Translation: Ahab ticked God off more than any other monarch in Israel's history. What made Ahab Israel's MDP (most despicable player) in God's eyes? He married a woman named Jezebel:

> It came about, as though it had been a trivial thing for him to walk in the sins of Jeroboam the son of Nebat, that he married Jezebel the daughter of Ethbaal king of the Sidonians. (1 Kings 16:31)

The marriage of Ahab and Jezebel was a political pact between Omri and Ethbaal that accounted for Israel's financial prosperity. But in spiritual terms, the marriage catapulted Israel into its darkest days. Like Solomon before him, Ahab's marriage to an idol-worshiping wife turned his heart away from the Lord.

Jezebel made a sport of hunting down and killing God's prophets (18:4). And at the top of her hit list—for reasons we will soon discover—was an ordinary man named Elijah.

Why is Jezebel the only queen named in the list of Israel's kings? She was the real power behind Ahab's throne. Ahab made no moves without first consulting Jezebel. We would say that she wore the pants in the family.

The fact that Ahab—a man with the backbone of a chocolate éclair when it came to Jezebel—allowed his wife to entice him into Baal worship is the reason that the writer of 1 Kings recorded that it was "a trivial thing" for Ahab "to walk in the sins of Jeroboam" (16:31). In other words, the sins of Jeroboam were child's play compared to the heinous sin of Baal worship introduced by Ahab and his wife Jezebel.

Baal was the sun, rain, and fertility god of the Canaanites—their chief god. His name means "lord" or "owner." Jezebel was the one who introduced Baal worship in Israel. Jezebel's father was the king of the Sidonians—a people at the center of Baal worship. And when she married Ahab, Baal worship was part of her dowry.

What made Baal worship so odious was the belief that Baal was greater than God, the Creator of heaven and earth. According to Baal worshipers, Baal controlled the environment and brought about climate change. Baal worship was accompanied with horrific sexual perversion, self-mutilation, and child sacrifice.

Idols of Baal were often made of hollowed-out sheet metal. Fires were placed either underneath the idol or within its belly, and children were placed either inside the belly of the idol, where they slowly roasted to death, or in the outstretched arms of the idol, where they slowly burned to death. Baal worshipers sacrificed their children to the god who promised to bring the warmth and rain needed for prosperity in an agricultural society.

This was the god Ahab and Jezebel worshiped and enticed the Israelites to serve as well. In fact, Ahab was so sold out to this pagan deity that he built a temple to Baal in the capital city of Samaria and erected a wooden likeness of Baal's female consort, Asherah (1 Kings 16:32–33). Ahab and Jezebel were such devout followers of Baal and Asherah that they regularly entertained up to 450 priests of Baal and 400 prophets of Asherah in their ivory palace (18:19; 22:39).

This was the world of ancient Israel—a depraved and dangerous place to live, especially if you worshiped the one true God. However, the darker the night, the brighter the light! It was against this dark background of immorality and idolatry that God would place His diamond of hope—an ordinary man named Elijah.

Extraordinary Attributes of an Ordinary Person

Elijah burst onto the scene when it appeared that God was in retreat. From a human perspective, God had been dethroned, and Baal—along with his puppet king, Ahab—now reigned over Israel. Evil ran rampant throughout the nation, unchecked and unchallenged.

But Elijah refused to sink into despair. He knew God would never be defeated. Though it seemed that things could hardly have been worse in Israel, God was not caught off guard or surprised by Ahab's wickedness. At just the right time—at Israel's zero hour—God raised up the right person.

Elijah was not afraid to stand toe-to-toe with the king of Israel. Don't misunderstand: Elijah was no spiritual superman. The New Testament writer James describes Elijah as "a man with a nature like ours" (James 5:17). That means Elijah was an ordinary person who struggled with the same issues that you and I battle. He experienced fatigue, got depressed, wrestled with temptation, and at times doubted the goodness and even the existence of God. Yet Elijah made an extraordinary impact on his world, becoming one of Israel's most famous heroes, because of three attributes that characterized his life.

Elijah Was a Man of Passion

When Elijah appeared in the pages of Scripture and introduced himself to Ahab in 1 Kings 17:1, he told the king that he served the *living* God. This was not only a dig at the dead god Ahab served but also an expression of Elijah's passion for the one true God. In fact, God was more alive to Elijah than were Ahab and Jezebel.

Furthermore, this power couple who thought they controlled Israel were as temporal as blades of grass that die within a year. But Elijah served the King who was eternal. He lived with an overwhelming sense of God's presence that fueled his passion for God. Twice Elijah said, "I have been very zealous for the Lord, the God of hosts" (1 Kings 19:10, 14).

Elijah was a man consumed with God. He was passionate about upholding God's reputation in an unbelieving world. Elijah's passion burned especially hot against Ahab, Jezebel, and the prophets of Baal who were deceiving Israel by denying the true God and elevating a false god.

Christian writer A. W. Tozer knew something of this passion and how it separates some Christians from run-of-the-mill believers—to say nothing of the rest of the world. Tozer wrote:

> The moment we make up our minds that we are going on with this determination to exalt God over all, we step out of the world's parade. We shall find ourselves out of adjustment to the ways of the world, and increasingly so as we make progress in the holy way.[3]

Elijah was such a man "out of step with the ways of the world" but in perfect step with the ways of God. And if we are to make a difference for God in our world, as Elijah did in his, then we need to continually fuel our burning passion for following Him.

Elijah Was a Man of Purpose

Elijah understood that it was God who set the direction of his life. It was God who called Elijah to be a prophet. It was God who placed His message in Elijah's mouth. And it was God who would ultimately hold Elijah accountable for his faithfulness to that purpose.

Because Elijah had a purpose that came from the Lord, he knew he had nothing to fear from Ahab. Elijah was a living illustration of Proverbs 28:1: "The wicked flee when no one is pursuing, but the righteous are bold as a lion."

In Elijah, Jesus's words in Matthew 10:28 were on full display: "Do not fear those who kill the body but are unable to kill the soul; but rather fear Him who is able to destroy both soul and body in hell."

Courage comes from the certainty of a calling. As someone has said, "Every man is immortal until his work on earth is done." Elijah—like all of us—had God-given work to do. And he knew that no one—Ahab, Jezebel, or even hundreds of false prophets of Baal—could touch one hair of his head until that work was finished.

Elijah Was a Man of Prayer

The foundational secret of Elijah's success was his belief in the power of prayer. We learn of this from James: "Elijah . . . prayed earnestly that it would not rain, and it did not rain on the earth for three years and six months. Then he prayed again, and the sky poured rain and the earth produced its fruit" (James 5:17–18).

The key phrase is "prayed earnestly," which can be literally translated "prayed with prayer." Don't misunderstand what James is saying. God does not answer our prayers because we squeeze our folded hands so tightly they turn white or because we spend so much time on our knees that they are bruised. To pray earnestly means praying habitually and continually, like breathing.

Do you have to remind yourself or have a doctor admonish you to take a breath? Hopefully not! For Elijah, prayer was not a painful discipline that had to be developed or a last resort after everything else failed. Instead, talking with God was as natural as breathing. And, like breathing, he prayed continually rather than sporadically.

The apostle Paul communicated the same idea when he commanded the Thessalonians to "pray without ceasing" (1 Thess. 5:17). The Greek word translated "without ceasing" was used to describe a persistent or hacking cough— one that seems to grab you by the throat and refuses to let go. Elijah prayed and prayed and prayed, speaking with the Lord throughout the day—like an uncontrollable cough. And that simple, continual practice of conversing with God was instrumental in the extraordinary accomplishments of this ordinary man.

The Secrets of True Significance

God can transform your life from ordinary to extraordinary, just as He did with Elijah. As far as God is concerned, there can never be enough Elijah-like men and women walking the earth, standing for His truth, and upholding His glory. How does such a transformation take place?

In the chapters that follow, we will explore the seven secrets of significance, which are resolves you and I must make in order to experience the incredible life God desires for us.

Secret #1: Discover Your Unique Purpose

Every follower of Christ has a general purpose in life—to bring God glory and to enjoy Him forever. But each of us also has a unique purpose that answers the question, "Why has God placed me in this world?"

Elijah's life offers clues to how we can answer that question in our own lives. Elijah's unique purpose was serving faithfully as a prophet of God, confronting a wicked king and queen, and calling his nation back to the worship of the true God. Your call is probably different, but, like Elijah, you have a specific purpose in life. In the next chapter, we will discover two questions that will help you determine God's unique purpose for your life.

Secret #2: Determine to Influence Your Culture

The first reaction of many Christians to an increasingly anti-Christian culture is to retreat, like a turtle pulling its head and legs into its shell. And though holy huddles— hanging out only with other Christians—offer safety and security, they communicate to the outside world an attitude of "us four and no more." To put it bluntly: holy huddles tell the world it can go to hell.

In contrast to the silo spirituality that so many Christians practice today, Elijah stepped out and determined to make a difference in his world. And what a difference he made! Elijah's example reminds us that God has left us on earth to influence the world, not to isolate ourselves from it.

Secret #3: Wait On God's Timing

No matter how old we are or how much life experience we have, no one likes to wait. We think of waiting time as wasted time. It's not—especially when we are waiting on God. God's most significant people learned how to wait, even if they had to wait a *long* time. Elijah had an extended period of waiting and training before his climactic showdown with the prophets of Baal.

You might be a student studying for a career that seems out of reach, a pastor ministering in obscurity, or a single adult wondering whether a mate will ever cross your path. But whoever you are and whatever you are waiting on, God hasn't forgotten you. Our heavenly Father is not interested in microwave Christianity or microwave Christians. It takes time to develop Elijah-like men and women.

Secret #4: Burn the Ships

If you decide to pursue an extraordinary life, then there will come a time when you must be prepared to go all in. As the saying goes, you must be willing to "burn the ships," eliminating all possibility of retreat. Hedging your bets and holding back is not an option when God is ready to move forward.

Elijah went "all in" when he challenged the priests of Baal to a winner-takes-all match on Mount Carmel. The stakes could not have been higher. Israel's future, not to mention Elijah's own life, hung in the balance. This was Elijah's burn-the-ships moment. In this chapter, you will discover how you can be ready for yours.

Secret #5: Unleash the Power of Prayer

Someone has observed that you can do much more after you have prayed, but you can do nothing of significance until you have prayed. Survey the Scriptures, and you will discover that those men and women who stood tallest for the Lord were those who knelt lowest before the Lord. And Elijah was no exception.

The New Testament writer James uses Elijah as Exhibit A of how to pray persistently, precisely, and powerfully. Using Elijah's prayer life as our model, we will learn how to experience God's power in our lives through prayer.

Secret #6: Learn How to Handle Bad Days

Elijah was not a super-saint but a normal person who even as a sold-out servant of God had to battle despair, depression, and doubt. One moment we find this man courageously standing for God on Mount Carmel, and soon after we find him curled up in a fetal position, wanting to die.

You and I are going to have experiences like that—periods of time when we doubt the goodness, the wisdom, or even the existence of God. Everyone who pursues an extraordinary life is going to have to deal with his or her share of bad days that include everything from flat tires and sore throats to genuine crises of faith. Elijah's life offers some practical and profitable ways to navigate these discouraging periods in our lives.

Secret #7: Live with the End in View

Perspective is one of the most difficult things to gain and maintain. With the hectic pace of life in the twenty-first century, it is tempting to get so caught up in today that we never think about tomorrow.

Not Elijah. He knew his time on earth was very limited. Elijah knew that when his work on earth was finished, God's work on earth would continue. So Elijah made provisions for his departure by training a successor. People who choose extraordinary lives live each day as if it were their last and make adequate preparations to ensure their godly legacy will outlast them. In this final chapter, we will discover how to do that by following Elijah's example.

A Majority of One

Someone once said, "One person with courage makes a majority." That was true in Elijah's day, and it is true in ours as well. On September 11, 2001, Welles Crowther, an ordinary young man, became a majority of one. He was simply known as the man with the red bandanna, and writer Peggy Noonan told his story on the fifteenth anniversary of the 9/11 terrorist attacks on New York City.[4]

Welles received the bandanna from his father when he was a child. Dressed in his first suit, Welles stood as tall as he could while his father placed a white handkerchief in his breast pocket and the red bandanna in his back pocket. As Noonan tells it, "One's for show, [his father] said, the other's for blow."

Welles worked as a junior associate for Sandler O'Neill, in the south tower of the World Trade Center, on the 104th floor. Whenever Welles took the red bandanna from his pocket, his coworkers would tease him about being a farmer. His usual reply was, "With this bandanna I'm gonna change the world."

The plane that struck the south tower ripped through floors 78 to 84. With his red bandanna tied around his face, Welles made his way down to the 78th floor, where he saw a group of people, some badly injured, waiting for the elevator. He picked up a woman and told the group to follow him to the stairwell. Eighteen floors below, the air began to clear.

He placed the woman on the floor and told the group to continue down. He then turned and went back up.

When Welles got back to the 78th floor, another group of people was there waiting. Through the fire and smoke, they heard a voice: "Everyone who can stand now, stand now. If you can help others, do so." And he guided another group to the stairwell.

No one knows how many trips Welles made to the higher floors or exactly how many people he saved. Recovery personnel discovered his body six months later, in the lobby of the south tower. He was found lying beside many firefighters, at their command post, and was only identified because of his red bandanna. Welles Crowther had made it down and could have run for his life. Instead, he gave his life for others.

God placed us on earth to do as Welles did—and as Elijah did—to rescue people. Our culture is decaying and dying. One day, this entire planet will be destroyed by fire, and many will lose their souls by following false gods who offer no hope of escape. Jesus Christ is the only Way of escape from this world into the next world, and He has given us a mission to point as many people to Him as possible, without regard for our own popularity, prosperity, or life. The secret to an extraordinary life is understanding God's purpose for our lives and then living it, just like Elijah.

When we pursue God's purpose, He will transform our ordinary existence into an extraordinary life. Nothing could be more significant than that.

SECRET #1

Discover Your Unique Purpose

In his poem "The People, Yes," Carl Sandburg sums up the history of humanity in three simple words: "Born, troubled, died."[1] Unfortunately, that depressing description is closer to the mark than most of us are willing to admit. I'm reminded of the Chicago sewer worker who described his life this way: "I dig the ditch to earn the money to buy the food to get the strength to dig the ditch." Get up, go to work, come home, eat dinner, watch television, go to bed . . . and the cycle continues.

Life is meant to be more than an endless and mindless treadmill. Jesus said, "I came that [you] may have life, and have it abundantly" (John 10:10). Jesus is in the business of saving and satisfying lives—of making life rich and rewarding. One way He accomplishes this is by giving each of us a unique purpose to fulfill during our brief stay here on earth. This purpose could be described as the specific story God wants to communicate to the world through your life.

Although the story God has created you to tell is unique, it is also connected to a larger story God is proclaiming to the entire universe.

The Bigger Story

When God decided to create human beings, He determined to create them in His image. Genesis 1:27 tells us, "God created man in His own image, in the image of God He created him; male and female He created them."

God then commanded His image bearers—Adam and Eve—to have children, rule over the earth, and create a thriving culture. Before sin entered the world, Adam and Eve experienced a deep, intimate relationship with the Lord.

From the beginning, the story God was communicating was that obedience to and fellowship with Him were the secret to experiencing abundant life. Theologians have summarized God's overarching purpose for each of us like this: "Man's chief end is to glorify God, and enjoy him forever."[2] Let's unpack what that general purpose means.

Glorifying God

Each of us was created to glorify God. The apostle John emphasizes this truth in Revelation 4:11 when he pictures the twenty-four elders—who represent the church in heaven—encircling God's throne and saying, "Worthy are You, our Lord and our God, to receive glory and honor and power; for You created all things, and because of Your will they existed, and were created."

The word *glory* comes from a Hebrew word that means "heavy." When we glorify God in our lives, we are showing Him to be heavy or substantial to others. He takes center stage. He becomes the big deal. The true weight of our lives is not measured by our temporary possessions—money, fame, achievement, awards, or degrees—but by the centrality of God in our lives.

God created you to glorify Him in everything you do. This is why the apostle Paul instructs us, "Whatever you do, do all to the glory of God" (1 Cor. 10:31). In other words, the overriding question we should use to evaluate every decision and every activity is this: "How will this action or this decision make God look bigger and better to others?"

Elijah grasped this primary purpose in life. His entire existence revolved around demonstrating to a largely unbelieving world that the God of Israel was the only true God.

Is that true of you? Can you honestly say that your priority in everything you do is to motivate others to follow God? Our story begins with making God the priority in our lives so that others will be encouraged to do the same.

Enjoying God

Yes, we have a duty to glorify God, but there is also an accompanying delight in doing so! In fact, as John Piper says, "God is most glorified in us when we are most satisfied in Him."[3] God wants our lives to glorify Him, but He also wants us to enjoy Him, just as David described:

> You will make known to me the path of life;
> In Your presence is fullness of joy;

> In Your right hand there are pleasures forever.
> (Ps. 16:11)

We spoke earlier of the unbroken fellowship Adam and Eve experienced with God. But the Lord wants to give us more than His presence; He wants to give us "pleasures." In Hebrew, this word means "sweetness" or "delight." What are the delightful gifts found in God's hand? David lists some of them in Psalm 103: forgiveness of sins, healing from sickness, deliverance from death, enrichment in life, and compassion for the oppressed. For all these—and more—David declared, "Bless the LORD, O my soul, and forget none of His benefits" (Ps. 103:2).

One way we enjoy God is by thanking Him for His blessings and mulling over His attributes. For example, when you go to a nice restaurant you (hopefully) do not wolf down your meal. You savor every course—the appetizers, the soup, the salad, the entrée, the dessert. You linger over the food, taking your time to relish every dish, taste every morsel, and enjoy every moment of the experience.

That is what God wants us to do with Him—to savor in our hearts and minds His blessings and character. Again, this is what Jesus had in mind when He said He came to give life abundantly (John 10:10)—that our relationship with God would be so rich we would want to spend every minute of every day in His presence, living to bring Him glory, and enjoying the unending benefits of His favor.

Elijah: A Case Study in Glorifying and Enjoying God

As I noted in the last chapter, Elijah was not a spiritual superman. He was a spiritual everyman—"a man with a nature like

34

ours" (James 5:17). Yet, even though he was an ordinary person, he understood he existed for an extraordinary purpose—to glorify God and enjoy Him forever. From the moment Elijah showed up on the scene, he said his whole purpose was to be "zealous for the LORD, the God of hosts" (1 Kings 19:10).

But to fulfill that purpose, Elijah had to demonstrate his zeal for God in concrete actions. To fulfill his general purpose, he had to discover his unique purpose in life. He had to tell the story God had specifically written for him.

The same is true for you and me. All of us are called to point people to God, but the path we follow to do that is unique for each of us. Every Christian has both a general purpose—to glorify and enjoy God—as well as a specific purpose (or "calling") through which we do so.

Elijah's specific calling was to serve God as a prophet to the nation of Israel. He would spend his life confronting the Israelites for forgetting the only true God. Whether it was through his courageous denouncement of the nation's wicked king and queen, his challenge to the false prophets on Mount Carmel, or his quiet faith in God's supernatural provisions, Elijah understood that all the puzzle pieces of his life were part of God's unique calling that, in turn, fulfilled his ultimate purpose of glorifying God. And it was his dogged pursuit of this purpose that made Elijah such a significant, successful, and satisfied individual.

When we read about Elijah in the Bible, his introduction is sudden and stark: "Now Elijah the Tishbite, who was of the settlers of Gilead . . ." (1 Kings 17:1).

Little is known of Elijah's life before his appointment as God's prophet. Nevertheless, we can piece together some clues as to how he came to understand his purpose in life.

His introduction tells us something significant about his background and his personality.

His Background

Names are a big deal. In our culture, we generally name our children after loved ones—a grandmother or grandfather, for example—or because we simply like the sound of certain names, especially how first names sound with our last names. But in the biblical culture, names were often given as a distinctive symbol for what parents wished for their child's future or were given as a descriptive indicator of their child's character. For example, the Old Testament patriarch Jacob's name literally means "heel catcher," which was appropriate since he "came forth with his hand holding on to [his twin brother's] heel" (Gen. 25:26).

The Hebrew word for Jacob could also mean "trickster." Jacob lived up to this meaning when he tricked his brother, Esau, out of his birthright (25:27–34), and tricked his father, Isaac, into giving him the blessing of the firstborn (27:1–38). Years later, God changed Jacob's name to Israel, which means "he strives with God," when Jacob wrestled with the angel of the Lord (32:24–28; Hosea 12:4).

If we look closely at Elijah's name, we'll discover that it is made up of three Hebrew words: *El*, which is short for *Elohim* (God), *Jah*, the abbreviation for *Jehovah*, and the letter *I*, the personal pronoun "my" or "mine." Putting all three together, Elijah's name literally means "My God is Jehovah" or "The Lord is my God."

Think about that. Every time his mother called him by name to wash up for supper, Elijah was reminded that one God ruled supreme and made an exclusive claim on his life. "Hurry up, 'The Lord is my God' and wash your hands before the meatloaf gets cold!" When his friends came to the house, it was as if they asked, "Can 'My God is Jehovah' come out to play?" After a lifetime of being reminded that he belonged to God alone, it makes sense that when Elijah appeared before Ahab, he would say, "As the LORD, the God of Israel lives, before whom I stand" (1 Kings 17:1). (By the way, parents, regardless of what we name our children, we should continually remind them of their duty and privilege to serve the living God.)

But Elijah's entrance on the scene in 1 Kings 17:1 gives us more than the name of the prophet who would confront Ahab and Jezebel. The verse also tells us where Elijah came from: Tishbe. What is interesting—and it gives us a clue as to how ordinary Elijah really was—is that his hometown is somewhat of a mystery. Archeologists have not found the exact location of Tishbe, but wherever it was, it was about as significant a place as Mud Lick, Kentucky; Oatmeal, Texas; or Boogertown, North Carolina. (Yes, these are real places!)

A friend of mine once owned a hunting cabin in the wilds of West Texas. On one hunting trip he invited his pastor to come along. After driving for hours, weaving this way and that, and bouncing over rut-filled roads, they finally arrived at the location. The pastor had been warned that the cabin was in the middle of nowhere, but when he got out of the truck and looked around, he said, "This is *truly* nowhere." My friend thought the comment appropriate, so he named his hunting lease "Truly Nowhere."

That's the kind of place Elijah was from—truly nowhere.

At some point, Elijah moved from Tishbe to the region of Gilead, just east of the Jordan River. It was a rough and rugged place, a place of solitude and silence. Dense forests covered its hills, and wildlife teemed in its valleys. No doubt the people who lived in Gilead were just as rough and rugged as the landscape—tanned, muscular, and leathery. And Elijah was one of them, dressing as a backwoodsman in coarse camel hair and leather (2 Kings 1:8). He was no spit-shined, polished, and sophisticated person of wealth and position. He was an ordinary, hardworking man. But it did not matter. God had a difficult mission for Elijah—a purpose that did not entail cocktail parties and diplomacy. God needed a rough and ready man—a nobody from nowhere to become God's somebody to confront a godless and wicked king.

It is not just Elijah's hometown that is a mystery, however. We know nothing of his family, his parents, whether he had siblings, or to which tribe he belonged. However, his parents—whoever they were—must have instilled in him an understanding that his purpose was to glorify the living God. They must have impressed upon him a love and fear of God—a passion to see God worshiped as the true Lord of Israel. They certainly taught him the Scriptures. The first thing Elijah said to King Ahab, after introducing himself, was "surely there shall be neither dew nor rain these years, except by my word" (1 Kings 17:1).

Elijah's message was one of judgment and was based on God's Word as recorded in Deuteronomy. Elijah declared that God would judge Israel for her idolatry. Moses had warned the children of Israel that God would "shut up the heavens so that there will be no rain and the ground will not yield its fruit; and you will perish quickly from the good land which the LORD is giving you" (Deut. 11:17). That was exactly what Elijah predicted. And for three and a half years it came about—"heaven [became] bronze, and the earth [became] iron, [and] the rain of [the] land [became] powder and dust" (Deut. 28:23–24; see James 5:17).

The false god Baal was believed to control the weather. But Elijah's "no dew, no rain" pronouncement was a direct challenge to the imaginary Baal under whose spell the Israelites had fallen. Ahab and Israel would see what sort of god Baal was. If he could not produce rain, then he would be found to be what he in fact was—a blind, dumb, and deaf hunk of metal.

Elijah's parents—though unknown and unnamed to us— taught their son well. The knowledge of God's Word they instilled in Elijah was instrumental in his discovery of God's unique purpose for his life. Elijah's parents remind me of my parents, now in heaven. My father was the reason that my mother came to faith in Jesus, taking her to a Billy Graham crusade in Dallas where she placed her faith in Christ. He and my mother joined First Baptist Church of Dallas—the church I have the honor of pastoring today. Two years after I was born, my dad traveled to Chicago for one purpose: to visit the Moody Bible Institute bookstore and to purchase the best collection of Christian books he could find for me. He invested $200—about one month's salary at the time—to ensure that I grew up knowing, loving, and fearing the Lord. And Elijah's parents did the same for him.

His Personality

If you like fire and brimstone type preaching then Elijah is your man. He was not one to mince words. As one of my mentors put it, Elijah was not a "mild-mannered man preaching a mild-mannered sermon, teaching people how to be more mild-mannered." Elijah's preaching was pointed, like a sharp stick shoved into someone's sternum. Appearing at Ahab's doorstep, Elijah went right to the heart of the matter: God's judgment was coming. He declared, "As the LORD, the God of Israel lives, before whom I stand, surely there shall be neither dew nor rain these years, except by my word" (1 Kings 17:1). Remarkable! This nobody from "Truly Nowhere" appeared before the king of Israel and predicted a national calamity.

When I read this verse, I think about my own experience preaching to the President of the United States and his family on the day of his inauguration. Although I knew the president and considered him a friend, there was something quite intimidating about staring into the eyes of one of the most powerful people in the world and delivering God's message, even though my message was one of encouragement, not condemnation.

By contrast, Elijah had a hard message to deliver to the king. "It is time to make a decision," Elijah told Ahab. "Who will it be: God or Baal? Until you abandon Baal and return to God, there will be no dew or rain unless I say so. Period." For Ahab and Jezebel, it was time to get rid of Baal and return to God—or Israel's rivers would dry up, crops would fail, and people would die.

This was Elijah's story, his God-ordained purpose for living. He heard the call of God and faithfully began to carry out his responsibilities as a prophet to the nation of Israel. God's assignment for Elijah was not easy, but it was clear: deliver a politically incorrect message of judgment to a wayward and wicked nation.

Discover God's Unique Purpose for Your Life

Your specific story is different than Elijah's, but it is just as significant and important. Elijah was a unique individual, never to come again. The same is true of you. You are a unique individual, never to come again. In the words of David, "The LORD looks from heaven; He sees all the sons of men" (Ps. 33:13). And what does God see in each of us? A life individually fashioned by Him (v. 15).

Every baby is a brand-new creation from the hand of God—uniquely created to accomplish a unique purpose. Peter affirmed this when he wrote, "God has given each of you a gift from his great variety of spiritual gifts. Use them well to serve one another. . . . Then everything you do will bring glory to God through Jesus Christ" (1 Pet. 4:10–11 NLT).

If you are going to have an extraordinary life—a life of significance—then you must discover your special purpose. But before we learn ways to uncover it, let's examine some of the benefits of understanding your purpose in life.

The Benefits of Discovering Your Purpose

I recently read a story about a group of analysts at Bank of America Merrill Lynch who concluded that there is a 20 to 50 percent chance that the world in which we live is not real—it is a virtual simulation, like the *Matrix* movies made popular in the late 1990s and early 2000s. (Their speculation made me wonder if my weekly deposits to their bank have disappeared into some imaginary virtual reality as well!)

You may chuckle at such an absurd idea, but many scientists and philosophers believe it is possible. They argue that the future of humanity will take one of three courses: "extinction before reaching a 'posthuman' stage, reaching posthuman existence but not simulating evolutionary history, [or] we are in the matrix already."[4] If we are in the matrix, they contend, we cannot know that we are in it.

In other words, we cannot know if what we call reality is really real. And if that is the case, then can we really say life has a purpose? This reminds me of something I read from Christian thinker Os Guinness:

> Out of more than a score of great civilizations in human history, modern Western civilization is the very first to have no agreed-on answer to the question of the purpose of life. Thus more ignorance, confusion—and longing—surround this topic now than at almost any time in history. The trouble is that, as modern people, we have too much to live with and too little to live for. Some feel they have time but not enough money; others feel they have money but not enough time. But for most us, in the midst of material plenty, we have spiritual poverty.[5]

Could anything be more spiritually bankrupt than believing that you are living in a computer simulated, virtual world— that everything you know and love is not real? I can only imagine what the apostle Paul would say to such nonsense— probably something like this:

> Live life . . . with a due sense of responsibility, not as men who do not know the meaning and purpose of life but as those who do. Make the best use of your time, despite all the difficulties of these days. Don't be vague but firmly grasp what you know to be the will of God. (Eph. 5:15–17 Phillips)

We are to live with the knowledge that life has meaning and purpose, "firmly [grasping] what [we] know to be the will of God." What a reassuring word in our complex and strange world! You are real, living in a real world, sent out by our real God to accomplish a real and unique purpose. Once you fully grasp this truth, it will serve as a prescription lens on life, correcting and clarifying reality. In fact, knowing your purpose—your story—clarifies three challenges we face in life.

Knowing Your Purpose Clarifies Priorities in Life

Paul said to "make the best use of your time"—make the most of your days on earth. Literally, this means to "buy up the time." Do not waste your life by wasting your time. As someone said, "Life is like a dollar bill. You can spend it any way you wish—but you can only spend it once."

Instead of spending your life on frivolous endeavors, invest your life in things that really matter—things that count for eternity. Practice the discipline of saying no not only to evil activities but also to unproductive activities. Unproductive things may not be bad in and of themselves, but they distract you from achieving your unique purpose in life.

For example, I could fill my time with counseling appointments. I pastor a large and diverse church, and people in our congregation have large and diverse problems. But counseling is neither my passion nor my giftedness—it does not fulfill my specific God-given purpose. Nevertheless, people need help, so we have pastors on staff whose purposes are fulfilled by counseling others. To have a significant life and tell the story God wants you to tell, you must never mistake the good for the best.

Knowing Your Purpose Clarifies Uncertainties in Life

Paul said we ought to be wise when it comes to under-standing God's will for our lives. Each of us faces daily decisions—some small, some large. Most have little impact on our lives, while a few have tremendous impact on our lives. Knowing and wisely applying our unique purpose to these decisions—especially major decisions—can save us years of regret.

For example, suppose you are offered a promotion in your company. While the prospect of a higher salary and more prestigious title are appealing to you, the promotion will require you to uproot your family and move to another city—and spend many more hours at work. Should you accept the promotion? It depends. If you still have children at home, your primary way of glorifying God and expand-ing His kingdom may be through rearing godly children. If the promotion would cause you to neglect that primary responsibility, then accepting it may be the wrong decision. However, if your children are grown and your new job would both maximize your gifts and expand your influence for God, then accepting the promotion might be exactly the right decision.

Knowing Your Purpose Clarifies Difficulties in Life

The apostle Paul was no Pollyanna. He knew life was filled with "difficulties," as he put it in Ephesians 5:16 (Phillips). In fact, as he wrote these words, Paul was in prison fac-ing possible execution. Had Paul's life purpose been that of most Christians today—peace, prosperity, pleasure, and the avoidance of pain—his "difficulties" of imprisonment and possible death would have been perplexing. "Why is God allowing this to happen to me when I've been so faithful to Him?" Paul could have lamented.

But firmly grasping God's purpose for his life provided Paul with a completely different perspective on his problems. As he wrote in his letter to the Philippians, he could "rejoice" in his circumstances, knowing that his difficulties were opportunities in disguise for him to fulfill his life purpose of sharing the gospel with as many people as possible (Phil. 1:18).

How so? Paul's imprisonment gave him the opportunity to share Christ with the Roman soldiers assigned to guard him, who in turn shared the gospel with the highest-ranking military officers in Rome (v. 13). Not only that, but ordinary Christians were being emboldened to share their faith because of Paul's example (v. 14). Had Paul's life purpose been self-focused, then he would have thrown himself a giant pity party in prison. But because Paul understood and embraced his unique purpose—to spread the gospel to the Gentiles— he declared, "In this I rejoice because Christ is proclaimed" (see v. 18).

Understanding your unique purpose gives you a different prism through which to view the difficulties that God allows or even brings into your life. When I think of that truth, I am reminded of the example of Staff Sergeant Travis Mills. He was on his third tour of duty in Afghanistan when he set down his rucksack on an undetected IED (improvised explosive device). When Mills came to—on his twenty-fifth birthday—he discovered he had lost all four limbs and the purpose of his life. As he tells the story in his book, *Tough As They Come*, Mills tried to persuade his wife, Kelsey, that she should divorce him; she could take all their possessions and start a new life with their baby daughter. Kelsey reminded him that's not how marriage works. She would stick by his side and see him through this trauma.

Mills questioned why God had allowed this to happen to him. He even demanded his sister-in-law remove a plaque she hung in his hospital room with the promise of Joshua 1:9 written on it: "Have I not commanded you? Be strong and courageous! Do not tremble or be dismayed, for the LORD your God is with you wherever you go." But, in time, Mills came to understand that God had a purpose for his life—even without his arms and legs.

Today, Travis Mills works through his foundation to assist wounded warriors and travels the country speaking to veterans' groups, large corporations, and civic organizations about never giving up and never giving in—about being brave and courageous. A man who heard Mills's testimony and message credits him with saving his life. I would say that is a significant purpose in life, wouldn't you?

Like Travis Mills, those with a clear focus on a purpose bigger than themselves see difficulties as opportunities both to grow in their own faith and also to glorify God to others.

The *STORY* God Wants to Tell through You

Since God made only one version of you—custom designed for a one-of-a-kind assignment—it is important to understand how to discover the unique purpose for which God created and gifted you. This is the story God wants to tell through you, so let's use the word *story* to help us.

S*tart with Scripture*

God's great desire for all of us is that we come to faith in Jesus Christ and then mature in our faith. This is the surest way for us to glorify God and enjoy Him. What does maturity look like? Paul gives us a clue in 1 Thessalonians 5:15–18:

> See that no one repays another with evil for evil, but always seek after that which is good for one another and for all people. Rejoice always; pray without ceasing; in everything give thanks; for this is God's will for you in Christ Jesus.

Seeking the best for others, rejoicing, praying, and giving thanks does not come by osmosis. This kind of maturity only comes through marinating our hearts and minds thoroughly in God's Word. Paul told Timothy:

> All Scripture is inspired by God and profitable for teaching, for reproof, for correction, for training in righteousness; so that the man of God may be adequate, equipped for every good work. (2 Tim. 3:16–17)

Scripture is given to *teach* us who God is and who we are—and how He has fashioned, equipped, and gifted us. The Bible provides lessons and instruction on life so we might develop the skills, knowledge, and insight necessary to identify and fulfill our purpose.

God's Word is also given for *reproof* and *correction*. When we sin we turn away from our purpose of glorifying God, and God uses His Word to point us back to the truth. Scripture highlights and rectifies errors and persuades us to conform to God's standard. When we do that—when we are living in the truth—the Lord reveals His unique purpose for us and blesses us as we seek to fulfill that purpose.

Scripture is also given to *train* us in righteousness. The Bible would only be a punitive book if all it did were rebuke and correct. But God uses His Word to gently guide us toward maturity—toward being the kind of believers described in 1 Thessalonians 5.

None of these benefits can be experienced apart from reading and applying the Bible. God's Word is His immediate means of communicating His will—including His unique purpose—to you. Do not misinterpret what I am saying. You will *not* discover your profession in the Bible (unless you are into fishing, tax collecting, or shepherding). Nor will the Bible reveal to you the name of your mate (unless it is Boaz or Mary). But saturating your mind with the commands of God and the unique stories of God's servants in the past is the beginning point for discovering God's specific purpose for your life in the present.

Talk to Others

Proverbs 13:10, 20 says, "Wisdom is with those who receive counsel. . . . He who walks with wise men will be wise." When it comes to discovering your unique purpose, it's wise to talk with those who know you best. They can see things you cannot see—both your abilities and your inabilities. All of us have blind spots, and if we are wise we will ask trusted family and friends to point out areas in our lives that are hidden to our eyes.

Theologians and pastors often refer to a person's unique purpose as a "calling," which one scholar defined as "an inner desire given by the Holy Spirit, through the Word of God, and confirmed by the community of Christ."⁶ You may think you have a knack for something. And as a believer growing in your faith and spending time in God's Word, you feel called to use that gift in a particular way. Good. You are on the road to discovering your special story. But to be sure you are on the right road, God provides an important road sign you ought not to ignore: the wise counsel of other people.

You see, "God has given us different gifts for doing certain things well" (Rom. 12:6 NLT), but we do not always appreciate or understand the gifts He has so graciously given. That's why we need other people in our lives—people who can guide and confirm what we believe to be our unique purpose.

My ninth-grade speech teacher, Nancy Fry, did this for me. She was a petite, older woman who barked like a drill sergeant and wore what appeared to be laced-up army boots to complete the image. Her students were scared to death of her—and for good reason! When timid students would take their turn to stand up before their peers and deliver their assigned speech, Miss Fry would often climb on the top of her desk at the back of the room and yell at the top of her voice, "Louder!"

But for some reason, Miss Fry took a special interest in me. She would work with me after school, and one day she said to me, "Robert, you are going to make a great preacher someday. You could sell anyone anything—and that's scary!" She was the first person outside of my family who envisioned success for me as a speaker. And while I could have used my speaking ability in any number of ways, I obeyed the Lord's leading and chose to dedicate that ability to preaching God's Word.

Years later, when I was just beginning my ministry, I received word that Miss Fry had passed away—and in her will she stipulated that she wanted me to conduct her funeral service. Knowing how particular she would have been about who spoke at her service, I considered that the highest compliment of all! I am so grateful that in those formative years of my life, when I was trying to determine God's unique purpose for me, God placed someone like Nancy Fry—and many others afterward—whom He used to steer me toward my life's calling.

However, God can also use the counsel of other people to point out our liabilities. When I had finished my Master of Theology degree from Dallas Theological Seminary, I was burned out on school, having spent three years in college followed by four years in graduate school. I had thought about pursuing a doctorate, but frankly, I was looking for an excuse not to.

One day I scheduled lunch with an older, more seasoned minister and told him my dilemma, laying out all the reasons I really didn't need a doctorate. "Look at pastor so-and-so," I said. "He doesn't have a doctorate, and he has a huge church and a thriving ministry." My friend looked at me and said, "That's right, Robert. But you don't have his looks or his voice. You'd better get your doctorate!" Ouch! I saw that not-so-gentle-reproof as God's leading and followed my friend's advice. Seeking counsel from those who know us is one of God's primary ways for us to discover His specific calling for our lives.

Obey Your Passions

Many people are shocked when they hear me say, "One of the primary ways God directs you is through the desires He puts in your heart. If you want to know what you *should* do, ask yourself the question, 'What do I *want* to do?'"

I can hear some people protesting, "Wait a minute! Doesn't the Bible say that our hearts are wicked, deceptive, and can never be trusted?" That's certainly true about our desires *before* we become a Christian. But one of the results of salvation is the transformation of our hearts—our desires—to conform to God's desires. The closer we move toward God, the more our desires reflect His desires for us.

If you are in a growing and intimate relationship with God, then the Bible teaches that He will mold your desires to conform to His plan for your life. To put it another way, when God controls your life, He controls your desires, just as David explained in Psalm 37:4–5:

> Delight yourself in the LORD;
> And He will give you the desires of your heart.
> Commit your way to the LORD,
> Trust also in Him, and He will do it.

Another word for desire is *passion*. To discover your unique purpose, ask yourself, *What am I passionate about? What needs do I see in the world that must be met?* Sometimes our passion arises from a deep hurt in our life. Candace Lightner lost her daughter to a drunk driver and as a result decided to devote her energies to removing the menace of drunk drivers from the nation's highways through the organization she founded, Mothers Against Drunk Driving.

Other times, our passion flows out of our desire to glorify God. When he was a teenager, one megachurch pastor was always looking for ways to share Christ with his fellow students.

One day he invited a non-Christian friend to go to church with him. The poorly presented music and mediocre message so embarrassed him—and so turned off his friend—that this young man determined to devote his life to creating a church where everything was done with excellence and where Christians could bring their unbelieving friends without apologizing. That experience was the beginning of a ministry that now has been copied by thousands of churches across the country.

Christian writer Frederick Buechner said, "The place God calls you to is the place where your deep gladness and the world's deep hunger meet."[7] One of the primary ways God reveals the unique purpose for our lives is through the passion He has placed in our hearts—a passion that will meet a very real need in the world.

Yet many Christians live under a black cloud of doubt, believing that their passion to accomplish their purpose is somehow sinful. They are convinced that the best way to discover God's will is to ask, *What is absolutely the most miserable thing I could imagine spending my life doing? That must be God's will for me!* They are convinced that God's plan for them should be the hardest, most distasteful existence they can possibly imagine. Nothing could be further from the truth! God is more interested in your discovering His unique plan for you than even you are. And one of the primary ways He reveals that purpose to you is through the desires He places in your heart.

Recognize Your Gifts and Abilities

God will not only give you the desire (passion) to fulfill His purpose for life but He will also endow you with the gifts and abilities you need for that purpose. The apostle Paul affirmed, "It is God who is at work within you, giving you the will [desire] and the power [gifts and abilities] to achieve his purpose" (Phil. 2:13 Phillips).

The common idea that "You can be whatever you want to be in life" is a feel-good sentiment that has no basis in reality. For example, many of us were told as children, "Anyone in America can become the president of the United States." Yet the truth is that most people do not have the gifts, temperament, or skills necessary to perform that job.

Although you cannot be anything you want to be, God has given you all the gifts you need to be everything *He* wants you to be. Just as understanding your desires is key to discovering God's purpose for your life, recognizing your gifts and abilities can help you determine the story God has designed you to tell.

The apostle Paul encouraged us to perform an honest assessment of our gifts and abilities when he wrote, "I say to everyone among you not to think more highly of himself than he ought to think; but to think so as to have sound judgment" (Rom. 12:3).

Paul is encouraging us to be realistic when it comes to evaluating our gifts. For example, if you feel like God is calling you to become a doctor but you have no gifts in science and pass out at the sight of blood, you might want to rethink your vocation! Perhaps you envision yourself preaching God's Word to thousands. Yet if you break out into a cold sweat when you face a large crowd and have the "gift" of putting people to sleep when you speak, you might consider another calling. I realize there are examples in the Bible of God occasionally calling people to roles for which they had no gifts, but usually God's purpose for us aligns with God's gifts to us.

This principle is clearly seen in Exodus 31, when the Lord tells Moses that He has uniquely gifted Bezalel as a skilled craftsman:

> I have filled him with the Spirit of God in wisdom, in understanding, in knowledge, and in all kinds of craftsmanship, to make artistic designs for work in gold, in silver, and in bronze, and in the cutting of stones for settings, and in the carving of wood. (Exod. 31:3–5)

God did not call Bezalel to be the leader of God's people—that was Moses's job. Nor did God call Bezalel to be the priest of God's people—that was Aaron's role. Rather, God called Bezalel to be the craftsman of God's tabernacle. If Bezalel had tried to lead the people and Moses had tried to carve the stone, both would have been a disaster.

"God normally calls us along the line of our giftedness," Os Guinness observed.[8] If you don't have a clear understanding of your gifts, ask yourself the following questions:

- What do I enjoy doing?
- What things do other people see me do and say, "You were born to do that"?
- What do I do that seems effortless to me?
- What is the common denominator in the three most satisfying and successful things I've done in my life?

Accurately assessing your gifts is key to discovering the purpose for which God has created you. Remember, God did not create you to tell someone else's story. Instead, He has gifted you to communicate a unique message through your life that will glorify Him.

Yield to the Leading of the Spirit

Saturating your mind with Scripture, consulting with others, following your passion, and determining your gifts are all vital in discovering your unique purpose. But living out your purpose requires surrendering your life to the control of God's Holy Spirit.

From the time I was a little boy, I felt that my life's work would be as an executive producer in the television industry. I was interested in communication and finances—both integral parts of that profession. I spent every spare moment I could reading professional journals and books about the television industry. I had no doubt this was how God wanted me to spend my life.

But all that changed one summer day when I was fifteen years old. After the noon service at our church's youth camp—as everyone was racing to be first in line for lunch—God communicated to me very clearly that He had a different plan for my life than I had thought. On that summer day God told me I was to be a pastor. (Sometimes people ask if God spoke to me audibly. I jokingly reply, "Actually, it was louder than that!")

None of my gifts or interests changed that day; they were just redirected toward another calling. But before I could start fulfilling my purpose, I had to surrender to God's Spirit and say, "Yes, Lord."

We must learn how to listen when God's Spirit speaks to us and then learn to obey—even when obedience seems absurd. For example, from a human perspective it was foolish for Abraham to strike out for an unknown land or to offer Isaac as a sacrifice.

It was idiotic for Joshua to march his army around Jericho with nothing but shouts and trumpets.

It was impractical for Gideon to go into battle against larger numbers with only three hundred men.

It was dangerous for Rahab to harbor the Jewish spies who scoped out Jericho.

It was risky for Elijah to confront the king and pronounce God's judgment.

But each of these men and women knew they had heard the unmistakable call of God and responded with total and unconditional obedience. Had they chosen not to surrender to God's plan for their lives, we would not be talking about them thousands of years later.

⦂⦂⦂⦂⦂

Pastor and author Max Lucado has a simple formula for discovering your purpose in life: "Use your uniqueness (what you do) to make a big deal out of God (why you do it) every day of your life (where you do it). At the convergence of all three, you'll find . . . your sweet spot."[9] Discovering your "sweet spot" is the first step to living an extraordinary life.

Determine to Influence
Your Culture

Evangelist Billy Graham was on the cutting edge of our culture for more than half a century. Thousands of people, including my own mother, came to faith in Christ after attending one of his conferences, reading one of his books, or watching him on television. He served as spiritual adviser to presidents and prime ministers, and without ever wavering—but always with wisdom and grace—addressed the social and moral issues of his day.

As far back as 1965, Graham hit upon a persistent problem confronting our culture. In *World Aflame*, he wrote:

> In a declining culture, one of its characteristics is that ordinary people are unaware of what is happening. . . . Modern man has become a spectator of world events, observing on his television screen without becoming involved. He watches the ominous events while he sips his beer in a comfortable

chair. He does not understand that his world is on fire and that he is about to be burned with it.[1]

That was me in the early part of my ministry. Although I was not sipping beer, I came home every day, sat in my comfortable chair, watched the news, and thought about how tragic the world was becoming. I reasoned that as long as I faithfully preached God's Word every Sunday, the fire that was consuming the world would not consume me or the congregation I served.

I soon found out how foolish I was.

In 1998, a member of my church who worked for our local public library brought two books to my attention—books promoting the homosexual lifestyle to children. Told from a child's point of view, *Daddy's Roommate* and *Heather Has Two Mommies* extolled the virtues of homosexuality and a family structure radically different than the one created by God and celebrated by the general culture. *Daddy's Roommate* had an illustration of a little boy's father in bed with another man as the boy explains that his father and his father's new roommate enjoyed "sleeping together."

"Pastor, what are you going to do about this?" my church member asked me.

Coincidentally, the sermon I was preparing for the next Sunday was on God's destruction of Sodom and Gomorrah in Genesis 19. On Thursday afternoon, I had already written my message and was going to press this point to the congregation: "We cannot afford to condone what God has condemned." Then it hit me—almost with as much force as the fire and brimstone that had rained down on those two wicked cities: *Robert, are you condoning what God has condemned by your reluctance to speak out?*

I initially determined not to make too big a stink about the books. I simply called the head librarian on my way home that Thursday afternoon and asked her to remove the books. I politely explained to her that the behavior promoted in these books (sodomy) was illegal in our state (though that has since changed), that the three major world religions all condemned such behavior, and that homosexual acts were largely responsible for the epidemic of the deadly disease AIDS. She listened quietly and then let me know in no uncertain terms that she would not be removing the books. The following Sunday I held up the books in the pulpit, explained my objection to them, and informed my congregation and television audience that I was not going to return the books to the library.

Thus began a two-year-long controversy that involved the local newspaper calling for my arrest and incarceration and a federal lawsuit against our city. Letters to the editor in our local newspaper were filled with denunciation. PBS even filmed a documentary on the dispute called *The Fundamental Fight*.

I am aware of Paul's admonition in Romans 12:18: "If possible, so far as it depends on you, be at peace with all men." But that experience in 1998 was my awakening to the fact that it is impossible to be at peace with a culture that is at odds with God. Those men and women who want to experience a truly significant life must be willing to confront their culture with God's truth.

Caring for Our Culture

We cannot afford to be unaware and uncaring about what is happening in our culture. From the beginning, God commanded Adam to cultivate and care for the world in which God had placed him. Genesis 2:15 tells us, "The LORD God took the man and put him into the garden of Eden to cultivate it and keep it."

This is a basic principle that many Christians have forgotten: God cares about what happens in His world. God's interests are not confined to the church but extend throughout all His creation.

Simply put, "culture is what human beings make of the world."[2] And in many ways, we have made the world a better place—certainly in transportation, communication, and medicine. Walking is good, but not if you have to get across town to buy groceries. Driving a car is better for that. Writing letters is good. But if you need a quick answer to help solve a business problem, then an email or phone call is preferable. And who would trade laser surgery for a sharp knife (and no anesthesia) from one hundred years ago?

Yet all our advances in technology have not stemmed the moral unraveling of our culture. On this front, we have made a mess of the world. No one can deny that our culture has deteriorated rapidly in the last one hundred years—especially in our own country.

While America was once a nation living under the Judeo-Christian ethic, we are now a nation living under the secular ideology of postmodernism and relativism. And we see the end results of these ideologies splashed on the front pages of our newspapers, in the lead stories of our television news, and in the headlines of our social media.

And like Elijah, whom God raised up in Israel's decaying culture, so God has placed us in our decaying culture to cultivate moral and spiritual goodness. As Paul reminded the Ephesian believers, "We are [God's] workmanship, created in Christ Jesus for good works, which God prepared beforehand so that we would walk in them" (Eph. 2:10). The word translated "workmanship" in this verse is *poieme*, from which we get our word "poem." At the moment of salvation, God creates a new work in us and we become God's masterpiece.

God does not write His poem in our lives for us to simply sit on a shelf. Rather, He composes our lives so that others might read His poem when they come into contact with us. The operative word is *contact*. If we are going to cultivate our culture with goodness, then we must penetrate our culture—as Elijah did—rather than isolate ourselves from it. (More about that later.) But first, we need to expand our understanding of the word *culture*.

Cultivating Our Culture

When people hear about the culture, they usually think about the national culture created in Hollywood, New York, or Washington, DC, and they become discouraged because there is little they can do to change it. But culture is not just national in scope; it is also local, made up of small communities and local activities. God is not expecting you to change Washington, DC, or Hollywood, except perhaps by voting with a ballot or your pocketbook. However, God *is* calling you to work for change in the areas in which you do have influence.

For example, if you are a stay-at-home mother with young children, you have a wonderful opportunity (and responsibility) to shape the culture of your home. In the Old Testament, Hannah prayed for years to have a son, promising God that she would dedicate him to the Lord's service if He granted her petition. After she gave birth to Samuel, she raised her boy to know the Lord. When she turned Samuel over to the care of Eli, God's priest, the Lord blessed Samuel and made him a great prophet and judge in Israel.

If you are a student, you have an opportunity to change the culture of your school—or at least your corner of it. When I was in junior high, a Christian teacher asked me to meet with her after school one day. She said, "Robert, have you ever thought that God has placed you here in this school for one reason—to be a witness for Christ to your other classmates?" Honestly, the thought had never crossed my mind! She continued, "I challenge you to make a list of five of your classmates who aren't Christians, begin to pray daily for their salvation, and sometime during the year share the gospel with them." For some reason, I decided to accept her challenge.

The first guy on my list was a boy named Nick. He was what we used to call a "hood." Nick looked and talked like someone from the cast of *West Side Story*. He was a tough guy whom most students were afraid of. But one day, I worked up the courage to ask Nick if I could talk with him after school. For whatever reason, he agreed.

We met in an empty classroom, and I shared with him the fact that God loved him and wanted to have a relationship with him. I explained who Jesus was and the forgiveness of sins He offered. Finally, I closed by saying, "Nick, is there any reason you wouldn't like to trust in Christ right now?"

"No, there really isn't. I'd like to do that," he said. And so, that fall afternoon, Nick became a Christian and the first person I ever led to Christ. Neither he nor I had any idea that Nick had a brain tumor that would take his life within nine months. That year I saw all five of my classmates on my list become Christians—including one girl who later became my wife!

I will be the first to admit that the five people I led to Christ did not compare to the hundreds of thousands of people Billy Graham has led to Christ. My influence did not extend to crowded football stadiums, world leaders, or Hollywood luminaries. Instead, my sphere of influence was confined at that time to a junior high school in Richardson, Texas.

The same is true for you. You may hold little sway over the larger culture of the United States, but you can impact your neighborhood, school, office, church, and home. And who knows, God may choose to expand the scope of your influence.

How *Not* to Influence Your Culture

On the whole, Christians are ineffective at dealing with culture. Most believers do not respond appropriately when it comes to changes in culture—especially when those changes are contrary to God's Word. When confronted with an anti-Christian environment, most Christians tend to fall into one of two categories: silo saints or spiritual sellouts. Elijah-like men and women avoid the trap of either one, because neither create the kind of change God desires in His world.

Silo Saints

Some Christians respond to an ungodly culture by retreating into their silos—primarily their homes and churches—hoping to shelter themselves and their families from spiritual pollution. Christians who choose to live only in their holy huddles are basically saying, "We are going to heaven; the world can go to hell." These silo saints might pop their heads up long enough to talk to non-Christians about salvation, but they do not want to impose their Christian values on the culture—so they tend to remain underground, isolated from their world.

Just this week I participated in a panel discussion at a seminary. One of the students asked me, "Dr. Jeffress, why do you feel that conservative Christians have the right to impose their views on a pluralistic society?" I reminded the student that someone's values will always be imposed on society; the only question is *whose* values would prevail. For example, until June 2015, the Supreme Court followed the Judeo-Christian principle that marriage was a sacred union between one man and one woman (*Murphy v. Ramsey*, 1885). But after the June 2015 ruling of *Obergefell v. Hodges*, the Supreme Court abandoned that principle for a new principle—a principle the Court is now imposing on the culture. Those who refuse to submit to this new definition of marriage are being labeled "bigots" and in some cases face government fines and bankruptcy.

Unfortunately, this student subscribed to the belief that anyone should be free to impose his or her values on culture—anyone, that is, except a Christian. Such silo spirituality quickly leads to compartmentalized Christianity—a false dichotomy between the sacred and the secular. For example, some people believe that the church is sacred but government is secular. They fear if these two forces come in contact with one another, then the results will be explosive. For some, this "fear" is nothing but a smokescreen for imposing a secular agenda on the nation without any opposition from Christians. If secularists cannot destroy Christianity, then their next best option is to contain it within the four walls of the church.

But God sees no divide between the sacred and the secular. God's sovereignty is not limited to religious people and religious institutions. God's sovereignty certainly wasn't limited at the time of Elijah. Drought came upon the land of Israel because the head of the civil institution (King Ahab) had established a foreign god (Baal) at the head of Israel's religious institution.

God is interested in all people and all institutions. The psalmist declared, "The LORD has established His throne in the heavens, and His sovereignty rules over all" (Ps. 103:19). While it is evident that not everyone acknowledges God's authority, God still desires that every person and every institution submit to His will. If you have difficulty believing that, then consider how Jesus instructed His followers to pray:

> Our Father who is in heaven,
> Hallowed be Your name.
> Your kingdom come.
> Your will be done,
> On earth as it is in heaven. (Matt. 6:9–10)

When we pray for God's will to be done on earth, we are not just referring to some future time in history when

Christ is literally reigning over this earth. This is also a here-and-now request. "Right now, God, we want Your will to be done in our world, our nation, our homes, and our individual lives."

Does God's will on earth include the murder of millions of unborn children through abortion, the persecution and marginalization of Christians around the world and in our own nation, the redefinition of marriage, or the oppression of the poor? Of course not! Yet this is what is happening on earth every day because God's people have bought into the myth of silo spirituality. They have formulated a theology that allows them to compartmentalize their faith instead of integrating it with the rest of their lives. The result is a culture increasingly untouched by God's righteous standards.

Spiritual Sellouts

Today we are witnessing a strange synthesis of the religious right and the secular left when it comes to the question of culture. Both agree that God does not care about culture. The secularists come to this conclusion because they do not believe in God, while Christians arrive at this conclusion because they believe God is above such concerns—that He is merely interested in the salvation of souls and the finer points of theological doctrine.

Beyond that, many Christians have also come to believe—as secularists believe—that sin is not really a big deal. In fact, the word *sin* is never used in our national discourse to describe behaviors that are outside of God's standards. And the avoidance of the word in our churches leads many

Christians to conclude that sin is merely a human flaw, easily overlooked. One Christian philosopher described the process of how sin becomes acceptable like this:

> As any sin passes through its stages from temptation to toleration, to approval, its name is first euphemized, then avoided, then forgotten. A colleague tells me that some of his fellow scholars call child molestation "intergenerational intimacy": that's euphemism. A good-hearted editor tried to talk me out of using the term "sodomy": that's avoidance. My students don't know the world "fornication" at all: that's forgetfulness.[3]

If we cannot call things what they truly are—molestation, sodomy, or fornication, for example—then we will forget that they are truly sinful. And if we no longer believe they are truly sinful, then we are only a small step away from fully accepting and approving sin.

If we are not careful, we can become swallowed up in the quicksand of our corrupt society, making it nearly impossible to tell Christianity apart from the larger culture. In the words of a friend, "The sins of the culture will become the sins of the Christian, and the sins of the Christian will become the sins of the church." Some Christians sell out spiritually by surrendering to the moral temptations of our culture. Other Christians sell out their faith to political correctness. Unlike Elijah, they remain silent instead of proclaiming God's truth about hot-button issues, fearful of being labeled a "religious fanatic" or losing a promotion at work or popularity in their school. And if they have a friend who *is* willing to stand up for truth, then they distance themselves from that person, not wanting to experience any of the negative fallout their friend experiences.

I had the honor and privilege of delivering a sermon in a private service with president-elect Donald Trump and vice president-elect Mike Pence on the day of their inaugurations. It was a day I will never forget. But the evening before was almost as memorable. That night, I walked into the Fox studios in Washington, DC, for an interview regarding the presidential service. My cell phone rang, and the caller informed me that CNN, NBC, and other outlets were breaking the news that president-elect Trump had selected an "inflammatory pastor," noted for his "anti-gay, anti-Muslim rhetoric," to deliver the sermon the next morning. I was sure that president-elect Trump's team would call me, encouraging me to decline the invitation. And I wouldn't have blamed them. They didn't need the negative publicity on such an important day. But Mr. Trump and his team didn't blink. Though they may not have agreed with all of my beliefs, they understood I represented the beliefs of millions of Christians in the United States.

Ironically, through the years, members and leaders have exited our church because they did not want to be associated with a pastor or a church that takes unpopular, biblical stands. This has deeply disappointed me, because in many ways these individuals were sold out more to the culture than to Christ.

The apostle Paul was deeply wounded by such "spiritual sellout." When he was sitting in a dungeon in Rome, he lamented about a close associate who had left him. He wrote, "Demas, having loved this present world, has deserted me and gone to Thessalonica" (2 Tim. 4:10). It is likely Demas feared that his association with a condemned man like Paul might implicate him in the eyes of the Roman authorities. Demas was not about to risk his reputation and freedom for Paul—or the gospel.

Sadly, Demas loved freedom more than the faith. Or, as is increasingly seen on college campuses—where free speech and the free exchange of ideas are supposed to be valued—Christians would rather remain mute than risk backlash from their peers and professors for speaking out for Christ.

Isolation vs. Influence

Identifying with the culture poses a clear and present danger for Christians. However, I am convinced that an even greater threat to influencing our culture is isolating ourselves from it. Even though many Christians have been sucked into the culture's value system, they know they are acting in a way contrary to the teaching of Scripture. No Christian I know will cite verses from the Bible to justify his or her immorality, greed, or bitterness.

Yet many Christians today actually pride themselves for isolating themselves from unbelievers or for refusing to lift a finger to effect any change in the world in which they live. For example, I am amazed by the number of Christians who have openly condemned me for my friendship with people they consider to be unbelievers. They say, "How could you allow yourself to be seen with someone who is so immoral? Don't you know that the Bible says we are to be holy?"

Interestingly, the Corinthians (some of the most corrupt believers of the first century) made a similar misapplication of Scripture that the apostle Paul had to correct:

I wrote you in my [earlier] letter not to associate with immoral people; I did not at all mean with the immoral people of this world, or with the covetous and swindlers, or with idolaters, for then you would have to go out of the world. But actually, I wrote to you not to associate with any so-called brother if he is an immoral person, or covetous, or an idolater, or a reviler, or a drunkard, or a swindler. (1 Cor. 5:9–11)

If you are going to isolate yourself from ungodly people, stay away from ungodly Christians—not ungodly non-Christians. It is not only impossible to separate yourself from unbelievers (unless you want to reside on Mars) but it is also illogical to do so. Just imagine a doctor who said, "I can't stand being around sick people with all of their germs! I'm going to only treat people who are well." That doctor would not be in business very long. As Jesus pointed out, "It is not those who are well who need a physician, but those are sick" (Luke 5:31).

Jesus has left us as His representatives in the world not only to bring healing to spiritually sick people but also to influence a spiritually sick culture. Before Jesus ascended into heaven, He prayed for both His current and future followers (including you and me) in this way:

Now I am departing from the world; they are staying in this world, but I am coming to you. . . . And the world hates them because they do not belong to the world, just as I do not belong to the world. I'm not asking you to take them out of the world, but to keep them safe from the evil one. They do not belong to this world any more than I do. Make them holy by your truth; teach them your word, which is truth. (John 17:11, 14–17 NLT)

Notice that Jesus asked God to keep us from isolation ("I'm not asking you to take them out of the world") and from identification with the world ("make them holy") so that we might influence the world. Admittedly, it can be quite a challenge to pull off the in-the-culture-but-not-of-the-culture philosophy. But Jesus demonstrated how to do it, as did Elijah.

Three Convictions That Will Transform Your Life

My mentor, the late Howard Hendricks, observed that when Elijah arrived on the scene in Israel, "the nation was on the skids."

> There was a mania of mediocrity. Seven thousand believers were huddled in a cave in silent protest: "We don't want to get involved." This man, Elijah, stands out like a spiritual colossus in the midst of a generation of perverts and spiritual pygmies.[4]

Our own generation could be described as perverted and populated by "spiritual pygmies." Yet the convictions that made Elijah a "spiritual colossus" in his generation can make us giants in our generation as well. Elijah embraced three convictions that can transform us into spiritual giants who can transform our world.

Conviction #1: God Is Alive and Active in the Culture

I pointed this out earlier, but it is worth highlighting again: Elijah claimed that he served the *living* Lord. Before pronouncing judgment on Israel, Elijah made sure Ahab understood whom he was dealing with: "As the LORD, the God of Israel lives" (1 Kings 17:1).

We live in a world filled with people—even Christians—who do not understand who God is. Recently, I was at a prayer gathering where the chaplain of a Christian hospital prompted everyone to bow their heads in "worship to the god of their own understanding." I was stunned. How could this man represent the Christian faith and open the possibility that there are many gods or many equally valid understandings of God? There is only one true God, and He has revealed Himself through His written Word and through the living Word—Jesus Christ. The apostle John made this clear in the first chapter of his Gospel.

> In the beginning was the Word, and the Word was with God, and the Word was God. He was in the beginning with God. . . . And the Word became flesh, and dwelt among us, and we saw His glory, glory as of the only begotten from the Father, full of grace and truth. (John 1:1–2, 14)

I am so convinced of the truth of Jesus's claim, "I am the way, and the truth, and the life; no one comes to the Father but through Me" (John 14:6), that I wrote a book on the subject. In *Not All Roads Lead to Heaven*, I state, "What you believe about the exclusivity of the gospel of Christ determines whether you will spend eternity in heaven or hell."[5]

Worshiping the god of your own understanding is the surest way to end up in hell. Elijah knew that. The nation of Israel had been on a long course of worshiping the gods of their own understanding. What we celebrate as "pluralism" and "inclusivism" in today's culture, God called "idolatry"— and He'd had enough of it! So He dispatched Elijah to Ahab to remind the king—and the people—that the living God was about to judge the nation.

We did not make the rules; God did (and He gave those guidelines for our benefit, not our detriment). Our assignment, like Elijah's, is to uphold the standards of the one true God regardless of the consequences. We do so believing that God is alive and active in the affairs of men and women, and He will hold our culture accountable if we retreat from the truth.

Conviction #2: You Are God's Ambassador to the Culture

You and I are God's representatives in the world. Paul said, "We are ambassadors for Christ" (2 Cor. 5:20). To be effective ambassadors for Jesus, we must first bring our opinions about the validity of other religions, same-sex relationships, abortion, capital punishment, or any other controversial subject under the authority of God's Word. Then, we are to articulate and represent God's views to those within God's kingdom and those living outside of it.

Elijah understood that he was the ambassador of the living Lord and that he received his marching orders from God alone. Whether Elijah was ordered to pronounce judgment, to retreat into the wilderness, to challenge the prophets of Baal, to confront a sinful king, or to call fire from heaven, he was a man who did God's bidding without compromise.

For that time and place in Israel's history, Elijah answered God's call to be His ambassador—and he made a significant impact on his culture. God is still looking for ambassadors who will make a difference in our time and place. As 2 Chronicles 16:9 reminds us, "The eyes of the LORD move to and fro throughout the earth that He may strongly support those whose heart is completely His."

Ambassadors do not speak on their own initiative or represent their own interests. Rather, they speak on behalf of and represent the rulers who commissioned them. Their loyalty resides completely with the ruler they serve, and in turn the ruler pledges his or her support and protection to these ambassadors. If we faithfully represent God's message to those inside and outside His kingdom, then we can be assured of His divine enablement and providential care.

This does not mean our assignment will be an easy one. In fact, most ambassadorships are not to the French Riviera, where you can sun yourself on the shores of the Mediterranean. Most ambassadors are sent to run-of-the-mill places, and a few to dangerous locations. But no matter where the Lord has placed you—in whatever sphere of influence—being an ambassador for Christ requires courage, especially if you are going to confront a culture that is growing increasingly hostile to God's message.

A few years ago, I received an invitation to fly to Hollywood and appear on *Real Time with Bill Maher*. I had seen Maher in a few interviews and knew of his hostility to Christian viewpoints, but I had never watched his program. I accepted the invitation and told a few of my friends, prayer partners, and deacons about my decision. "Are you out of your mind?" they asked. "Bill Maher will eat you alive!" I thought that was a little hyperbolic, until I watched a few episodes.

As I prayed about whether to cancel my appearance, I thought of the potential I had to speak God's truth to millions of people who might not ever enter a church. I finally concluded if the apostle Paul could go to Mars Hill to reason with the skeptics, then surely I could travel to Maher's studio in Hollywood to speak to unbelievers!

On a Friday, my wife, daughter, and I flew to Hollywood. Although I have done thousands of radio and television interviews, I had never been as apprehensive about any of them as I was that day. Before the car picked us up at the hotel to travel to the studio, my wife, daughter, and I got into a circle and prayed that, whatever happened, God would be glorified. Hundreds of my prayer partners in Dallas were praying as well.

When the interview started, Bill poked some fun at me, and there were a few groans and boos from the audience. But as the interview progressed, I could feel God's Spirit taking charge, giving me the opportunity to share the gospel message that Jesus Christ was the only way to salvation. By the end of the segment, the audience applauded. Staff members from the show later told me they had never seen Bill treat a Christian with so much respect.

After the show, Bill invited my family and me to the after-show party. We stood and talked for about a half an hour. At the end of our conversation, Bill said, "You know, Pastor, I don't believe one thing you believe. But you are a great representative of your faith." Years later, I still run into non-Christians who saw that broadcast and say it caused them to think differently about faith issues. Had I stayed in my cocoon in Dallas and not taken the risk of engaging the culture, I would have forfeited that opportunity to affect others in the culture.

Most people don't face the quandary of whether or not to appear on a national television program. But all of us decide every day whether we are going to take a risk and speak God's truth to our world—in a classroom, at work, in a conversation with a friend or family member. Those who choose an extraordinary life submit themselves to the King's commands found in Matthew 5:

> You are the salt of the earth; but if the salt has become taste-less, how can it be made salty again? It is no longer good for anything, except to be thrown out and trampled under foot by men.
>
> You are the light of the world. A city set on a hill cannot be hidden; nor does anyone light a lamp and put it under a basket, but on the lampstand, and it gives light to all who are in the house. Let your light shine before men in such a way that they may see your good works, and glorify your Father who is in heaven. (Matt. 5:13–16)

In Jesus's day, salt served as a preservative for meat. Salt did not prevent decay but delayed it. Salt gave the meat a longer shelf life, but it eventually had to be thrown away. Jesus says that as His ambassadors we are like a preserva-tive that delays the decay of our world. But salt cannot delay the decay of meat if it remains in the saltshaker. Only when the salt leaves the confines of the shaker and penetrates the meat can it preserve it.

No ambassador worth their salt remains in the security of their country's embassy when they are in a foreign land. Sure, it is safer there. But for ambassadors to represent their leader's policies to others, they have to come in contact with other people—including those who may disagree with or misunderstand the ruler he or she is representing.

Jesus also said we were the "light of the world" (Matt. 5:14). It is no accident Jesus also used that phrase to refer to Himself: "I am the Light of the world" (John 8:12). Now that Christ has ascended into heaven, we are to function as His light—illuminating the way to God through faith in His Son, Jesus Christ.

But no light is useful if it remains hidden. Before light can dispel darkness, it has to come in contact with darkness. A few weeks ago, we lost power in our house. Fortunately, I had a flashlight in a kitchen drawer. But that flashlight was of no use to me as long as it remained in the drawer. It could not cut through the darkness until it confronted the darkness.

Elijah was salt and light to the nation of Israel, preserving and illuminating the truth of the living God when he confronted Ahab. Our calling and responsibility are the same. By our words and actions, ambassadors of Christ must preserve the truth, cause others to thirst for God, and illuminate the way to God through faith in Christ.

But if we are not careful, we can become discouraged in our duty as Christ's ambassadors. Our decaying and darkening world may appear to be beyond hope, causing us to remain isolated in the shaker or keep our light hidden in the drawer. That is why we need to stand firmly on a third conviction.

Conviction #3: God Is Able to Change the Culture

While we are called to be faithful ambassadors of Christ to our generation, ultimately we are not the ones who influence culture—God is. God is the one who wills and works according to His good pleasure (Phil. 2:13). And though He does not need us, God invites us to partner with Him in cultural change. Our responsibility is to make sure our salt remains salty and our light remains bright. How do we do that? We follow the same pattern laid down by Elijah.

First, *trust in the power of God's Word.* Elijah knew and trusted in the Word of God. When he prayed that it would not rain, he prayed a promise that God had already spoken. In Deuteronomy 11 and 28, the Lord warned the nation of Israel that if they turned aside and worshiped other gods, then He would turn off the faucet of heaven. They refused to believe God when He uttered those words in Moses's day, and they refused to believe Elijah when he repeated that pronouncement. But Elijah believed.

The same Word that Elijah knew and believed is still in effect today. Writing some eight hundred years after Elijah, the author of Hebrews declared, "The word of God is living and active and sharper than any two-edged sword, and piercing as far as the division of soul and spirit, of both joints and marrow, and able to judge the thoughts and intentions of the heart" (Heb. 4:12).

The Word of God is living and active because it is spoken by the living and creative Lord. God's Word cuts with exact precision, separating natural (fleshly) attitudes and motives from supernatural (spiritual) attitudes and motives. God's Word is sharper than any surgeon's scalpel.

It does spiritual surgery—something our culture is in dire need of today.

Think a moment about that surgeon's scalpel. The surgeon uses it to cut into a person's flesh. In the days before anesthesia, that was extremely painful! But the surgeon's motive for inflicting temporary pain was to bring about permanent healing. In the same way, God's Word is a knife that may hurt, but in the hands of the Great Physician it brings healing.

When you are simply sharing your opinions with other people, your power to change their attitudes and behavior is limited to your persuasive ability. But when you are proclaiming God's message from His Word, you are wielding an incredibly powerful instrument that can bring healing to individual lives and to the world.

Second, *practice the power of prayer*. James 5:17 attributes the lack of rain in Israel for those three and a half years to Elijah's prayer (1 Kings 17:1). This is why James could conclude, "the effective prayer of a righteous man can accomplish much" (v. 16). Elijah's righteousness was not self-righteousness. His righteousness was the result of knowing and obeying God's Word and from his time spent in prayer. This was what made Elijah so influential in his culture.

Unbelievers in our world have seen plenty of fakes and phonies. What they have not seen nearly enough is authentic and winsome Christianity lived out with wisdom and grace. If we are to influence our culture, we must begin on our knees. Show me a believer who is effective in public, and I will show you a believer who is effective in private. Show me an individual communicating persuasively to this generation, and I will show you an individual communicating passionately with God.

Third, *depend on the power of the Spirit.* The Holy Spirit is not mentioned by name in the story of Elijah, but the Spirit's fingerprints are all over the page. As we will see in later chapters, from the call for Elijah to retreat to the brook Cherith, to the raising of the widow's dead son, to the victory on Mount Carmel, to the still small voice in the wilderness, and to the chariot of fire that took Elijah to heaven, the Spirit of God hovered over Elijah's life.

Elijah's empowerment by the Holy Spirit was instrumental to his extraordinary life. Yet you and I have something Elijah never possessed: the permanent indwelling of the Holy Spirit. In Old Testament times the Spirit came upon and enabled followers of God to accomplish a specific task, but the Spirit was always temporary, never perpetual in a person's life. The Spirit came and went as God desired. This is why David, after his sin with Bathsheba, prayed, "Do not take Your Holy Spirit from me" (Ps. 51:11).

But when Jesus came, He promised a change in the Holy Spirit's ministry. Just before Jesus's arrest, trials, and death, He assured His disciples:

> I will ask the Father, and He will give you another Helper, that He may be with you forever; that is the Spirit of truth, whom the world cannot receive, because it does not see Him or know Him, but you know Him because He abides with you and will be in you. (John 14:16–17)

The idea of abiding and indwelling is that the Spirit takes up permanent residence in the life of every believer. And what will He do after establishing His home? Jesus said the Spirit "will convict the world concerning sin and righteousness and judgment" (John 16:8). The Spirit's job is to work through believers like you and me to convince others of their sin and their need for a Savior.

Don't miss this: God's Spirit performs His work not apart from Christians but through Christians. It is not that God *needs* us to accomplish His ultimate purpose in the world. He could have chosen any number of ways to communicate His message to a lost world (think skywriting or thunderous messages from heaven every day at noon). In fact, such direct communication from God to the entire world could have ensured that the message did not get muddled through fallible humans. But God chose to allow us to partner with Him in His effort to reconcile the world to Himself by pointing people to the Light of the World—Jesus Christ.

Additionally, the Holy Spirit is referred to as the One who restrains evil in the world (2 Thess. 2:6–7). The Holy Spirit is like the Hoover Dam, holding back a flood of chaos that will one day engulf the world. Again, the Holy Spirit does not perform that function apart from Christians but through Christians who are willing to stand up and push back against ungodliness in our world.

When you speak out at a school board meeting against a proposed immoral curriculum for students, when you oppose a proposal to legalize drug use in your state, when you vote against a candidate who supports late-term abortion, the Holy Spirit is working through you to restrain evil in the world.

You Never Know Whom You Are Influencing

Elijah's efforts to influence his culture were neither convenient nor comfortable. They never are—not when you are trying to stand for God in a sinful and corrupt generation. But even if you have to stand alone, I urge you to stand without bending, because you do not know whom you are influencing.

John Quincy Adams, the sixth president of the United States, was one of the earliest and most vocal proponents of the abolition of slavery in the United States. After his presidency, Adams served in the House of Representatives, where he almost singlehandedly fought and won a nine-year battle against the House's "gag rule" preventing congressmen from debating the slavery question. After his victory, Adams stunned the House—and the nation—by immediately demanding an extension of constitutional liberties to black Americans by abolishing slavery. The House voted him down. And regrettably, he would go to his grave without achieving the great goal of abolition.

However, while Adams made his impassioned but fruitless pleas for freedom, a relatively unknown congressman from Illinois was sitting at the back of the chamber, soaking in Adams's words. His name was Abraham Lincoln. Moved and emboldened by Adams's courage, Lincoln, in time, became the guiding hand behind the Emancipation Proclamation and the ultimate triumph of Adams's hope, when the Thirteenth Amendment was passed and ratified.

Lincoln, and Adams before him, knew that significance is not found in selling out to or isolating yourself from the culture. Significance is found in engaging the culture. Those who want to experience an extraordinary life are those who are willing to compassionately but boldly confront an ungodly world and say, "Thus says the living Lord."

John Adams reminds us that one person with courage is a majority.

Elijah reminds us that one believer empowered by the Word of God and the Spirit of God can truly change the world.

SECRET #3

Wait On God's Timing

Theodor Geisel did not particularly like children. But as Dr. Seuss—his literary alter ego—he knew how to reach children at their level. His whimsical drawings, silly made-up words, and memorable rhymes made him a staple of children's literature. Children learned about the ups and downs of life through characters such as the Cat in the Hat, Horton the elephant, the Lorax, and the Grinch.

One of Dr. Seuss's most interesting books is *Oh, the Places You'll Go!* It is the story of a boy starting out on the adventure of life. With shoes on his feet and a brain in his head, he can choose which paths to follow. But no matter which path he chooses, he eventually ends up in the waiting place.

The waiting place is where the doldrums extend over the horizon. It is a dreary and depressing place—at least the way Dr. Seuss describes it. Everyone is waiting for something insignificant to occur, like watching paint dry or grass grow.

According to Dr. Seuss, the waiting place is not the place anyone should aspire to be. Yet, according to God, the waiting place may be the perfect place to be.

> [God] gives strength to the weary,
> And to him who lacks might He increases power.
> Though youths grow weary and tired,
> And vigorous young men stumble badly,
> Yet those who wait for the LORD
> Will gain new strength;
> They will mount up with wings like eagles,
> They will run and not get tired,
> They will walk and not become weary.
> (Isa. 40:29–31)

When life grows dreary or you become weary of the rat race, God has strength to spare—and to share. God's abundance of strength can replace your abundance of weakness. All that is required is for you to "wait for the LORD"—for His replenishment of supernatural strength.

Those who desire to experience an extraordinary life learn the value of waiting on God's timing. Waiting time does not have to be wasted time. God often calls on us to take a timeout, because waiting has always been a part of God's plan for those He uses in a powerful way. God's most extraordinary servants have had to learn that significance is developed not on the playground of activity but during the quiet recesses. For example,

- Noah waited 120 years before feeling the first drop of predicted rain.

- Abraham and Sarah waited more than twenty years for the birth of Isaac.
- Moses waited forty years on the backside of the desert before leading the exodus.
- Paul waited three years in the Arabian desert before beginning his ministry.

"In life, God will always work sovereignly, strangely, and slowly," pastor and author Steve Farrar says. "He will take time, but He will not waste time. His delays are not necessarily His denials. And when He delays, He often doubles the mercy."[1] It is during these divine downtimes that God is at work transforming our lives.

Or, to put it in the words of Rick Warren: "When God wants to make a mushroom, he does it overnight, but when he wants to make a giant oak, he takes a hundred years. Great souls are grown through struggles and storms and seasons of suffering."[2]

Why God Makes Us Wait

Extraordinary people are grown through struggles and suffering—through waiting. If you find yourself in the waiting place, before pulling your hair out in frustration because God's clock seems to run at a glacial pace, consider these reasons that God makes us wait.

Waiting Reminds Us of Our Need for God

Most of us are eager to move quickly from a past failure to the next big thing God has planned for us. But after we experience a major failure in life, God often calls for a divine time-out so that we might reflect on the cause of the failure and renew our relationship with God.

At other times, however, God calls us to wait not because of failures but because of successes. When we are experiencing the blessings of God, we sometimes conclude that we deserve the success we are experiencing at work, in relationships, or in ministry. In Texas, we call this "getting too big for your britches." Before God can continue to use us, He sometimes has to bench us to remind us of our need for Him.

In his short career as the University of Texas's head football coach, Charlie Strong had to bench one of his all-star players, Malik Jefferson. Touted to become a Big 12 Defensive Player of the Year, the "Predator," as Jefferson was called, got too big for his britches after an outstanding performance in the 2016 season opening game against Notre Dame. In the weeks that followed, the Predator looked more like the prey, as offenses ran over and through him. Coach Strong benched him—and Jefferson got the message. You win and lose as a team, but each individual on the team must do his job. "I wasn't trying to get better," Jefferson later said. "I thought everything would be handed to me, and I had to realize you have to work for things."[3]

After a few weeks on the bench, Jefferson came back into the huddle and became the Predator once again.

Whenever we experience success in life, it is important for us to remember that whatever we accomplish *for* God, we accomplish *because of* God. As Paul reminded the Philippian Christians, "It is God who is at work within you, giving you the will and the power to achieve his purpose" (Phil.

2:13 Phillips). Occasionally, we must wait in time-out—or ride the bench—for God to remind us of that important truth.

Waiting Allows Us to Recharge Our Physical, Emotional, and Spiritual Batteries

Success gives us a shot of adrenaline—and like the Energizer Bunny, we believe we can go on and on and on. Unfortunately, if we keep going without taking a break, we discover that success can be draining. Eventually, even vigor gives way to weariness and stumbling—what an avid hiker friend of mine calls "dumb feet." At those times, when a hiker's feet are stumbling on the trail, threatening to send him careening off the mountain, he needs to sit down, drink some water and eat a snack, and allow his feet to rest.

Jesus's disciples experienced something like spiritual "dumb feet" after their rousing success of preaching, healing, and driving out demons. Jesus had divided His disciples into teams, and after a period of ministry they came to report "all that they had done and taught" (Mark 6:30). They had been faithful and done well. But Jesus knew that successful ministry leads to a never-ending cycle of ministry, until the inevitable comes—burnout. If time is not taken to rest and recharge, it is easy to develop spiritual "dumb feet." So Jesus told His disciples, "Come away by yourselves to a secluded place and rest a while" (v. 31).

We all experience times when we need to pull back from work and the hubbub of our daily schedules and take a break.

And if we will not do it voluntarily, then the Lord just might make us do it involuntarily.

Waiting Can Prepare Us for an Even Bigger Mission

After I finished college and married my wife, Amy, the legendary pastor Dr. W. A. Criswell hired me to serve as the youth pastor of First Baptist Church of Dallas. I was elated to have the opportunity to work under Dr. Criswell at the first megachurch in America, ministering to hundreds and hundreds of teenagers. Yet I knew God's ultimate plan was for me to serve as a senior pastor.

During the seven years I was on staff at First Dallas, I talked with pulpit committees of some fairly large congregations. However, nothing ever came of these discussions. Then, one day, I received a call from Lee Graham, chairman of the search committee of First Baptist Church of Eastland, Texas—a small town ninety miles west of Dallas. I had no interest in going to Eastland. Amy, on the other hand, was interested in at least having a conversation with Lee and the committee members. I finally agreed to meet with the committee. After the meeting, I was not that impressed, but Amy said, with tears streaming down her face, "Robert, I believe we are supposed to go to this church."

Within a month, we moved into the little parsonage of this county-seat church. I cannot describe the culture shock of moving from a major metropolitan city like Dallas to a small, rural town that claimed a population of 5,200. We had a highway that ran through the center of town, right by our home. On Friday afternoons, my younger daughter and I would sit outside on our porch and watch the cars go by—about one every twenty minutes. That was our entertainment.

Honestly, the first several years I was there, I did everything I could to go to a larger church. But God had a different plan for me. During the seven years I was in Eastland God taught me priceless lessons about leadership, ministering to people, and study (I had plenty of time for that!). As I look back over my spiritual journals from those years, I realize what a gift that experience was and how God was preparing me for my next assignment.

Elijah experienced something similar in his life. He had accomplished his first mission—to pronounce the judgment of no rain or dew on Israel (1 Kings 17:1)—a mission in and of itself that was no small thing. But compared to his next public assignment, which would be confronting 850 frenzied, sword-wielding Baal worshipers, his confrontation with Ahab was a relatively small challenge. After all, Ahab was a passive and henpecked man. Elijah had little to fear from the king. However, that could not be said of his wife Jezebel! She was the real threat. Ahab may have been a snake, but he was only a garden-variety snake. Jezebel was a true viper.

So, before throwing Elijah into Jezebel's pit with her Baal-worshiping priests, God sent His prophet to a waiting place to prepare him for the mission to come—just as He will probably do with you at some point in your life.

Training Camp for God's Servant

"Elijah was a man with a nature like ours," James 5:17 informs us. He had the same weaknesses and fears we do. He

91

stood against the corruption and idolatry of his day—the same kind of corruption that is present in our day. And Elijah did so with the same resource readily available to each one of us: faith. I am not talking about some undefined optimism that everything will turn out okay in the end. Elijah needed the kind of faith that could look a corrupt king or queen in the eye, declare God's judgment on their wickedness, and then enter a winner-take-all contest in which he would be outnumbered 850 to 1. That kind of steely faith can only be hardened and purified after it has endured God's crucible of testing.

Pastor and author Chuck Swindoll notes that Marine Corps recruits undergo a crucible of testing to earn the title United States Marine and the right to wear the eagle, globe, and anchor emblem (or EGA, as Marines call it). New recruits are shipped to either Paris Island or Camp Pendleton, where they suffer through thirteen weeks of drill instructors running, marching, and pushing them until they begin to think and function like Marines.

But that is just boot camp—the easy part. The "fun" is not over yet. Next, these Marines-in-training have to endure a fifty-four-hour marathon of forty-mile hikes, obstacle courses, and combat exercises—all accomplished on very little food and very little sleep. The Marines call it "the Crucible." The Crucible is what makes a Marine a Marine. Recruits who finish the Crucible are awarded their EGA and finally have the right to call themselves United States Marines.

Elijah would ultimately become an even more formidable warrior than any Marine, but God had to put him through a vigorous training program—first at the boot camp of Cherith and then through the crucible of Zarephath.[4]

Basic Training by the Brook

After Elijah's initial confrontation with Ahab, God told the prophet to leave Samaria and go to the wilderness. "The word of the LORD came to him, saying, 'Go away from here and turn eastward, and hide yourself by the brook Cherith, which is east of the Jordan'" (1 Kings 17:2–3).

Why would God send the one man in all of Israel willing to stand up to the godlessness that had gripped the nation to sit beside a small creek in the desert? I do not think it was for Elijah's protection. God was more than capable of ensuring that no harm came to His prophet without hiding him in the desert.

Instead, God reassigned Elijah to the wilderness for two other reasons. First, Elijah's withdrawal from the national scene was itself a judgment against the nation of Israel. The Hebrew word for "hide" in verse 3 could be translated, "Go away from here and turn eastward, and *remove* yourself by the brook Cherith."[5] In other words, for the time being, Elijah was to leave his public ministry behind.

One theologian has said that Elijah's temporary removal from the national life of Israel was God's judgment against the nation.[6] Just imagine what our country would be like if suddenly God told every preacher of His Word to stop preaching and go hide for a few years. Without the proclamation of God's Word, our nation would soon collapse under the weight of its own sin. The Old Testament prophet Amos predicted a day would come when the Israelites would experience a famine of the Word of God (Amos 8:11–12). Israel suffered under a physical famine by the word of Elijah; now they suffered under a spiritual famine without the word of Elijah.

But judgment was only one reason that God commanded Elijah to "hide" himself by Cherith. God would also use this parenthesis in Elijah's ministry to prepare him for a great future mission. By isolating him in that uncomfortable place, God was teaching Elijah to trust Him in ways he had never trusted before. This deepening of Elijah's faith was not optional but essential for the future assignment God had in mind for His prophet.

My own Cherith experience was my first pastorate, in that small county-seat town. During those seven years, I felt cut off from family members and lifelong friends in my hometown of Dallas. I was suddenly removed from the security of ministering in my home church, where people were willing to overlook the mistakes and shortcomings of a novice minister. Although not removed completely from ministry like Elijah, I was in a place of obscurity where I was forced to trust God like I never had before.

Perhaps you are in a similar place in your life in which you feel cut off from others and even from God. Your Cherith may be the result of

- the loss of a significant relationship due to death or desertion of another person,
- a moral failure in your life that continues to produce painful consequences,

- a poor decision in your finances or your career that has separated you from your dreams, or
- fulfilling the mundane—and often unrewarded—responsibilities of caring for your family.

Although your present circumstances make you feel cut off from the life you dreamed of, God is using this experience to cut down your reliance on anything or anyone other than Him so you might learn to trust God completely. Learning to depend upon God fully is vital for anyone who wants to experience an extraordinary life.

Skills for Spiritual Success

During Elijah's boot camp experience, God taught his servant three vital skills necessary for spiritual success—skills we must develop as well if we want to experience a significant life.

Cherith Teaches Us to Walk with God Daily

The path God calls us to walk is one of faith and obedience, not sight and independence. Paul encouraged the Corinthian believers with this truth: "we walk by faith, not by sight" (2 Cor. 5:7).

We used to live close to a lake. Every morning as I drove to our church in downtown Dallas, I often had to navigate through the fog produced by that large body of water. When the fog was especially thick, traffic crept along at a snail's pace. I had to drive "by faith, not by sight." And that meant slowing down.

God is not in the habit of revealing His entire plan for our life all at once. If He did, we would race forward without ever feeling the need to slow down, listen to His voice, and wait on His direction. While God does not unravel His entire blueprint for our lives, He can always be trusted to reveal to us the *next* thing we need to do. Every Christian who wants to experience an extraordinary life needs to answer the question, "What is the *next* thing God wants me to do?"

For Elijah, God's answer came through a simple command: "Go away from here and turn eastward, and hide yourself by the brook Cherith, which is east of the Jordan" (1 Kings 17:2–3). God did not reveal to Elijah what every day would be like at Cherith, the next phase of his training at Zarephath, or the daunting contest that awaited him on Mount Carmel. The Lord simply revealed to His servant what he was to do *next*.

What was true in Elijah's life is true in yours. Usually, God only reveals as much of His plan for your life as you need today. Do not worry about what He has in store for you in the next year, the next month, or even the next day. "Tomorrow will care for itself," Jesus said. "Each day has enough trouble of its own" (Matt. 6:34).

Cherith Teaches Us to Obey God Completely

When God recalled Elijah from the palace and redeployed him to the wilderness, he did not balk. Elijah did not dig in his heels and remind the Lord that He was the one who had dispatched him to Samaria on this risky mission in the first place. Nor did Elijah protest the unreasonableness of going into hiding when his influence was making such a difference in the culture. Instead, when the Lord told Elijah to pack his backpack for a camping trip, he obeyed instantly: "So he went and did according to the word of the LORD, for he went and lived by the brook Cherith, which is east of the Jordan" (1 Kings 17:5).

When our daughters were young, Amy and I tried to teach them the value of obeying the first time, every time. It did not always work. Sometimes, our commands were met with either "Why?" or an outright "No!" I remember once being on top of a mountain on a family vacation when my five-year-old started running toward the edge. Our cries for her to stop went unheeded, and the only reason she did not go over the side of the mountain was that I could outrun her (at least back then!).

Of course, it is not just children who struggle with obedience. I think about the honest confession of my friend and mentor Dr. Howard Hendricks, who said, "The Lord and I have a running argument. I constantly attempt to impress him with how much I know. He constantly seeks to impress me with how little I have obeyed."[7] If a godly leader like Howard Hendricks struggled with obedience, then why should you or I be surprised by our difficulty in obeying God immediately and completely?

However, Elijah not only preached God's Word to others but also practiced God's Word himself. When God spoke, Elijah listened and obeyed. God's prophet in hiding was a living illustration of what the New Testament writer James had in mind when he exhorted Christians to be "doers of the word, and not merely hearers who delude themselves" (James 1:22).

Immediate and complete obedience is often difficult, but it is also necessary to experience God's favor.

Cherith Teaches Us to Trust God Absolutely

God promised that He would take care of Elijah at Cherith. Though the means of God's provision seemed unusual, Elijah trusted God without reservation. The Lord said to Elijah, "It shall be that you will drink of the brook, and I have commanded the ravens to provide for you there" (1 Kings 17:4).

After Elijah found a spot to set up camp, the Lord dispatched ravens to feed His hungry prophet. Twice a day, morning and evening, those big black birds brought Elijah bread and meat, and he drank from the clear, clean water of Cherith (v. 6).

Every day Elijah experienced the truth one of Israel's kings had written years earlier:

> Trust in the LORD with all your heart
> And do not lean on your own understanding.
> In all your ways acknowledge Him,
> And He will make your paths straight. (Prov. 3:5–6)

If Elijah had chosen to "lean on his own understanding," then he would not have retreated to Cherith after his initial successful encounter with Ahab. Instead, he would have embarked on a speaking tour throughout Israel! He would have called the people back to faithfulness, cajoling the nation to repent from its idolatry. He probably would have immediately challenged the prophets of Baal to a showdown on

Mount Carmel. After all, Elijah was a hot commodity in Israel. Everyone was talking about this up-and-coming unknown prophet who had the courage to confront the most powerful person in the nation.

But that was the very thing God *did not* want Elijah to do—not at that time, anyway. God wanted His prophet to regroup, rethink, and renew his soul. And in Elijah's process of waiting for his next assignment and trusting the Lord to provide for his needs, God would refine and strengthen his faith.

Cherith seems like an odd place for a successful prophet to wait, but it was exactly the place where God wanted Elijah.

The Waiting Place

What about you? Are you where God wants you to be right now—even if it is in the waiting place? If so, He will provide. Not necessarily all at once, but day by day. Learn the lesson Elijah learned: trust the Giver of gifts more than the gifts themselves.

Notice the Lord did not send Elijah to a river but to a brook. Anyone who has ever been to Israel, especially east of the Jordan, knows just how dry and dusty it can get in that wilderness. Water is a life-or-death commodity. At any moment, the water in the brook could evaporate.

But this is how God often works. He rarely places us in the lap of luxury, where abundance threatens to turn our affections away from Him and toward the world. And He never places us next to rivers when He is testing us, preparing us for something significant. In those cases, He places us next to a trickling brook, a place where we can learn to trust the One who blesses and not the blessing.

Also, notice that God fed Elijah from the beaks of ravens. Ravens are considered the clown jesters of the bird world. They love to slide down snow banks and play games. In the wild, they play catch-me-if-you-can with wolves. Maybe because ravens are practical jokers, they are not the most reliable creatures on which to depend for your sustenance! Yet the Lord chose ravens to provide for Elijah's daily meals. Every day Elijah was forced to trust God to use these most unlikely and unreliable creatures to provide for his needs.

A colleague of mine underwent a two-year Cherith-like experience when he was laid off from his job. Though his wife taught school, her income was not enough to pay the mortgage, buy groceries, and keep three kids in college. They had to completely trust God for the difference and walk in faith day by day. He was able to cobble together enough work to cover their bills . . . until the bottom fell out of their hot water heater. They did not have the money to cover this additional expense. But God had shown Himself faithful thus far in paying their bills, so they believed He would show Himself faithful in replacing their hot water heater. And He did! God sent one of His ravens to provide the necessary funds to buy a new hot water heater and to pay the plumber to install it.

Maybe you are in a Cherith-like situation in which you are being forced to trust God to provide for your material or emotional needs. Remember, the same God who created the brook and directed the ravens that sustained Elijah is in control of the people and the circumstances that can meet your most pressing need.

God could have used His servant Obadiah to care for Elijah. After all, Obadiah had already hidden one hundred prophets in a cave and given them bread and water (1 Kings 18:4, 13). But God provided Elijah with an even better cuisine: bread, water, and *meat*!

That is the way it is with the Lord. When we are forced to trust Him only, He is able to provide "far more abundantly beyond all that we ask or think" (Eph. 3:20). But to bless us with abundance, God must first put us in a place where we are solely dependent on Him. That way, when God's blessings start flowing into our lives, there is no doubt about their source.

We do not know how long Elijah camped by the brook Cherith, perhaps up to six months. However, we do know that as the drought and famine deepened in Israel—the same one Elijah had predicted—the brook transformed from a steady flow to a trickle, from a trickle to a few muddy pools, and from a few muddy pools to a parched and rocky creek bed (1 Kings 17:7).

After the water ran out, Elijah's response was remarkable. He did not take matters into his own hands. He did not pack his bags and look for another brook. He remained right where he was, sitting beside the dried-up Cherith, because that was where the Lord had called him. He would wait until God called him to some other place, until "the word of the LORD came to him" again (v. 8).

This is a hard lesson we all must learn. Trusting God means remaining where God has placed us until He tells us to move. While I was experiencing my own Cherith in that small west Texas town, there were many times—especially in the early years—when I was looking for any opportunity to leave. But a wise mentor asked me, "Do you believe God led you there?" "There was no doubt He did," I replied. My mentor responded, "Then the same God who led you there will lead you from there—when He's ready."

If you are convinced God has called you to a particular place—a job, a church, or a relationship—then stay there until God moves you. As another wise friend said to me in a different situation, "Sometimes it takes more faith to stay somewhere than it takes to go somewhere." Elijah had the faith to stay at Cherith and learn invaluable lessons that would prepare him for an extraordinary life.

But his Cherith experience did not last indefinitely—and neither will yours. Eventually, God was ready for phase two of His servant's training regimen.

Crucible by the Sea

No sooner had Elijah survived God's boot camp by the brook Cherith than the Lord commanded him to go to "Zarephath, which belongs to Sidon, and stay there" (1 Kings 17:9). And there in Zarephath Elijah would face a period of even more intense training for his future mission.

To reach Zarephath, Elijah had to travel across almost one hundred miles of hostile territory. The trip was especially dangerous since Queen Jezebel had put a price on his head—and bounty hunters were looking to collect.[8] However, worse than that, Zarephath was ground zero for Baal worship. Located just eight miles south of Sidon—Jezebel's hometown—Zarephath was the site of a smelting plant that produced the metal to manufacture the idols of Baal. The name *Zarephath* comes from a Hebrew verb meaning "to melt" or "to smelt." The noun form of the word means "crucible."

While Cherith represents the *testing* of Elijah's faith, Zarephath represents the *refining* of Elijah's faith. In the refining process, gold or other metals are melted under intense heat. Impurities rise to the surface and are removed. Then the molten liquid is poured into a mold of the object the craftsperson wishes to make. And in the case of what was being manufactured in Zarephath, that object was the idol Baal.

The purpose of Cherith was to cut Elijah down—to test whether he would walk with the Lord daily, obey the Lord completely, and trust the Lord absolutely. The purpose of Zarephath was to "melt" Elijah down so that any impurities in his faith could be removed and he might be poured into the mold God had designed for him.

What God did for Elijah He must do for anyone who desires to be significantly used by Him. Just as the Lord tests our faith in our own personal boot camps, He refines our faith in our own personal crucibles. Specifically, God refines three vital qualities for anyone desiring to live an extraordinary life: humility, contentment, and gentleness.

Zarephath Refines Our Humility

Just as God did not send Elijah to a river but to a brook (at Cherith), so the Lord did not send Elijah to a wealthy sea merchant but to a poor widow (at Zarephath). "Arise, go to Zarephath, which belongs to Sidon, and stay there; behold, I have commanded a widow there to provide for you" (1 Kings 17:9).

Zarephath was not just another test of obedience; it was also a test of humility. To be cared for by a poor widow who did not have enough to meet her own needs must have been a humbling assignment for a man who only months earlier had stood in the presence of the king of Israel. But this experience was a lesson in Humility 101—a basic course for anyone wanting to be used mightily by God.

Beyond developing humility in Elijah, the Lord was accomplishing something else by sending His prophet to a Gentile widow. This was yet another sign of God's judgment against the Israelites. After all, on his one-hundred-mile journey from Cherith to Zarephath, Elijah passed countless widows in Israel, yet the Lord did not permit any of them to care for His servant. That honor went to a *Gentile* widow. This was precisely the point Jesus made in Luke 4:25–26: "I say to you in truth, there were many widows in Israel in the days of Elijah, when the sky was shut up for three years and six months, when a great famine came over all the land; and yet Elijah was sent to none of them, but only to Zarephath, in the land of Sidon, to a woman who was a widow."

God extended the privilege of knowing Him—and the abundance of life that comes through a relationship with the living Lord—to a Gentile widow. But God could only extend that invitation through a messenger like Elijah, who was willing to humble himself to become God's mouthpiece.

The humbling experience of having to entrust his care to a poor widow (and a Gentile widow at that!) forced Elijah to empty himself of pride so he could be the vessel God could use for His purpose. Even Jesus "emptied Himself" of the privileges of heaven to be God's instrument to bring salvation to the world (Phil. 2:5–8).

If God's plan for His servant Elijah and His Son, Jesus, included experiences that forced them to empty themselves of any positions or privileges they could boast about, then do not be surprised when God designs similar experiences for you.

Zarephath Refines Our Contentment

Once Elijah arrived at the gates of Zarephath, he saw a woman collecting wood. The prophet, no doubt thirsty and famished after his one-hundred-mile trek, had a simple request: "Please get me a little water in a jar, that I may drink. . . . Please bring me a piece of bread in your hand" (1 Kings 17:10–11).

Providing water was no problem, but offering Elijah bread—well, that was a *big* problem. It just so happened that the widow had been preparing the last meal for her son and herself before they ran completely out of food. After that, she and her son would slowly starve to death.

Today we have Social Security and other agencies to care for the needs of widows. For Christians, caring for widows is an indication of how healthy our faith is. James said, "Pure and undefiled religion in the sight of our God and Father is this: to visit orphans and widows in their distress" (James 1:27). Our church has a vibrant ministry to our nearly four hundred widows.

But in Elijah's day there were no financial safety nets for widows—and no churches. Nevertheless, Elijah assured the widow that God would provide. But God's provision would come only after the widow demonstrated her faith by her obedience to God's command. Many times, we try to make a deal with God: "If You will meet my need, *then* I will obey your command." God's response? "No, you go first! You obey my command, and *then* I'll meet your need!"

It was the same with the widow. Elijah relayed God's instruction and promise to her. God wanted her to use her last portion of flour to feed Elijah. Then God would keep her flour bowl full so that she and her son would have plenty to eat. She obeyed, and her bowl ran over with flour!

> She and [her son] and her household ate for many days. The bowl of flour was not exhausted nor did the jar of oil become empty, according to the word of the LORD which he spoke through Elijah. (1 Kings 17:15–16)

According to James 5:17, the drought lasted "three years and six months." If Elijah stayed at Cherith for the first six months, then he spent the remaining three years at the widow's home in Zarephath, where he ate the same meal every day. Now, I like salmon and broccoli for lunch, but I do not think I would like it *every* day. But God promised only to keep the widow's bowl full of flour and her jar full of oil—and that was it. He made no promise that her pantry and refrigerator would be filled with hamburger meat, sirloin steaks, or Häagen-Dazs ice cream! There wasn't even enough flour and oil to last beyond the needs of that day. Instead, God provided just enough food—the same food—to meet their needs for each day.

This was exactly how God provided for the people of Israel in the wilderness. He provided enough manna for each day, and everyone ate until they were satisfied . . . until they became dissatisfied and grumbled against the Lord. The daily menu consisted of manna—manna soup, manna soufflé, and ba-manna bread. They wanted something different, so God sent them quail. And then they got sick of quail, complained again, and were struck with a severe plague while the quail "was still between their teeth" (Num. 11:33).

Elijah did not make that mistake. He refused to grumble against the Lord for providing the same meal at breakfast, lunch, and dinner every day for three years. Instead, he allowed those years in Zarephath to teach him how—as the apostle Paul would write many centuries later—"to be content in whatever circumstances I am" (Phil. 4:11).

Contentment doesn't come easily for any of us (which is why Paul said he had to learn to be content). All of us naturally have an insatiable desire for "more" or "different." As long as we are consumed with earning more money, living in a better neighborhood, working at a higher paying job, or having a more supportive mate, we will never focus on fulfilling the unique purpose God has for our lives. It took three years of bread and water at Zarephath to quench Elijah's desire for "more" and "different."

Do not be surprised if God plans a similar experience in which you are forced to develop the invaluable quality of contentment.

Zarephath Refines Our Gentleness

After teaching Elijah how to be content with His provisions, God turned up the heat and put His servant through one more refining experience. The widow's son died unexpectedly, and she was quick to blame her new houseguest for the tragedy. "What do I have to do with you, O man of God?" she asked. "You have come to me to bring my iniquity to remembrance and to put my son to death!" (1 Kings 17:18).

I do not know exactly what sin she had in mind, resulting in her son's death. Perhaps her son had been the result of an immoral relationship. Or maybe she had been a Baal worshiper prior to Elijah's arrival. Whatever the case, she believed God was punishing her for some sin. And Elijah's presence became a twisting of the knife in her heart. After all, he was a "man of God," and she was a sinful woman.

Elijah did not rebuke her for her sin or her lack of faith. He did not say, "You got that right, sister. I *am* a man of God and you are a sinner!" Rather, Elijah put into practice Proverbs 15:1: "A gentle answer turns away wrath." This firebrand who earlier had confronted Ahab and pronounced judgment on Israel's idolatry gently said to her, "Give me your son" (1 Kings 17:19).

Elijah carried the dead body to the upper room and laid him on the bed. He wept before the Lord, pleading, "O Lord my God, have You also brought calamity to the widow with whom I am staying, by causing her son to die?" (v. 20).

Elijah then stretched himself out over the body—nose to nose, toes to toes—as if to transfer his life to the boy. Then he prayed, "O Lord my God, I pray You, let this child's life return to him" (v. 21). He did this three times. The third time, the Lord answered, and "the life of the child returned to him and he revived" (v. 22).

How did Elijah know God would answer his prayer? He didn't. Until this time no one had ever come back to life after death. This was the first time God had resuscitated a dead body. Elijah did not have precedent to rely on. No *How to Pray Someone Back to Life* manual was available for purchase. All Elijah had was faith—the unshakable belief that nothing is impossible for the living Lord.[9]

However, what is most striking to me is not so much Elijah's audacious request and God's supernatural answer but the manner in which Elijah made the request. The widow blamed Elijah for her son's death—and by implication she blamed the God Elijah represented.

Yet Elijah refused to respond in anger to the unfair accusation. Instead, he dealt gently with her anguish and took up her case before God. He prayed, "O LORD my God, why have you brought tragedy to this widow who has opened her home to me, causing her son to die? . . . O LORD my God, please let this child's life return to him" (1 Kings 17:20–21 NLT).

It takes a gentle and compassionate person to absorb someone else's anger—especially when you are innocent of their charges—and to make their grief your own. Yet this is what Elijah did. When he took her boy out of her arms, he took her grief—her anger, confusion, and doubts—and made them his own. And he poured them out before the only One who could do something about it.

The miracle of restored life, coupled with Elijah's gentleness, caused the widow to embrace the Lord and His Word. She said, "Now I know that you are a man of God and that the word of the LORD in your mouth is truth" (v. 24).

Once again, we see Elijah living out the unique purpose for which God had placed him on earth: proving to the world that "the Lord is God"—just as Elijah's name predicted.

The Gift of Gentleness

Gentleness—a genuine compassionate concern for others—is the mark of anyone who wants to be used of God in an extraordinary way. Author Peggy Noonan illustrates what gentleness looks like in an encounter her former boss President Ronald Reagan had with a widow.

Frances Green was an eighty-three-year-old widow living on Social Security. Every year, she sent one dollar to the Republican National Committee. One day she received an RNC fund-raising letter inviting her to visit the White House and meet President Reagan. She failed to notice the suggestion of a sizable donation. She thought the RNC had sent her the invitation because they appreciated her annual dollar.

Scraping together every cent she could, she took a four-day train trip from Daley City, California, to Washington, DC. She arrived at the White House gate at the appointed time, but the Secret Service guard could not find her name on the list and would not let her in. Heartbroken, she did not know what to do. A compassionate Ford Motor Company executive who witnessed the exchange pulled her aside and asked her to meet him at the White House gate on Tuesday morning at nine.

When Tuesday arrived, it was a busy news day—that morning Attorney General Ed Meese had resigned and a military action was taking place abroad. The Ford executive, having provided White House officials with the information about Frances the day before, gave Mrs. Green a tour of the White House and then took her to the Oval Office, sure that the president would have no time for her. But when the Ford executive peeked in, Reagan waved him in. Frances Green followed.

When Reagan saw Mrs. Green, he called out, "Frances! Those darn computers, they fouled up again! If I'd known you were coming I would have come out there to get you myself." They sat in the Oval Office and talked of California and days gone by.

Noonan, Reagan's biographer, wrote, "If you say on a day like that it was time wasted, there are a lot of people who'd say, Oh no it wasn't. No it wasn't."[10] Time is never wasted when we exhibit gentleness or contentment or humility or trust or obedience—qualities that can only be learned during our time in Cherith and Zarephath.

And qualities that are essential to experiencing the extraordinary life.

Burn the Ships

Spanish explorer and treasure seeker Hernán Cortés landed in Mexico on April 22, 1519—Good Friday—in search of gold and to claim the land for God. Setting foot on the beach, Cortés established Villa Rica de la Vera Cruz (Rich Village of the True Cross). Arriving in Mexico at the height of the Aztec kingdom, whose powerful king was Montezuma, Cortés devised a bold plan to fill Spanish coffers and convert the people to Catholicism. He would march his men into the country, conquer Tenochtitlan, Montezuma's capital city, and take Montezuma dead or alive.

But this was no simple task. The distance from Villa Rica to Tenochtitlan was some two hundred cactus-filled and snake-infested miles. Cortés and his men would have to traverse unfamiliar ground, surrounded by hostile natives, with no supply line to provide food and water. Success was sketchy; failure was likely.

With the dangers of the unknown before them, Cortés did the unthinkable to keep his men from fleeing to the safety of

Cuba. He ordered the master of his ships to sail nine of the twelve vessels onto the beach. And then, according to legend, Cortés gave the order to burn the ships.[1] The expedition "had nothing to rely on," Cortés later wrote, "apart from their own hands, and the assurance that they would conquer and win the land, or die in the attempt."[2]

"Burn the ships" has become a metaphor for any decision where retreat is no longer an option. It is a point of no return. Although these kinds of decisions do not come along every day, when they do, they are life-changing. For example:

- Should I marry this person and forsake all others?
- Should I have children and forgo my life of complete independence?
- Should I accept this new job offer in a different city that may or may not work out?
- Should I commit my life completely to obeying God regardless of the short-term consequences?

Answers to any of these questions can be life-altering. But your answer to the last question carries eternal consequences. And since your answer to this question is irrevocable on the other side of the grave—the ultimate point of no return—you want to get it right on this side of the grave.

A Culture in Chaos

Getting the burn-the-ships question about your commitment to God correct is becoming more of a challenge in our current culture. Globalization and multiculturalism have introduced us to all sorts of weird, wild, and wacky religious ideas. And secularism has been unrelenting in its assault on traditional biblical beliefs, drumming into the uninformed the idea that Christianity should be confined to one's personal life and that Christians should cease trying to change public opinion or behavior.

In our postmodern and post-Christian culture, citizens no longer share common ideas of right and wrong based on God's unchangeable Word. Our society is not only unaffected by God's truth but it is completely unfamiliar with it. No wonder our culture is drowning in violence, immorality, and utter disregard for God. As Proverbs 29:18 warns, "Where there is no revelation [literally, a word from God], people cast off restraint" (NIV).

God placed His servant Elijah in the middle of a similar culture. The pagan influence of Ahab and Jezebel flourished in a nation that had arrogantly separated itself from its spiritual heritage. This is not to say that the people were not spiritual. But their spirituality can be better described as mysticism—a synchronistic blend of God worship and Baal worship—rather than biblical orthodoxy.

Just this week, a television reporter told me after an interview, "I'm a very spiritual person. I just don't know anything about the Bible." That was the Israelites. Their faith was rooted not in theological truth but in fear and fanaticism, which led them to the altar of Baal. Because the Israelites rejected what they knew to be true and embraced what they knew to be false, God punished them with three and a half years of drought and famine. The people of Israel were living illustrations of Jeremiah 2:19:

"Your wickedness will punish you;
   your backsliding will rebuke you.
Consider then and realize
   how evil and bitter it is for you
when you forsake the LORD your God
   and have no awe of me,"
      declares the Lord, the LORD Almighty. (NIV)

God is not one to be trifled with. When it comes to making decisions about your relationship with Him, it is best to burn your ships and commit yourself completely to Him, just as Moses and Jesus commanded: "The Lord our God is one Lord; and you shall love the Lord your God with *all* your heart, and with *all* your soul, and with *all* your mind, and with *all* your strength" (Deut. 6:4–5; Mark 12:29–30).

Elijah's Burn-the-Ships Message—Follow God Completely

Jesus's message in Mark 12:30 was the essence of Elijah's message in 1 Kings 18:21. Standing on Mount Carmel, getting ready to do battle with the prophets of Baal, God's prophet said to the people, "If the LORD is God, follow Him."

The overarching issue in 1 Kings 18 is the question, "Who is the true God: the Lord or Baal?" Remember, the Israelites had not totally rejected God. Instead, they were trying to blend the worship of God with the worship of Baal. They wanted to experience the best of both religions rather than embrace one or the other completely.

The Israelites were like many Christians today who think of the world's religions and philosophies as a spiritual buffet from which they can pick and choose. Accept what is most appealing; reject what is least appealing. Scratch beneath the surface of many Christians' faith and you will find it to be a strange mixture: one part biblical Christianity, two parts mysticism, one part positive thinking—all sprinkled with a pinch of American patriotism.

Elijah declared that the Israelites could no longer straddle the fence. It was time for a burn-the-ships decision: "How long will you hesitate between two opinions? If the Lord is God, follow Him; but if Baal, follow him" (1 Kings 18:21).

Elijah challenged the Israelites to decide what they really believed and to commit themselves to it totally. He was saying to the people, "If the Lord is God, then obey all His commands and forsake Baal completely. But if you think Baal is God, then commit yourself to him and forget trying to follow the Lord."

Like the Israelites, many Christians today are trying to straddle the fence between following God and following their idol of choice—not necessarily some figurine made of wood or metal, but people or objects we love more than we love God. Popular idols today include money, sex, career, and relationships. None of these is wrong in and of itself—until it becomes the major focus of your life.

Most Christians are not comfortable totally forsaking God and devoting all their attention toward their idol, so—like the Israelites—they try to worship both of their "gods." The result? They never fully experience the benefit of either "god" because of a halfhearted commitment. If Elijah were speaking to us today, he would say, "If money, sex, or your career is what you really love, then give yourself completely to it and forget all this Jesus stuff. But if you believe God is who He says He is, then devote yourself completely to Him. It's time to burn the ships."

After enduring three and a half years of God's judgment of drought, the people of Israel were still trying to follow Baal and God. So the Lord sent Elijah with a message: there would be a winner-takes-all showdown between God and Baal, to see who was really God. Before that climactic battle on Mount Carmel, however—which we will look at in detail in Secret #5—Elijah encountered Obadiah, Ahab, and the people of Israel. Each illustrates a different response to the burn-the-ships challenge of total commitment.

Elijah: Faithful and Fearless

Until you are completely committed, you can experience no true greatness or significance in life. Someone once said, "Set yourself on fire for God, and people will come from miles around to see you burn."

Elijah was a man who burned white-hot for God. After being refined by the Lord at Cherith and Zarephath, Elijah faithfully and fearlessly followed Him.

Elijah Followed God Faithfully

Elijah followed God faithfully. He had a steely resolve to transform his culture rather than conform to his culture (Rom. 12:1–2). How did Elijah keep from being conformed to the world? He made obeying God—rather than pleasing people—the focus of his life.

Elijah was more concerned about what God thought than about what Ahab thought. That laserlike focus kept Elijah from becoming a conformer to culture and turned him into a transformer of culture.

Elijah Obeyed God Fearlessly

Elijah also obeyed God fearlessly. Once Elijah was sure he had heard God's voice, he moved forward without looking back. Elijah's chariot did not have an "R" on the transmission—it moved in only one direction: forward! For Elijah that meant obedience to whatever call the Lord placed on him, whether to confront an evil king, to hide himself by a brook, or to live with a Gentile widow and her son. That fearless obedience would eventually lead Elijah to the summit of Mount Carmel and a showdown with the prophets of Baal.

For you, following God fearlessly may mean moving forward by:

- taking the first step and picking up the phone to heal a fractured relationship,
- breaking off a relationship that is hazardous to your spiritual health,
- saying yes to a job offer that is risky but obviously from God, or
- making a sacrificial financial gift to God's work even though it seems absurd.

When I think of someone who illustrates Elijah's total commitment to faithfully and fearlessly follow God, I think of William Borden. His father made a fortune in the silver mines of Colorado, which young William would inherit one day. But a trip around the world—a high school graduation gift from his father—changed all that. On his journey William saw the magnificent sights of Europe, the Middle East, and Asia, but also the despair and brokenness of many people who lived around the world. God was at work in William's heart. And a growing sense of calling became clear—he would sacrifice an affluent life as a businessman in Chicago for a plain life as a missionary in China. When a friend suggested that William was throwing his life away, he wrote in his Bible, "No reserves."

William went on to study at Yale University, where he threw himself into evangelizing his fellow students and helping the poor and destitute in New Haven, Connecticut. It was at Yale where his missionary zeal focused on the Muslim Kansu people in China. Graduating from Yale, William was offered many lucrative jobs, including one in the family business. He turned them all down and wrote in his Bible, "No retreats."

William enrolled at Princeton Seminary to further his theological studies. And with his eyes firmly fixed on the Kansu people, upon graduation he sailed for China. Because he was hoping to work with Muslims, he stopped in Egypt to study Arabic. While in Egypt, William contracted cerebral meningitis. Within a month he was dead. He was twenty-five years old.

It is said that when William's mother discovered his Bible after his death, she found the phrases he had written and dated in the back: "No reserves. No retreats." But there was a third phrase. As he lay dying in an Egyptian hospital, Borden had written, "No regrets."

William Borden had burned his ships—his wealth, his position, and his privilege—in favor of saying yes to Jesus's call.

Elijah had done the same. He answered God's call and never turned back. But not everyone in Israel was as committed to faithfully and fearlessly following God. Obadiah, King Ahab's servant, was faithful to the Lord, but his commitment to God was compromised by fear.

Obadiah: Faithful but Fearful

Some people are truly committed to following God, but they want to keep their commitment solely between themselves and the Almighty. Why does anyone else need to know? They have deluded themselves into thinking that they can be more effective representatives for God in their school, workplace, or family if they operate as secret saints. That was the case with one of Elijah's contemporaries, a man named Obadiah (not to be confused with the prophet of the same name who has his own book in the Old Testament).

As one of King Ahab's servants, Obadiah was tasked with watching over the king's household, which included Ahab's palace, estates, and livestock (1 Kings 18:3). We might think of him like the chief usher of the White House. All housekeeping, cooking, serving, and groundskeeping staff answered to him.

When Elijah first encountered Obadiah, he was searching for water and food for Ahab's livestock—not an easy task given the severe drought that had devastated the land. Baal—King Ahab's deity of choice—was supposed to be the weather god, the one who should have brought rain to end the drought. Yet there had been no rain for over three years.

However, during this same period, Obadiah had secretly provided water, food, and protection for one hundred of God's prophets—prophets that Queen Jezebel was trying to exterminate (v. 4). Obadiah's name means "servant of Jehovah," and he served God faithfully, but he did so fearfully—in secret.

Elijah had one simple request for Obadiah: "Go, say to your master, 'Behold, Elijah is here'" (v. 8). But instead of running off and finding the king, who had been looking for Elijah for three and a half years, Obadiah shook in his sandals.

> What have I done to deserve this? Ahab will kill me. As surely as your GOD lives, there isn't a country or kingdom where my master hasn't sent out search parties looking for you. . . . The minute I leave you the Spirit of GOD will whisk you away to who knows where. Then when I report to Ahab, you'll have disappeared and Ahab will kill me. (1 Kings 18:9–12 Message)

Obadiah was afraid that if he reported to the king that he had found Elijah—public enemy number one—the prophet would disappear, and Obadiah would be left to endure the king's wrath. But beyond that, Obadiah did not want to reveal to Ahab that he was a follower of God. Obadiah had found a comfortable compromise between his faith and his work. He lived a double life as a faithful follower of God (secretly) and a faithful servant of Ahab (publicly). Obadiah had not yet burned his ships and declared his commitment to God openly. And now that Elijah was forcing him to do so, Obadiah feared for his life.

Like Obadiah, it is easy to rationalize our compromises and try to remain a secret follower of God, often telling ourselves:

- "If I challenge my teacher about his inaccurate portrayal of Christian beliefs, I might offend him and other students."

- "If I protest this ungodly policy at work, I could lose my job and not be able to provide for my family—as the Bible commands."
- "If I am open about my commitment to Christ, I might turn off my spouse and lose my opportunity to influence him or her."

Obadiah's fear had so diluted his faith that his life had lost its effectiveness. Whenever our faith "loses its saltiness," as Jesus said (Matt. 5:13 NIV), we become useless in transforming the world around us.

Ahab: Faithless and Fearless

Because the capital city was the heart of Baal worship in Israel, "the famine was severe in Samaria" (1 Kings 18:2). It was so severe that Ahab feared he would lose his livestock. Looking for food and water for his royal herd, Ahab sent Obadiah in one direction while he went searching in the opposite direction. He said, "Perhaps we will find grass to keep the horses and mules alive, and not have to kill some of the cattle" (v. 5).

Just as a golfer bends down and plucks a blade of grass and lets it go to see which way the wind blows, so Ahab's words reveal the direction of his heart. Yes, animals are important, but they are not more important than people. As tragic as the deaths of the nation's livestock were, the human suffering was nearly unimaginable. Families slowly and painfully died of starvation and dehydration. Disease ran rampant throughout the nation. Children walked around with sunken eyes, sunken cheeks, and bloated bellies.

Israel's situation at the time was like the severe famines we have seen hit modern-day Ethiopia or Somalia. And just like the despots and tyrants in some countries today, Ahab saw how much his people suffered . . . and did nothing. His concern was for his cattle, not his people.

What a contrast to David, who thought only of his people when the Lord punished the nation because of David's lack of trust in God. Confessing his iniquity, David prayed, "Behold, it is I who have sinned, and it is I who have done wrong; but these sheep [the people], what have they done? Please let Your hand be against me and against my father's house" (2 Sam. 24:17).

David's prayer is the appropriate response of a sinful—but regenerate—leader. That was not Ahab. Ahab knew the drought and famine were the result of divine judgment for leading the people into idolatry. But he did not soften his heart and repent like David. Rather, he hardened his heart toward God and toward God's people, caring only for his livestock. It is true: when the wicked rule, the people suffer. And Ahab's people suffered greatly.

As the drought deepened, Ahab's hatred of God and His prophets intensified. Instead of repenting of the sin of idolatry, Ahab multiplied his wickedness by allowing Jezebel to commission bounty hunters to murder God's prophets (1 Kings 18:4). The days were desperate and dangerous. And it was in these dark times when "the word of the LORD came to Elijah . . . saying, 'Go, show yourself to Ahab'" (v. 1).

It is the mark of an unrepentant and proud sinner to blame someone else for the fact that he or she is suffering divine punishment. And that is exactly what Ahab was and what he did. When he met Elijah, he cursed God's prophet: "Is this you, you troubler of Israel?" (v. 17).

The Hebrew word translated "troubler" means "to bring calamity." Sometimes the word is used to refer to a snake.[3] When Ahab called Elijah a "troubler," it was another way of saying, "Is this you, you sorry snake in the grass?"

You can understand why Ahab reacted this way. After all, it was Elijah who, three and a half years earlier, had pronounced that no rain would fall and no dew would come. Creeks had dried up. Cisterns were empty. The rotting carcasses of animals littered the land. Flies filled the air. And the cemeteries were overflowing with dead bodies. No wonder Ahab greeted Elijah with poisonous words: "You viper that poisons everything! You are the cause of all this trouble—all this drought, disease, and death."

It took courage for Elijah to confront Ahab. It took even more courage to shift the blame back to Ahab, where it squarely belonged. "I have not troubled Israel, but you and your father's house have, because you have forsaken the commandments of the LORD and you have followed the Baals" (1 Kings 18:18).

Ahab—and all of the Israelites—needed a reminder that the God of heaven is the supreme God. And Elijah was just the man to deliver the message. Elijah commanded Ahab to gather the people, the 450 prophets of Baal, and the four hundred prophets of Asherah and meet him on top of Mount Carmel for a demonstration of divine power—a test to see whether the Lord or Baal was the true God.

The People: Faithless and Fearful

Because God controls His foes as well as His friends, Ahab complied with Elijah's command to gather the people for the showdown in Samaria. Once everyone had gathered at Mount Carmel, Elijah challenged the Israelites: "How long will you hesitate between two opinions? If the LORD is God, follow Him; but if Baal, follow him" (1 Kings 18:21).

The Hebrew word translated "hesitate" means to "hop" or "limp." Literally, Elijah said, "How long will you hop between two forks [in the road]?" Some translate the word as "totter," like a drunkard who weaves to one side of the street and then to the other side.

The people of Israel had not rejected God and accepted Baal completely. Rather, they embraced the false notion that they could worship both God and Baal. They had adopted a both/and mind-set. In other words, they thought they could sacrifice their children to Baal on Friday and sacrifice a lamb to Jehovah on Saturday!

Honestly, Baal worship offered some attractive alternatives to God worship. First, it carried official and royal approval—signed and sealed by the king and queen. Power is persuasive, especially power wielded at the point of the sword. So if you want to get along, go along.

Second, Baal worship appealed to felt needs. Baal was the god who brought rain, which produced grain, oil, and wine. He supposedly healed the sick and raised the dead. And he was the god of human and animal fertility. Of course, Baal never actually accomplished any of those things—and the three-and-a-half-year drought proved that.

However, Baal worship appealed to something more powerful than felt needs—it satisfied carnal desires. As one scholar notes, Baal allowed worshipers to worship with all of their glands. Married or not, Baal followers would engage with a temple prostitute who helped them worship body and soul.[4]

Hopping between God and Baal, the people had their feet planted solidly in midair. They were double-minded, which is dangerous, and double-hearted, which is disastrous. As Jesus bluntly noted, "He who is not with Me is against Me, and he who does not gather with Me scatters" (Matt. 12:30). So Elijah challenged the people to burn their ships of double-mindedness and double-heartedness and make an either/or decision: either the Lord is God or Baal is God. Period!

This was not a new and strange message. Ever since the beginning of time, God has made it clear that He alone is God and that His people must obey His commands completely. Hundreds of years earlier, Joshua issued this challenge to the Israelites, whom he had led into the Promised Land:

> Now, therefore, fear the LORD and serve Him in sincerity and truth; and put away the gods which your fathers served beyond the River [Euphrates] and in Egypt, and serve the LORD. If it is disagreeable in your sight to serve the LORD, choose for yourselves today whom you will serve; whether the gods which your fathers served which were beyond the River, or the gods of the Amorites in whose land you are living; but as for me and my house, we will serve the LORD. (Josh. 24:14–15)

How did the people response to Elijah's burn-the-ships message? With deafening silence! "The people did not answer him a word" (1 Kings 18:21). It's easy to remain apathetic to God's call for a full-time commitment. And the people chose *easy*.

One of my concerns for future generations of Christians is that, like the Israelites, they will become apathetic when it comes to their dedication to God—not fully committed to anything, including their relationship with Jesus, but always dabbling in a little bit of this and a little bit of that. Put another way, I'm concerned the next generation will make Christianity something less than it should be by embracing cultural values that are antithetical to Christianity.

Many modern-day believers are like the people during Elijah's day, trying to walk down both sides of the street at the same time. With one foot in the world and one foot in the church, carnal Christians are more concerned with self-gratification than self-denial. They do not struggle with sin; they surrender to sin. But Jesus has a better way. He calls us to burn our ships—to "take up [our] cross and follow [Him]" (Matt. 16:24).

Jesus's Burn-the-Ships Message—Follow Me Completely

Elijah's burn-the-ships message was repeated in the New Testament by John the Baptist, a prophet who came "in the spirit and power of Elijah" (Luke 1:17). John the Baptist served as the forerunner and proclaimer of Jesus's ministry (Mal. 4:5–6; Matt. 11:14; 17:10–13). John's bold message was exactly Elijah's message: burn your ships and follow God.

Jesus picked up John's (and Elijah's) message and personalized it: "Follow Me." This is the call to discipleship—to see Jesus as more important than anything or anyone else in life; to deny yourself and crucify your sinful habits; to go anywhere and do anything at any time Jesus commands. This is the call to a radical commitment to Christ, where He is the beginning and end of all your hopes and dreams.

This challenge became real for me when I was a teenager. I had played the accordion since I was five (please, no accordion jokes!). Through the years, I earned quite a bit of money playing for weddings, bar mitzvahs, and local Oktoberfest celebrations where the accordion is king.

At the same time, I also volunteered at a small church on weekends. One Sunday evening, the pastor shared with the congregation his vision for establishing a bus ministry to bring inner-city kids to church. Obviously, to have a bus ministry you have to have a bus. The church had none. And the church had no money to buy one. So the pastor announced that a special offering would be collected the following Sunday to purchase a bus.

This created a quandary for me. I believed in the pastor's vision—to bring inner-city kids to the church so they could hear the gospel of Jesus—but what could I do? Yes, I had gained a tidy sum from playing my accordion, but it would not be nearly enough to buy a bus. And besides, I had worked hard for that money. I had other plans for it.

As I was praying about what I should do, the Lord grabbed me by the ear and said, "Go all in—burn your ships." So I did. When Sunday came around, I placed a check in the offering plate for the complete balance of my checking account—$500. And I never regretted it. Today, as I look back on that experience, I realize that $500 is not that much money, but at that time in my life it represented everything I had. Far more valuable than the money I gave that day, however, was learning how to listen to—and obey—the voice of God.

That is the kind of commitment Christ calls us to: to burn our ships and follow Him completely. But exactly what does that entail? What does it really mean to follow Jesus? Well,

Jesus answers that question and tells us that following Him—being a true disciple of His—involves four aspects of our lives.

Get Your Priorities Straight

From the beginning of His ministry, Jesus called His disciples to follow Him (Mark 1:17; John 1:43). As His ministry progressed and His fame increased, others began to express a desire to follow Jesus. After Jesus healed Peter's mother-in-law, a scribe—an expert in the Jewish law—said to Him, "Teacher, I will follow You wherever You go" (Matt. 8:19).

Jesus's reply was remarkable because He neither encouraged nor discouraged the scribe. Rather, Jesus challenged the man to count the cost of completely following Him. He said to the scribe, "The foxes have holes and the birds of the air have nests, but the Son of Man has nowhere to lay His head" (v. 20).

This did not mean that Jesus was penniless and homeless. Rather, Jesus was letting the scribe know that the call and demands of His ministry forced Him to live as a nomad. His ministry kept Him on the move, and if the scribe wanted to be Jesus's disciple, then he, too, would be moving about from place to place.

Most people do not want to live out of a suitcase. Instead, we are taught from a young age that a central priority in life ought to be finding a stable and well-paying job and working toward the American dream of home ownership. There is absolutely nothing wrong with that—and fortunately, most of us can follow Jesus without living as a vagabond.

But sometimes following Jesus requires us to pull up stakes and move to a new town across the state or to another state. And for a few of us, following Jesus requires us to move to a new country. Being committed to following Jesus meant I had to move to Eastland, Texas, and Bill Borden had to move to China. It is simply a matter of determining what is most important in life—following Jesus wherever He may lead or planting yourself in one location that appears to be safe and secure.

Another man approached Jesus with a commitment to discipleship, but this man wanted to bury his father first (Matt. 8:21). He asked Jesus to wait for him before leaving on His next ministry assignment. Jesus's response to the man was to grab his gear and go—"Follow Me"—and let those who are spiritually dead (who have no interest in following Jesus) bury those who are physically dead (v. 22).

Jesus was not being insensitive to the man's commitment to his family or to honor his father. But when other commitments conflict with our commitment to Christ, true disciples must always follow the Lord. When our commitments do conflict, more times than not, the struggle is not between something evil and something good but between something good and something better.

Again, it is a matter of getting our priorities straight. We do not necessarily have to become gypsies or forsake our families. But if the choice comes down to following Jesus or putting our security and families first, then our allegiance to Jesus and His will must take priority. This is why William Borden is such a great example of one who burned his ships. His priority was Jesus first—all others second.

Get Rid of Your Prejudices

Jesus had a notorious reputation—at least among the cultural elites of His day. The Pharisees often criticized Him for keeping company with "tax collectors and sinners" (Matt. 9:11). Little has changed since the first century. Tax collectors were just as despised then as IRS agents are today. But in Jesus's day, Jewish tax collectors were considered traitors because they worked for the Roman government. Tax collectors were also often corrupt, charging more taxes than required and pocketing the difference.

From the Pharisees' perspective, Jesus was guilty by association. Their underlying accusation against Jesus was this: How could He, if He claimed to be a good Jew who followed the law, befriend turncoats and thieves?

Jesus's response to the Pharisees' criticism was to do the unthinkable—to call a social pariah to become one of His own disciples! "As Jesus went on from there, He saw a man called Matthew, sitting in the tax collector's booth; and He said to him, 'Follow Me!' And [Matthew] got up and followed [Jesus]" (v. 9).

Jesus was making an important point about what it means to follow Him completely: "God is no respecter of persons" (Acts 10:34 KJV). Like God, who saw the heart of David, Jesus "sees not as man sees, for man looks at the outward appearance, but the LORD looks at the heart" (1 Sam. 16:7).

We are the ones who test someone's fitness to follow Jesus by their race, their education, their social status, their gender, and even their politics. For instance, we just *know* that someone who is politically liberal could never follow Jesus wholeheartedly. So convinced are we that Christ must be a political conservative that we conclude that all Christians are conservatives and all conservatives are Christians. I know that is a bit of an overstatement, but many of my conservative friends cannot believe that a liberal could really love Jesus. May I introduce you to Kirsten Powers?

Powers is an antiabortion evangelical liberal pundit for CNN previously for Fox News. In an article she wrote for *Christianity Today*, she said, "If there was one thing in which I was completely secure, it was that I would never adhere to any religion—especially to evangelical Christianity, which I held in particular contempt." But through conversations with and the prayers of her then-boyfriend and others, Powers went to hear Tim Keller preach at Redeemer Presbyterian Church in New York City. After eight months of listening to Keller preach the gospel, she began to feel her commitment to the one thing she was "completely secure" about beginning to crack.

"My whole world was imploding," she wrote. "How was I going to tell my family or friends about what had happened? Nobody would understand. I didn't understand. (It says a lot about the family in which I grew up that one of my most pressing concerns was that Christians would try to turn me into a Republican.)" Then one day, after attending a Bible study, her life changed forever. She said, "The world looked entirely different, like a veil had been lifted off it. I had not an iota of doubt. I was filled with indescribable joy. . . . The Hound of Heaven had pursued me and caught me—whether I liked it or not."[5]

Paul made it clear in Galatians 3:28, "There is neither Jew nor Greek, there is neither slave nor free man, there is neither male nor female; for you are all one in Christ Jesus."

Our commitment to Christ is determined by our faith in and obedience to Christ, not our politics, our intellect, or our skin color. People from every tribe, tongue, and tone will populate heaven. So, if in the life to come we are going to live with people who are different from us, shouldn't we start trying to get along with them in this life? This requires us to lay aside our prejudices and view our fellow disciples as Christ views them—as brothers and sisters in the faith. Jesus declared, "By this all men will know that you are My disciples, if you have love for one another" (John 13:35).

Get Your Pleasures Aligned

We often define "pleasures" in terms of living in a palatial home, eating fine meals, and driving a luxurious car. In other words, we think pleasures can be purchased—which is probably why the rich young ruler had such a hard time accepting Jesus's challenge to sell everything he owned, give the money to the poor, and follow Jesus (Matt. 19:21). The desire to control our lives goes back to humanity's original sin in the Garden of Eden, when Eve "saw that the [forbidden] tree was good for food, and that it was a delight to the eyes, and that the tree was desirable to make one wise" (Gen. 3:6). So she picked a piece of fruit and ate it. Today we call her sin self-centeredness—the lust to satisfy our selfish desires without any concern for the well-being of others or the commands of God.

Claiming ultimate control over our lives is the very definition of selfishness. But that attitude is antithetical to following Christ. Jesus said, "If anyone wishes to come after Me [as a disciple], he must deny himself, and take up his cross and follow Me" (Matt. 16:24).

Discipleship requires self-denial. Some people erroneously equate self-denial with pushing aside an extra piece of dessert or giving up a favorite television program to read their

Bible. If only it were that easy! Denying ourselves means aligning our desires with God's desires. And whenever there is a conflict between what we want and what God wants, God wins every time. As Jesus said in the Garden of Gethsemane, "Not as I will, but as You will" (Matt. 26:39).

Jesus tells us that, if we want to be burn-the-ships kind of disciples, we must submit to His power over our lives. We must surrender our desire to control our lives to God's control. As someone has said, the essence of discipleship is not a makeover of your life but a takeover of your life. Like Jesus, we must say to God, "Not as I will, but as You will."

Get a Handle on Your Possessions

Placing your desire to control your own life under God's will for your life requires a radical readjustment in your thinking. But it is necessary if you are going to live an extraordinary life for God. However, don't be surprised if, after you commit yourself to self-denial, Jesus asks you to demonstrate that commitment in a tangible way.

When a wealthy young man approached Jesus with a question about eternal life, Jesus tested his level of commitment to God by telling him to "keep the commandments," specifically, the sixth, seventh, eighth, ninth, and fifth commands (19:17–19). The fact that the young man claimed to have kept all of them revealed his pride. And the fact that the young man still questioned what was necessary for salvation revealed his despair in not finding it through living a good life. So Jesus answered, "If you wish to be complete, go and sell your possessions and give to the poor, and you will have treasure in heaven; and come, follow Me" (v. 21).

Now, don't misunderstand Jesus here. Jesus is not teaching that salvation comes through selling your possessions and giving everything away. If that were the case, then Jesus would be teaching that salvation comes through good works, which would defeat the whole purpose of His death and resurrection and our need to place faith in Christ. Jesus's conversation with this wealthy man revealed who or what was actually in control of the young man's life. This man had allowed gold to become his God. If this man was truly willing to follow Jesus, then he must let go of all rivals to Jesus's authority in his life.

Does Jesus require us to get rid of our possessions? Not necessarily. There is nothing wrong with having money and possessing the things money can buy. Abraham, Job, David, Lydia, Joseph of Arimathea, and others in the Bible were wealthy individuals who led God-honoring lives. The Bible never terms money as "evil" but does single out "the love of money" as a root cause of "all sorts of evil" (1 Tim. 6:10).

We live in a materialistic society where our creature comforts rival our commitment to Christ. The temptation to make and horde money exerts a powerful pull on almost all of us. Therefore, we must be careful to get a handle on our possessions, seeing them simply as gifts from God to enjoy responsibly. However, the moment your house is no longer a pile of wood and brick, or a fine meal is no longer fuel for your body, or your bank account is no longer digital numbers in a computer, then you have to question whether your possessions control you or whether you control your possessions.

The test of my burn-the-ships commitment to Christ comes when He asks me to open my wallet or to walk away from a lucrative business deal. It was a struggle for me to give up that $500 for a bus ministry, but I am glad I did. It could not have been easy for Bill Borden to turn his back on the family fortune to minister to Muslims in China. And though he did not complete his mission, he had "no regrets."

Burning the ships to follow Jesus completely is not for the faint of heart. It requires courage. For Elijah, burning the ships meant having the courage to confront Ahab and challenge the Israelites to choose God or Baal. For you, burning the ships means deciding once and for all who is in control of your life: you or God.

A Declaration of Discipleship

A Zimbabwean pastor knew what it meant to burn his ships and follow Jesus to the very end. Just before his martyrdom, this young man wrote his declaration of discipleship:

> I am part of the fellowship of the unashamed. I have the Holy Spirit's power. The die has been cast. I have stepped over the line. The decision has been made; I am a disciple of *His*! I won't look back, let up, slow down, back away, or be still.
>
> My past is redeemed; my present makes sense; my future is secure. I am finished and done with low living, sight walking, small plannings, smooth knees, colorless dreams, tamed visions, world talking, cheap giving, and dwarfed goals. . . .
>
> My face is set, my gait is fast, my goal is heaven, my road is narrow, my way rough, my companions few, my guide reliable, my mission clear. I cannot be bought, compromised, detoured, lured away, turned back, deluded, or delayed. I will not flinch in the face of sacrifice, hesitate in the presence of the enemy, ponder at the pool of popularity, or meander in the maze of mediocrity.

I won't give up, shut up, let up, until I have stayed up, stored up, prayed up, paid up, and preached up for the cause of Christ. I am a disciple of Jesus. I must go until He comes, give until I drop, preach until all know, and work until He stops me. And when He comes for His own, He will have no problems recognizing me. My banner will be clear.[6]

That's the kind of burn-the-ships commitment God requires from anyone who wants to experience an extraordinary life.

SECRET #5

Unleash the Power of Prayer

A local Baptist church opposed the construction of a bar in their little town and began an all-night prayer vigil, asking God to intervene. Later that evening, lightning struck the bar, burning it to the ground. The owner of the bar brought a lawsuit against the church, claiming that the church was liable for the bar's destruction. The church hired an attorney, claiming they were not responsible. When it went to trial the judge said, "No matter how this case comes out, one thing is clear. The bar owner believes in the power of prayer and the church does not."

We may chuckle at that story, but I do hope you are part of a church that believes in the power of prayer. In prayer, we get to engage in a conversation with the God of the universe, as well as seek His guidance and His forgiveness. But beyond all of that, through prayer we have the opportunity to move the hand of God to perform the supernatural.

I remember some years ago in a previous church we planned to build a new worship center. However, the only way we could make it work was to purchase a small street from the city that bisected our property. The city was opposed to allowing our church to purchase the street, and the project appeared doomed.

I had tried to cajole the city into granting the request or to find an alternative to using the street. Nothing worked. Then I had a novel idea—Why not pray about the matter? Early one morning I asked about one hundred of my church prayer partners to join me in our sanctuary to ask God to change the city officials' hearts about the street. A few hours later, out of the blue, the city manager called the chairperson of our building committee to discuss selling the street, and within a few weeks the deal was done.

"When all else fails, pray!" is far too often the credo by which most of us live. Not Elijah. For this mighty prophet of God, prayer was as normal and necessary as breathing. Elijah had unshakable faith in the power of God—power that could only be accessed through prayer.

If you want to live a truly extraordinary life like Elijah—and I suspect you do, or you wouldn't have made it this far in this book—then, like Elijah, you will learn how to harness the incredible power of God that flows into our lives through prayer.

Showdown on Mount Carmel

We have now come to the part in Elijah's story that many people are familiar with—the winner-take-all battle with the prophets of Baal on top of Mount Carmel. When most people read the story, they focus on the frenzied and futile antics of the 850 prophets of Baal and Asherah or the miraculous fire from heaven that consumed Elijah's sacrifice to Jehovah. We will look at both of these realities briefly, but the heart of this story is Elijah's prayer that brought rain from heaven.

Certainly Elijah is to be commended for his boldness in confronting the false prophets of Baal and Asherah. I have stood on Mount Carmel and reflected on the sheer guts it must have taken for Elijah to engage in a contest in which he was outnumbered 850 to 1. But the reason we are still talking about this incident almost three thousand years later is not because of Elijah's courage but rather his reliance on the power of prayer.

In this chapter, we are going to discover how we can tap into the same divine power that permeated Elijah's life. We will look at the prelude, prerequisites, principles, and practice of powerful praying that are foundational to a significant life.

The Prelude to Powerful Praying

The prophets of Baal and Asherah were devout followers of their faith. They were as sincere in their beliefs as Elijah was in his—but they were sincerely *wrong*. Nevertheless, they were determined to prove that Baal was the only true god. The purpose of their lives was to glorify Baal, and the contest on Mount Carmel was just the way to do that.

As we saw with secret #4, Elijah told Ahab to gather the Israelites and Baal's prophets on Mount Carmel, which lies between God's land (Israel) and Baal's land (Phoenicia). At one time, there had been an altar to Jehovah on the summit of the mountain, but since the reign of Ahab and Jezebel it had been torn down and the mountain renamed "Baal's Bluff," giving Baal the home-field advantage in this contest to see who was God.[1]

Baal's apparent advantage was due to more than the mountain's nickname. *Carmel* means "Garden Land." It overlooks the Jezreel Valley, which when in full bloom is a patchwork quilt of green fields. But during the three-and-a-half-year drought, the valley had become brown and brittle. Carmel was known for its sudden storms of lightning and thunder— representations of Baal's divine power and booming voice, according to those who worshiped him. And since Baal was worshiped as the fire god, the contest of fire should also have been to Baal's advantage. A well-timed lightning strike could easily ignite the dry grass and start a fire, proving that Baal was alive and well.

The rules for the contest were simple. On one side, the prophets of Baal—all 850 of them—were to take an ox, cut it up, and place it on an altar. On the other side, God's solitary prophet, Elijah, would do the same. (Remember, God's other one hundred prophets were too afraid to show their faces and were in hiding.) Neither side was to set their sacrifices on fire. Rather, Elijah issued this challenge: "You call on the name of your god, and I will call on the name of the LORD, and the God who answers by fire, He is God" (1 Kings 18:24).

After the preparations of the sacrifices, Baal's prophets began their incantations and chants, crying out for Baal to send fire. Hour after hour—from morning until midday—the prophets danced around the altar. "But there was no voice and no one answered" (v. 26).

Of course no one answered! Baal had no voice box by which he could answer, no hands by which he could throw a lightning bolt to consume the sacrifice, and no heart by which he could sympathize with the obvious distress of his servants. Baal had nothing, because Baal *was* nothing. He was simply the figment of the godless imaginations of those who had rejected the knowledge of the one true God.

What was true of Baal is true of all false gods—anyone or anything that is loved more than the Creator of the universe. False gods are named "Baal," "Asherah," and "Buddha." They are also named "money," "sex," and "career." Regardless of their names, all false gods are impotent, just as the psalmist declared:

> Their idols are silver and gold,
> The work of man's hands.
> They have mouths, but they cannot speak;
> They have eyes, but they cannot see;
> They have ears, but they cannot hear;
> They have noses, but they cannot smell;
> They have hands, but they cannot feel;
> They have feet, but they cannot walk;
> They cannot make a sound with their throat.
> (Ps. 115:4–7)

At noon, when the sun shone at its brightest, Baal—the sun god—should have been able to ignite a simple fire and consume the sacrifice. But nothing happened. So Elijah thought he would have a little fun with Baal's prophets: "Call out with a loud voice, for he is a god; either he is occupied or gone aside, or is on a journey, or perhaps he is asleep and needs to be awakened" (1 Kings 18:27).

"Speak a little louder," Elijah taunted. "If Baal is up in heaven, he may have a hard time hearing you!" Or perhaps Baal was "occupied" with other matters. Maybe he was deep in thought or distracted, not paying attention to all the hulla-balloo on Mount Carmel. Or perhaps he had "gone aside"—a euphemism indicating that Baal was in the restroom. "Baal can't be bothered because he's sitting on a celestial com-mode!" Elijah teased.

Of course, Baal was not preoccupied, on vacation, or in the bathroom. He simply did not exist. But that didn't stop his prophets from crying out even louder from noon until three o'clock in the afternoon. For three intense hours, they worked themselves into a frenzy, even cutting themselves to gain the attention of Baal. But nothing worked. Finally, their wails grew silent, and they lay on the ground exhausted. And still, "no voice, no one answered, and no one paid attention" (1 Kings 18:29).

Now it was Elijah's turn. Taking twelve stones, represent-ing the twelve tribes when Israel was unified, he "repaired"—literally, "healed"—God's altar (v. 30). Under the authority and authorization of God, Elijah "built an altar in the name of the Lord" (v. 32).[2] He dug a trench around the altar, wide and deep enough to hold twenty-two quarts of seed.[3] Then he arranged the wood and the ox for the sacrifice.

To add a little dramatic flair to the contest, Elijah com-manded his men to find four large barrels, fill them with water from the Mediterranean Sea, and pour the water over the altar.[4] If it wasn't challenging enough for God to consume the sacrifice with fire, Elijah upped the ante. He ordered the men to drench the sacrifice three times, until the whole altar was soaked and the water was running into the trenches. By purposefully stacking the deck, Elijah was setting the stage for a dramatic demonstration of the power of the only true God.

The prelude to a powerful answer to our prayers is a seemingly impossible situation that motivates our prayers. God does not despair over our difficult circumstances—He delights in them! Why? The more difficult our situation is, the greater the opportunity God has to demonstrate His incomparable power. If you want to see God do something big, ask Him for something big!

The Prerequisites to Powerful Praying

Pagans think a certain way, so they pray a certain way. The prophets of Baal believed their god would pay attention to their request only if they engaged in a flurry of tortuous and religious mumbo jumbo. Christians often believe the same about our God—that long, tedious hours spent on our knees, pouring our hearts out before the Lord, is what it takes to get God's attention. Not so.

Jesus explained why His followers do not have to pray like pagans (known as "Gentiles" in His day): "When you are praying, do not use meaningless repetition as the Gentiles do, for they suppose that they will be heard for their many words. So do not be like them; for your Father knows what you need before you ask Him" (Matt. 6:7–8).

Sometimes, as I listen to Christians drone on and on when they pray in public, I wonder if God is as bored as I am. I'm sure He's not, but I sometimes picture Him in heaven looking at His watch, wondering when this is going to end! God is not moved to act by the number or the choice of words we offer. However, the Bible does offer three prerequisites for unlocking the power of prayer.

A Right Relationship with God

When James wrote, "The effective prayer of a righteous man can accomplish much" (James 5:16), he could have been referring to Abraham, the friend of God, or David, the man after God's own heart. But he was not. James was describing Elijah. Elijah is a model of powerful praying because Elijah is a model of righteousness.

Many people trip over the word *righteousness*. They assume, since they are not perfect, this verse means that God will not hear their prayers. But righteousness does not mean perfection. Instead, the Bible uses the term *righteousness* in two ways.

Sometimes the word *righteous* refers to "judicial righteousness." At the moment we trust in Christ as our Savior, God declares us to be in right standing before His holy bench. To put it another way, the instant we acknowledge our lack of perfection and our complete reliance upon Jesus Christ for forgiveness, God declares us "not guilty" in the great courtroom of heaven.

Because Jesus has already endured the punishment we deserve, we never need to fear that God will one day dredge up our sins and hold us accountable for them. Perhaps you are familiar with the concept of double jeopardy—the legal notion that a person cannot be tried for the same crime after he or she has been acquitted of it. If you are declared "not guilty" for robbing a store, you can never be charged for that crime again.

Christ willingly endured the punishment we deserve; we have been acquitted from sin, and our death sentence has been commuted. We never have to worry about divine double jeopardy. That is why Paul confidently declared, "Therefore there is now no condemnation for those who are in Christ Jesus" (Rom. 8:1).

But having a right standing before God means more than never having to face His judgment for sin. Judicial righteousness also radically changes our relationship with God. Instead of being slaves of sin, we are now children of the King, with all the privileges that accompany that relationship.

Let me illustrate how that truth relates to prayer. If a child in our church came up to me after a service and said, "Pastor, would you give me three hundred dollars to buy an Xbox?" my reply would be, "Go ask your parents!" As much as I may like that child, he or she is not a family member and I am under no obligation to answer that request.

However, recently, one of my girls asked me to help her and her husband with a down payment for their home. I listened carefully to her reasoning and determined that her request made sense, so I happily gave her the funds. Obviously, I wouldn't do that for someone else's child, but I was thrilled to do that for my child.

When you become a Christian, your status changes from being outside God's family to being a member of God's family. In Galatians 4, the apostle Paul explains that when we enter God's family through faith in Christ, we have the same rights as God's beloved Son, Jesus. He writes, "Because you are sons, God has sent forth the Spirit of His Son into our hearts, crying, 'Abba! Father!' Therefore you are no longer a slave, but a son; and if a son, then an heir through God" (Gal. 4:6–7).

Abba is an Aramaic word denoting the intimate relationship between a father and his child. It could be translated "Daddy" or "Papa." Because of our right standing before God, we do not have to approach Him with our requests as some distant deity but as a daddy who loves us. And since He views us as family members, we can know He listens just as carefully to our requests as He does to the requests of His Son, Jesus Christ.

Does that mean that God automatically says yes to everything we ask of Him? Of course not! God even said no to His Son, Jesus, on occasion. In the Garden of Gethsemane, Jesus pled with His Father to spare Him from the experience of the cross. When God refused to offer an alternative way to provide redemption for the world, Jesus acquiesced to His Father's plan, saying, "Not My will, but Yours be done" (Luke 22:42).

Realizing that God might not grant our request should not keep us from making the request—no matter how outlandish it may seem. Because of our right standing with God, we approach our heavenly Father with our requests—whatever they are. As the apostle John explained, "This is the confidence which we have before Him, that, if we ask *anything* according to His will, He hears us" (1 John 5:14).

God answered Elijah's prayers because he was a righteous man. But Elijah's righteousness extended beyond his judicial standing before God. Elijah's life also represented the second meaning of righteousness used in the Bible—which just happens to be the second prerequisite to answered prayer.

Obedience to God's Commands

When the late author and pastor Norman Vincent Peale was a young boy, he found a cigar and decided to experiment with what his father had forbidden. When Peale saw his father approaching, he attempted to hide the cigar and distract his dad by pointing to a sign advertising a circus that was coming to town. "Dad, do you think we could go to the circus together?" Peale's father replied, "Son, I've learned never to petition your father while you're holding smoldering disobedience in your hand!" Good advice for all of us when approaching our heavenly Father with our prayer requests. Willful disobedience and powerful praying just do not mix.

Elijah understood this principle. That does not mean the prophet was perfect. James made it clear that Elijah was no plaster saint but instead "was a man with a nature like ours" (James 5:17). Because he was no spiritual superhero, he had his share of slip-ups, mess-ups, and screw-ups. Nevertheless, God regularly and powerfully answered his prayers. Why? Because Elijah was a righteous man. Scripture makes it clear, "The effective prayer of a *righteous* man can accomplish much" (v. 16).

Righteousness, therefore, refers not only to our right standing before God (judicial righteousness) but also to our right acting before God (ethical righteousness). Judicial righteousness describes what God does for us by declaring us not guilty and placing us in His family. Ethical righteousness refers to how we obey God after we become part of His family. Make no mistake about it: obedience to God's commands is a prerequisite for answered prayer. As Peter said, "The eyes of the Lord are toward the righteous, and His ears attend to their prayer, but the face of the Lord is against those who do evil" (1 Pet. 3:12).

Ethical righteousness does not mean we act perfectly all the time—that is impossible. But living righteously denotes both the *desire* and the *direction* of our life. A truly righteous person—the kind of person God listens to—has made pleasing God the primary *desire* in his or her life. That does not mean that person can always pull it off, but at least he or she wants to. Having the desire to obey God requires cultivating a distaste for sin.

But beyond our desires, righteousness also refers to the *direction* of our life. I am glad that God does not evaluate my life by the major blunders I have made. Aren't you? Instead, God looks at the general trajectory of our lives—are we moving closer to Him or farther away from Him? Fortunately, God did not judge the whole of Elijah's life by his one colossal failure of faith after Mount Carmel (an event we will examine in the next chapter). Instead, God declared His servant to be righteous because Elijah acknowledged his failure, received God's forgiveness, picked himself up, and resumed his walk with God.

What about you? Is your primary desire in life to please God? Are you determined to root out any disobedience in your life, or do you still cherish secret sins? Is the general direction of your life moving closer to or farther away from God?

Your answers to these questions reveal whether you are a righteous person and can expect powerful answers to your prayers.

An Unshakable Faith

Throughout the Bible there is an inseparable link between faith and answered prayer. Here are just a few examples:

- "If you have *faith* the size of a mustard seed, you will say to this mountain, 'Move from here to there,' and

it will move; and nothing will be impossible to you"
(Matt. 17:20).

- "Without *faith* it is impossible to please [God], for he
who comes to God must believe that He is and that
He is a rewarder of those who seek Him" (Heb. 11:6).
- "If any of you lacks wisdom, let him ask of God, who
gives to all generously and without reproach, and it will
be given to him. But he must ask in *faith* without any
doubting" (James 1:5–6).
- "The prayer offered in *faith* will restore the one who
is sick, and the Lord will raise him up, and if he has
committed sins, they will be forgiven him" (James 5:15).

But what does it mean to pray "in faith"? This is where
many Christians get it wrong. They have been taught that
faith is a synonym for *positive thinking*. They believe that
if they can conjure up enough positive persuasion that God
will do what they want Him to do, then God will reward
their positive belief with a positive answer. Their prayers are
reminiscent of the little engine that could: "I think God will,
I think God will, I think God will!"

That is not faith; that is presumption. Prayer is not forcing
God's hand to do what we want Him to do. Faith is believing
God will do what He has promised to do. As we will see in
the next section, Elijah could confidently pray for God to
send fire on Mount Carmel because he was following God's
command to engage in such a contest.

When you pray for a raise in your salary, physical healing
for your child, or a promotion at work, you may or may not
be praying according to God's will. That does not mean

you should not ask for those things. In those cases, praying with faith means boldly asking and quietly trusting in God to do what is best.

But when we pray for the reconciliation of a broken relationship, power in sharing the gospel with an unsaved person, or victory over an alluring temptation, we can have the confidence in knowing—as Elijah did—that we are praying according to God's revealed will. And that confidence provides power to our prayers.

The Principles of Powerful Praying

Unlike the prophets of Baal, Elijah did not need to engage in hysterical antics. No incessant pleading, no cutting, and no dancing around the altar. Instead, the prophet of the true God approached the altar and, with reverence and confidence, offered this simple, sixty-two-word prayer:

> O Lord, the God of Abraham, Isaac and Israel, today let it be known that You are God in Israel and that I am Your servant and I have done all these things at Your word. Answer me, O Lord, answer me, that this people may know that You, O Lord, are God, and that You have turned their heart back again. (1 Kings 18:36–37)

Elijah's attitude and prayer reveal three principles of powerful praying—principles guaranteed to bring the fire of God's power down from heaven when we pray.

Approach God with Confidence

Remember the rules of the challenge: the deity who consumed the sacrifice with fire was the true God. The prophets of Baal had their chance, and all that came from heaven was thundering silence. It was now Elijah's turn to approach the altar (1 Kings 18:36).

When I hear a friend say something that borders on the blasphemous, I sometimes joke, "Let me move out of the way. I don't want to get hit by lightning when God zaps you." But that is not what Elijah said or did. He did not move away from the altar; he moved toward it. By his actions he was saying, "God's a dead-eye shot. The sacrifice will burn; I won't." What confidence Elijah had in the Lord!

When you have an intimate relationship with God, your confidence to speak with Him about anything grows. Paul reminded the Ephesian believers that they had "boldness and confident access through faith" to come to the Lord (Eph. 3:12). And the writer to the Hebrews tells us that our faith in Christ is our VIP pass to the throne room of heaven and that we ought to "have confidence to enter the holy place" (Heb. 10:19).

Because of my jam-packed schedule, and for security reasons, people off the street cannot pop in to see me in my office. Requests for appointments are carefully screened before they are scheduled. But my wife and daughters know they can come into my office at any time for any reason—even if it is just to say hi. Why? Because they are the people I love and trust most in the world. They are family!

We can have that same confidence and access when we come before our heavenly Father. We do not need to have a preapproved agenda or even an appointment. We can confidently come into God's presence whenever we want because we are family.

Pray According to God's Will

Have you ever wondered how Elijah dreamed up this contest with the prophets of Baal and Asherah? Was he feeling especially aggressive one morning after a couple extra shots of espresso in his coffee? No. Elijah tells us the source of the challenge in his prayer: "Let it be known that You are God in Israel and that I am Your servant and *I have done all these things at Your word*" (1 Kings 18:36).

God is the One who gave Elijah specific instructions about the contest on Mount Carmel. Though he received God's commands privately, Elijah believed them with certainty, which ignited the power of his praying.

When we pray for God to do what He has already promised to do, we too can pray with absolute confidence. The apostle John writes, "This is the confidence which we have before Him, that, if we ask anything according to His will, He hears us" (1 John 5:14).

Maybe you are thinking, *If God would be that specific in revealing His will to me, then I could pray like Elijah and experience dramatic answers to my prayers too.* I understand that sentiment. There are items on my prayer list right now that I am asking God for daily—sometimes hourly. These requests are all good things related to my family, my church, and my ministry. But I cannot say with absolute confidence that they are part of God's plan for my life. So I keep asking with confidence—with the assurance that God will do what is best, not that God will necessarily say yes to my requests.

However, there are other requests on my list that I know with absolute certainty God is going to answer, because these requests are based on His divinely revealed will. For example, this morning I prayed with confidence that God would empower me to stay morally pure because this is God's will: "For this is the will of God, your sanctification; that is, that you abstain from sexual immorality" (1 Thess. 4:3).

One recent Sunday morning I had very little confidence in the effectiveness of the sermon I was about to preach, not because of the sermon but because of the calendar. It was a holiday weekend, and I was certain few would be in church. Additionally, I assumed those who were there would be too distracted by the festivities of the season to listen attentively. But before the service, I knelt before God and said, "Lord, this message is based on Your Word, and You promised in Isaiah 55:11 that Your Word would 'not return to [You] empty, without accomplishing what [You] desire.'"

When I walked into our worship center, it was jam-packed. As I preached I sensed God's power behind every word. And when I invited people to trust in Christ as their Savior, I was genuinely surprised at the number of people who visibly responded to my invitation on a holiday weekend.

There is nothing wrong in praying for the things we are interested in. We can know that our heavenly Father listens attentively to our requests and answers according to His loving and perfect will for our lives. But when we pray about the things God is interested in, then we can be assured He will answer positively and powerfully. That truth leads to a final principle for powerful praying.

Focus on Glorifying God

Elijah had dedicated his life to proving that the Lord was the only true God. Remember, as we saw earlier, Elijah's name meant "The Lord is my God." It should be no surprise that central to Elijah's prayer on Mount Carmel was the desire that all of Israel might conclude that the Lord, not Baal, was God. He prayed, "O LORD, the God of Abraham, Isaac and Israel, today let it be *known* that You are God. . . . Answer me, O LORD, answer me, that this people may *know* that You, O LORD, are God" (1 Kings 18:36–37).

Elijah's desire was to demonstrate God's glory to the world. It ought to be our desire as well. And one way we can demonstrate God's glory is by declaring God's holiness.

As a child, I loved singing the hymn "Holy, Holy, Holy" in church—not because of its theological content but because it was one of the shortest songs in the hymnal. Any Sunday night we sang it, we were sure to get out of church early!

But as I grew older, I came to love the hymn because it represents a transcendent truth about the nature of God— that His holiness is beyond comprehending. The hymn is based on Isaiah's vision of the heavenly throne in which he heard the angels crying out, "Holy, Holy, Holy is the LORD of hosts, the whole earth is full of His glory" (Isa. 6:3).

The repetition of a word—*holy*, in this case—is one way the Hebrew language emphasizes the importance of a word. The word *holy* comes from the Hebrew word *quodesh*, meaning "separate," "cut from," or "apart." When we say God is "holy," we are saying God is "separate" or a "cut above" anyone or anything else in creation, which is why He alone is worthy of worship.

Elijah's prayer on Mount Carmel was that God would use him to demonstrate God's holiness to the world. That request was in alignment with one of God's great eternal purposes throughout history: the declaration of His holiness—His separateness—so that people will worship Him.

God is still looking for men and women who, like Elijah, are passionate about declaring His holiness to the world. When I was in high school, I read the biography of George Müller, the founder of a great orphanage in Bristol, England. He recorded in his prayer journal over fifty thousand specific prayers that were answered by God. Once, he had run out of money and was not able to purchase milk for the children in his orphanage. Instead of panicking, he started praying. While he was still on his knees, he heard a knock at the door. He arose from his prayer and opened the door to a man who explained that his milk cart had broken down in front of the orphanage. The man wondered if Müller's orphanage could use the milk before it spoiled![5]

Müller, like Elijah, had unlocked the foundational secret of powerful praying: focus on glorifying God.

The Practice of Powerful Praying

Most people look on the contest between God and Baal as the climax of 1 Kings 18. Not so. In many ways, it is merely a prelude to the last few verses of the chapter. The chapter opens with a divine promise: "Go, show yourself to Ahab, and *I will send rain* on the face of the earth" (1 Kings 18:1). Elijah obeyed, and even though God subsequently consumed the animal sacrifice with fire, He had not yet brought the promised rain.

So, just as Elijah had prayed for the drought to begin and fire to fall, he now prayed for the drought to end and rain to fall:

Elijah went up to the top of Carmel; and he crouched down on the earth and put his face between his knees. He said to his servant, "Go up now, look toward the sea." So he went up and looked and said, "There is nothing." And he said, "Go back" seven times. . . . In a little while the sky grew black with clouds and wind, and there was a heavy shower. (1 Kings 18:42–43, 45)

Elijah's prayer on Mount Carmel during the dramatic contest illustrates the importance of approaching God with confidence, praying according to God's will, and focusing on God's glory. Elijah's second and rain-producing prayer reveals four practical principles for praying effectively and powerfully.

Pray Privately

Recently, I was answering questions from a group of engaged couples in our church. One person asked, "Pastor, would you tell us how you and Amy have learned to pray together over the years?" I decided to be honest with them. "We haven't and we don't. In fact, except for a few rare instances in which one of our children was facing a crisis, we don't pray together regularly." You could have heard the proverbial pin drop. I knew what they were thinking: *Nothing builds spiritual unity in a marriage more than praying together.* Maybe, but the purpose of prayer is not building unity in marriage or even building unity among Christians. Prayer is a conversation with our heavenly Father, a conversation more times than not best conducted privately.

When we are praying aloud in front of others, it is far too easy to become distracted by the wrong concerns: the choice of our vocabulary, the length of our prayers, or the reaction of others to what we are saying. That is why Jesus advised that we pray in private: "When you pray, go into your inner room, close your door and pray to your Father who is in secret, and your Father who sees what is done in secret will reward you" (Matt. 6:6).

That does not mean we should never pray in front of others. Jesus occasionally prayed publicly, often before He performed a miracle, such as the feeding of the five thousand or the raising of Lazarus from the dead. But the secret of Jesus's extraordinary life and ministry was the priority He placed on private time spent in conversation with His Father. In fact, the day after the busiest day of His ministry, we find these words: "In the early morning, while it was still dark, Jesus got up, left the house, and went away to a secluded place, and was praying there" (Mark 1:35).

If anyone could have made a case for sleeping in the next day after a jam-packed day of ministry, it could have been Jesus. But the Lord's alarm went off early, and He prayed. My mentor, the late Howard Hendricks, used to say, "If prayer was so essential for Jesus, the perfect Son of God, how much more vital is it for people like you and me!"

Jesus had a regular time ("in the early morning") and a location ("a secluded place") where He regularly met with God—and so should we. While talking with God throughout the day should be as natural and frequent as breathing, there needs to also be an uninterrupted time and place where we meet with God.

It really does not matter when or where you make your regular appointment with God. You may not be a morning person—that's fine. Your time can be after lunch or before you go to sleep. Your location may be a favorite place in your backyard or in a comfortable chair by your bed. When I was younger, there was a park by our home where I often met with the Lord. Now it is by the couch in my office at work. Although I pray publicly—sometimes in front of thousands of people—it is those private appointments with God that have nurtured my relationship with Him.

The same was true for Elijah. Yes, he prayed publicly for God to send the fire from heaven and consume the sacrifice—and God did just that. But it was in the solitary moments with God that the Lord answered Elijah's prayer for rain.

My friend David Jeremiah notes that only one-ninth of an iceberg is visible above the water; the other eight-ninths is below the surface where no one can see it. Our prayer life should be the same way. Only a fraction of our praying should be done publicly. Those who have uncovered the secret of powerful intercession do the bulk of their praying in private.

Pray Honestly

In his secret, second prayer, the text records that Elijah "crouched down on the earth and put his face between his knees" and called down the rain (1 Kings 18:42). The Hebrew word for "crouched" is the idea of someone stretching on or throwing themselves to the ground. It is the same verb used in 2 Kings 4:34 when Elisha "stretched himself" over the lifeless body of a young boy and prayed for the Lord to raise him from the dead by sending breath. In the same way, Elijah stretched himself over the ground and prayed for the Lord to raise the land from the dead by sending rain.

Why is Elijah's posture during this prayer significant? This was no folded-hands, "now I lay me down to sleep" kind of prayer. Instead, Elijah was passionately pouring out to God what was really in his heart—that God would end the drought and send rain.

Too often we censor our prayers, thinking, *God wouldn't want me to ask for that.* So instead we offer up "safe prayers," not prayers that could be labeled as "selfish prayers." We pray for missionaries or starving children in faraway lands. Yet the apostle Paul encouraged us to pray about anything and everything that truly concerns us. He wrote, "Be anxious for nothing, but in *everything* by prayer and supplication with thanksgiving let your requests be made known to God" (Phil. 4:6).

Yes, we should pray for those things we know God desires: the conversion of unbelievers, God's glory in the world, reconciliation of broken relationships, and our own moral purity. But we should also be honest with God about the other things we desire.

- Do you need a raise in your salary?
- Would you like your boss to commend you for your hard work?
- Are you ready for God to bring you a mate?

Tell God what is really in your heart—not just what you think should be in your heart. After all, He already knows! Just make sure you add to that request—no matter how audacious it seems—a sincere addendum: "Not my will, but Your will be done."

Pray Specifically

Few of us experience immediate and dramatic answers to our prayers on a regular basis. But Elijah did, and here is one reason why: he prayed with laserlike specificity. When James encouraged Christians to pray for healing for those who were ill, he encouraged them to pray specifically, noting, "The effective prayer of a righteous man can accomplish much" (James 5:16). Then, in the next verses, James illustrates what an "effective prayer" is by Elijah's example:

> Elijah was a man with a nature like ours, and he prayed earnestly that it would not rain, and it did not rain on the earth for three years and six months. Then he prayed again, and the sky poured rain and the earth produced its fruit. (vv. 17–18)

Whenever Elijah prayed, he pleaded with the Lord to grant very specific requests: the drought in Israel for three years, the raising of the widow's son from the dead, the fire to fall from heaven on Mount Carmel, and the rain to pour on Israel again.

I have a sneaking suspicion that the main reason we are hesitant to pray with specificity is that we do not want to embarrass God or disappoint ourselves when He does not answer our requests. So we pray generally ("bless this" and "bless that") without ever experiencing the exhilarating joy of answered prayer or the disappointment of unanswered prayer. There is nothing extraordinary about that kind of living.

Let me encourage you to do something I have done for years. I keep a prayer journal in a spiral notebook. I divide each page into two columns, labeled "My Requests" and "God's

Answers." Through the years, I have recorded all my requests to God (and used them as a guide for my praying). When God answers that request with a yes or no, I record it under "God's Answers." Occasionally, when I am discouraged, I flip through my journal and the cloud of discouragement dissipates as I remember God's supernatural intervention in my life. But I am equally encouraged when I read some of the "no" answers to my prayers and see how God had a better plan for my life than I could have ever imagined.

Perhaps one reason you are not experiencing dramatic answers to your prayers is that you are not boldly asking God for anything. Remember, "you do not have because you do not ask" (James 4:2).

Pray Persistently

Sometimes God answers our specific request immediately, just as He did when Elijah prayed for Him to consume the animal sacrifice on Mount Carmel. Other times God delays His answer, just like He did when Elijah prayed for the rain to return to Israel. Look at the account again:

> Elijah went up to the top of Carmel; and he crouched down on the earth and put his face between his knees. He said to his servant, "Go up now, look toward the sea." So he went up and looked and said, "There is nothing." And he said, "Go back" seven times. It came about at the seventh time, that he said, "Behold, a cloud as small as a man's hand is coming up from the sea." (1 Kings 18:42–44)

Just imagine what might have happened—or not happened—had Elijah stopped asking God for rain after the first or sixth time, reasoning, *This isn't working. Rain is obviously not part of God's will.* Elijah and the entire nation would have missed God's supernatural blessing had he not persisted in prayer.

The same is true for you and me. One reason we miss out on an extraordinary life is that we give up too easily in our praying.

If you want to experience an extraordinary life, then it is essential to learn how to pray at all times and not lose heart (Luke 18:1). Do not just pray when the answer seems possible but also when the answer seems impossible. And do not just pray a "one and done" prayer. Keep on praying until God answers with a definitive yes or no—just as Elijah did while alone with God on the top of Mount Carmel.

When we are faced with an impossible situation, there are many steps we can take—and should take—to change our situation. But those who choose an extraordinary life have learned the truth expressed by A. J. Gordon: "You can do more than pray, after you have prayed. But you can never do more than pray until you have prayed."[6]

SECRET #6

Learn How to Handle Bad Days

My father was a spiritual giant in my eyes, yet he also battled depression in his later years. In the depths of despair and fearing he would spend the rest of his life alone after the death of my mother, he rushed into a second marriage that turned out to be a disaster. He died shortly afterward.

As we look through the Bible, we discover that many of God's choicest servants also suffered from discouragement and depression. Both Moses and Jonah once asked God to take their lives (Num. 11:10–15; Jon. 4:3). Even the apostle Paul at one point during his ministry "despaired even of life" (2 Cor. 1:8).

Yes, many of God's greatest servants wrestled with discouragement, including Elijah. When James wrote that Elijah was "a man with a nature like ours" (James 5:17), he may have had in mind 1 Kings 19, where we see this champion of God stumble and fall into a pit of anguish.

165

The portrait of Elijah in 1 Kings 19 stands in stark contrast to the picture we saw in 1 Kings 18. In chapter 18 we see Elijah at his best, but in chapter 19 we see him at his worst. Placed side by side, the differences between the two depictions are startling.

Two Portraits of Elijah

1 Kings 18	1 Kings 19
"The hand of the LORD was on Elijah" (v. 46).	"He was afraid and . . . ran for his life" (v. 3).
Elijah was full of faith.	Elijah was full of fear.
Elijah bravely confronted 850 false prophets.	Elijah cowardly fled from one woman.
Elijah prayed for God to glorify Himself.	Elijah prayed for God to take his life.
Elijah became the leader of the people.	Elijah abandoned the people.

Unlike the fictitious characters of mythology who are presented as flawless, the real-life people in the Bible are presented just as they were—warts and all! The reason Scripture records the foibles of people like Elijah is to encourage us to avoid their mistakes. Seeing where they stumbled—especially when they experience difficulties and discouragements—helps us learn to handle our own bad days. And few lives provide more insight into how to do that than Elijah's.

By focusing on Elijah's bout with discouragement and depression, we not only learn what bad days look like but also learn some warning signs when bad days are approaching, along with practical steps we can take when those inevitable bad days arrive.

What Bad Days Look Like

Bad days are like a vacuum: they suck the joy out of life. Fortunately, for most of us, bad days consist of troubles that are manageable and then over. For example, misplacing your car keys when you are running late or discovering you have a flat tire clearly count as "bad days." Days like this are certainly annoying and aggravating, but they quickly end. That is not what we are focusing on in this chapter.

I'm using the term "bad days" to refer to seasons in life when difficulties and disappointments linger and pile up—one after another—until they become almost unbearable. These seasons of despair often start with unexpected and grim news, followed by troubles for many days afterward. These kinds of days sometimes come because of our own wrong choices and the consequences that follow. For example, someone who is sexually promiscuous might find out that he or she has contracted a sexually transmitted disease or AIDS.

Sometimes bad days are not of our own making. Those who endure long-term illnesses, devastating physical disabilities, or mental instability due to chemical imbalances suffer at no fault of their own. And though it is not true, they sometimes conclude that God has cursed them. Whenever I hear someone assume that their difficulties—or someone else's—are the result of God's curse, I remind them of the movie *Lone Survivor*, the story of a Navy SEAL team sent to capture an Al-Qaeda leader in an Afghan village. When the mission goes terribly wrong, one of the team members says, "It's feeling like a cursed operation." Marcus Luttrell, who survived the actual mission and wrote the book the movie is based on, responded, "It's not a cursed op. There's no curses. It's just Afghanistan, that's all."[1]

The same is often true about difficult seasons we experience. "It's just the world we live in, that's all." It's a world that is contaminated by sin and populated by sinners—so is it any wonder that we get battered and bruised during our brief stay on this planet? While every difficulty we experience cannot be directly attributed to God's curse on our individual lives, the general state of the world is the result of God's curse on the earth after Adam and Eve's rebellion against God: "Against its will, all creation was subjected to God's curse" (Rom. 8:20 NLT).

Whether because of your own wrong choices or because of living in a sin-infested world, you are going to experience bad days and bad seasons in life. No one is exempt from them, even those who choose to live an extraordinary life. And when bad days come, do not be surprised if they are accompanied by three painful emotions: discouragement, restlessness, and foolishness.

Discouragement

When we become discouraged, all we feel like doing is staying in bed and pulling the covers over our heads. Bad days can rob us of the courage needed to live an extraordinary life. If those days persist, then discouragement dissolves into depression. And if depression lingers long enough, we may come to believe that life has lost its meaning.

British philosopher and Nobel laureate Bertrand Russell lived a long and interesting life, championing human rights, nuclear disarmament, and free speech. By human standards,

Russell was a man of significance. But he was also a man without God, which created a pall of gloom over his existence. For all his success, the meaninglessness of life was a recurring theme in his writing. In his autobiography, Russell described the desolation that often accompanies human life: "We stand on the shore of an ocean, crying to the night and emptiness; sometimes a voice answers out of the darkness. But it is the voice of one drowning, and in a moment the silence returns."[2]

I told you Russell was a gloomy man.

Elijah was not a theological atheist like Russell, but during a particular "bad day" in his life, he behaved as a practical atheist—acting as though God was nonexistent. While some Israelites turned back to God after Elijah's triumph on Mount Carmel, the majority continued to worship Baal—and Elijah grew discouraged. He believed he had failed in his mission, so he prayed for the Lord to take his life.

Comparing himself to those of an earlier generation, Elijah lamented, "I am not better than my fathers" (1 Kings 19:4), meaning that his ministry was no more effective than that of the prophets who went before him. He could preach until his lungs collapsed and perform miraculous signs until his arms fell off, but the people's hearts remained unchanged. They continued in their rebellion against God and persisted in their worship of Baal.

The same discouragement that filled Russell and overtook Elijah can consume us as well. Anyone who attempts to evaluate his or her life without God's perspective, whether an unbeliever like Russell or a believer like Elijah, will experience discouragement—the loss of courage to continue pursuing an extraordinary life.

Restlessness

When life does not turn out as envisioned, some people turn to nonstop activity—either to divert their minds from the pain or to find a sense of purpose in life. As a young man, Theodore Roosevelt had a restless spirit brought on by tragedy. On Valentine's Day, 1884, Roosevelt's mother died of typhoid fever, and his wife died from complications after giving birth to their daughter just two days earlier. Devastated, Roosevelt opened his diary, placed a large black X through that date, and wrote, "The light has gone out of my life."[3] He deposited his infant daughter, Alice, with his sister and ran away to the badlands of the Dakotas to soothe his broken spirit.

In the Dakotas, disheartened and depressed, Roosevelt engaged in an exhausting swirl of activities—breaking horses, rounding up and branding cattle, and hunting down cattle thieves. Years later, writing about his time as a rancher in the western wilds, Roosevelt said, "Black care rarely sits behind a rider whose pace is fast enough."[4] In other words, get on a fast enough horse and you can ride out of the darkness. For Roosevelt, the cure for discouragement and depression was action.

Elijah also chose action as the remedy for his discouragement. Staring down a death threat from Queen Jezebel, Elijah ran from Jezreel in Israel to Beersheba, the largest village on the southern border in Judah—a distance of 120 miles. And then he ran from Beersheba to Mount Horeb in the Sinai wilderness—an additional two hundred miles.

When bad days come, we might not physically run away, as Roosevelt and Elijah did, but we might flee emotionally and spiritually. We might throw ourselves into our work, logging long hours at the office to avoid difficulties at home. We might spend more time and attention on hobbies so we do not have to work out the problems in our marriage or family. We might lose ourselves in watching television—mindlessly flipping through channels—or spend hours on social media to avoid having a conversation with a loved one.

But diversionary activity is not God's cure for bad days. When we find ourselves in adverse circumstances, the Lord encourages us to "be still"—to rest in the power of His provision and protection—and to "know that [He is] God" (Ps. 46:10 NIV). Nevertheless, when faced with difficult and discouraging days, being still is the last thing on our minds. Often, we are more interested in running from our problems than working out a solution to them.

Foolishness

Unfortunately, running from rather than confronting our problems can lead to unwise decisions. I cannot tell you the number of times I have seen people make foolish decisions because of the wrong response to a bad day or bad season of life. In the first church I pastored, I met with our personnel committee to confront our church custodian about his unsatisfactory job performance. Instead of vowing to do a better job, the custodian became infuriated, stood up, and announced, "I'm quitting this sorry job!" With that, he threw his ring of church keys at one of the committee members and stormed out of the conference room. We all sat there stunned until we heard a gentle knock at the door. It was the custodian, meekly explaining that he needed his key ring back since his car keys were on it. Talk about ruining a dramatic exit!

Running from our bad days can cause us to foolishly abandon our jobs, our friendships, or even our families. Do not think that sweeping your bad days under the rug or running from the real source of your problem is doing anything constructive. All you have done is postponed facing your bad day.

That's precisely what Roosevelt did when he ran away to the Dakotas. As a wealthy New Yorker with a bright political future, he was foolish to think he would be content living apart from his infant daughter and becoming a rancher. Roosevelt would have to deal with the death of his mother and wife in a more constructive way. So he returned to New York, resumed his political career, remarried, and reared a family.

Elijah made a similar foolish choice when he fled into the desert to escape Jezebel. God had not told Elijah to pack his bags and skip town. What did Elijah think he was going to do in the desert—preach to lizards and snakes? As a prophet called to declare the reality and power of God to an unbelieving world, what message was Elijah communicating by tucking tail and running from one disgruntled queen?

Contrary to his prayer for death (1 Kings 19:4), Elijah did not really want to die; he wanted to escape. (Had he really wanted to die, he could have stayed where he was and Jezebel would have happily taken care of that for him!) When bad days accumulate and press in on us, we sometimes say things we really do not mean. Like a frightened and wounded animal, we lash out, often at those closest to us. We tell friends we are sick of them. We tell loved ones we hate them. And we tell God we want to die. Bad days—if not confronted and handled wisely—can lead to foolish words and foolish decisions.

Warning Signs That Bad Days Are Coming

Paul told the Corinthian believers that the stories in the Old Testament—like those about Elijah—were "written [down] for our instruction," to serve as a practical example for us to follow. Therefore, Paul advised the Corinthians to apply those examples to their own lives, warning those who might disregard the lessons of history: "Let him who thinks he stands take heed that he does not fall" (1 Cor. 10:11–12).

Paul's warning applies to us as well. At the very moment we think we are the strongest, we are really the weakest, because that is the time when we let down our guard, making us more vulnerable. I have read that mountain climbers are much more prone to accidents on their descent rather than their ascent. As they make their way down from the peak, they are tired and less cautious after the victory of reaching the summit, making them more prone to stumbling.

When Elijah descended Mount Carmel after his great victory, he had every reason to believe that the entire nation would abandon Baal and return to God. But when that didn't happen, Elijah was knocked for a loop. He should have anticipated what would happen next. But Elijah ignored the warning signs that bad days were just over the horizon.

What are the factors that can contribute to a bad day or bad season of life? There are many I could mention, but Elijah's experience illustrates four critical factors.

Being Physically and Emotionally Exhausted

For three and a half years, Elijah lived on the edge. He had been hunted down as public enemy number one, had roughed it in the wilderness of Cherith, and had come close to starvation at Zarephath. From the time he left the widow's home, Elijah had been in perpetual motion—confronting Ahab, engaging in spiritual combat on Carmel, praying intently for rain, and running a half marathon from Carmel to Jezreel. Elijah was physically and emotionally exhausted. But rest and relaxation did not factor high on Elijah's list of priorities. I can understand that. My schedule is busy with preaching, teaching, pastoring, Bible conferences, writing, and appearing in news interviews. I thrive on a go-go-go routine. So did Elijah. But God's prophet had come to the end of his physical and emotional rope, which weakened his emotional and spiritual immune systems, leading to discouragement and even depression.

The same thing happened to me just last week. I returned home after a trip to Washington, DC, that was jam-packed with activities and interviews. My adrenaline had been flowing nonstop for about ninety-six hours. The day after my return, I fell into an emotional funk that resulted in thoughts and questions I do not even want to admit! I could not figure out what was wrong with me until I realized that I was simply exhausted. Then I remembered an observation my friend Howard Hendricks often made: "Sometimes the most spiritual thing you can do is take a nap!" After getting some much-needed rest, I regained my emotional and spiritual equilibrium.

"Burning the candle at both ends," as the old proverb goes— especially if you are burning the candle to build a bigger bank account or a bigger ego—is not healthy. Or, to put it another way, "You will break the bow if you keep it always bent."

Though Elijah did not work for money or fame, his bow had been bent for a long time, so it is no surprise he broke emotionally when Jezebel exerted pressure on him.

What about you? How long has your bow been bent?

Do anxious thoughts rob you of sleep?

Do your children get on your nerves easily?

Do minor setbacks turn into major emotional outbursts?

Do you use alcohol, prescription drugs, or endless television viewing to deaden the pain of disappointment?

The relationship between physical exhaustion and depression is indisputable. But we cannot dismiss the spiritual component either. Satan would love to use our discouragement as an entry point into our lives. Jesus described Satan as a thief who "comes only to steal and kill and destroy" everything important to us—including our joy (John 10:10). And physical exhaustion is one of his simplest tools to accomplish that goal.

Focusing on Challenging Circumstances Rather Than a Powerful God

When Ahab returned home from Mount Carmel after his showdown with Elijah, I imagine him coming into the palace haggard and dejected. Hearing the door open, Jezebel runs to get the report of what happened.

> "Praise Baal! I knew Baal would defeat the false god of the Israelites. You're rain-soaked—proof that Baal is the true god."
>
> "Well, I wouldn't necessarily say that."
>
> "What do you mean? Baal is the god of rain—and it is raining. The drought is over, and the land will flourish again because of Baal's great power!"
>
> "I'm not so sure Baal had anything to do with the rain. In fact, I'm convinced he didn't."

175

"Well, if not Baal, then who? What happened on Carmel?"

"The worst happened."

"What do you mean? Tell me everything—and be quick about it!"

Then "Ahab told Jezebel all that Elijah had done, and how he had killed all the prophets with the sword" (1 Kings 19:1).

After absorbing the news, Jezebel grew incensed. She sent a message to Elijah: "The gods will get you for this and I'll get even with you! By this time tomorrow you'll be as dead as any one of those prophets" (v. 2 Message).

In truth, Jezebel probably did not really want to kill Elijah. If she did, why would she send a messenger to him instead of a death squad? She probably wanted to discourage Elijah, hoping he would flee the city. If he did, she would discredit Elijah and his God in the eyes of the new converts. A revival without a leader is bound to fail.

Because Elijah was physically and emotionally exhausted, when he received word of Jezebel's threat "he [became] afraid and arose and ran for his life" (v. 3). Suddenly, Elijah became spiritually nearsighted, focusing on Jezebel's threat rather than on God's power, which he had just seen demonstrated on Mount Carmel. This happens to us as well. Whenever our focus shifts from our God to our circumstances, we inevitably stumble into a bad day or season of life.

Once Elijah took his eyes off the God who answered by fire and obsessed over the queen who threatened his life, Elijah began to drown emotionally. But instead of calling for the Lord to save him, Elijah cried out, "O Lord, take my life!" (v. 4).

Sometimes I will ask a friend, "How are you doing?" Often the reply is, "Well, I'm all right I suppose . . . under the circumstances." My first thought is, *What are you doing under there?* Yet that is where far too many Christians spend their days: smothering spiritually under the heavy weight of a prodigal child, a life-threatening illness, or mounting debt. As believers in an all-powerful God, the last place we should be living is "under the circumstances."

The only way we will ever escape the emotional oppression of real-life challenges is to shift our focus to another reality: the power of God. I am not suggesting we ignore the realities of the difficulties we face. Rather, I am suggesting we choose to live "above the circumstances." Let me explain what I mean.

Last night, it was dark and snowing as the airplane in which I was sitting began to roar down the runway at the Detroit airport. On the ground an oppressive atmosphere— even a potentially dangerous one—enveloped me. However, within minutes the plane rose into the air and soon I found myself surrounded by sunlight and unlimited visibility. It was still dark and snowing below me, but I had been lifted up to another reality that existed parallel to the reality below.

When we face oppressive challenges, God does not encourage us to deny reality. He instead encourages us to focus on another reality: His supreme power over our challenging circumstances. Centering our attention on God lifts us up and allows us to live above the turbulence and limited visibility of everyday life. As the prophet Isaiah promised, "Thou wilt keep him in perfect peace, whose mind is stayed on thee: because he trusteth in thee" (Isaiah 26:3 KJV).

Unfortunately, in Elijah's mind, Jezebel's power to destroy was more powerful than God's power to defend. His emotional bow had been bent for so long, all it took was one threat to break him. Elijah had bravely confronted 850 false prophets, but one angry person sent him running! That is what happens when we change our focus from God to our circumstances.

You can respond to seemingly impossible circumstances with either faith or fear. Perhaps right now you can only see the difficulty of your circumstances: cancer, a lost job, a prodigal child, marital troubles, or financial pressure. But alongside that reality is another reality: God's heavenly arm—though unseen—is surrounding and protecting you.

Holding On to Unrealistic Expectations

Winning is thrilling—and addictive. The downside of success is that it can create the unrealistic expectation that we will succeed all the time. And when we don't, we go into an emotional funk. Consider

- the author who hits the bestseller list with his or her first book and is disappointed when the next one bombs,
- the pastor whose church experiences remarkable growth for five years followed by several years of stagnant attendance,
- the entrepreneur whose at-home business is recognized as the top seller in the industry for three years but falls off the charts the next year, and
- the investor who experiences double-digit growth in his portfolio for ten years followed by a 50 percent decline the next year.

Elijah also experienced a tremendous victory at Mount Carmel, which led him to think he was on a winning streak. After he defeated the prophets of Baal, the people cried out, "The LORD, He is God; the LORD, He is God" (1 Kings 18:39) and the rain fell. Elijah, the conquering hero, must have thought that he would turn all Israel back to God. But it was not to be. Jezebel's death warrant crushed Elijah's hope of a great national revival. But his hope that the entire nation would turn to God after only one demonstration of power was unrealistic. Flashes in the pan rarely produce enduring change.

Like Elijah, we believe sudden success establishes a new pattern of life. We mistakenly assume that a coveted promotion at work, a new romantic relationship, a successful investment, or a meaningful experience with God means we will never taste failure again. That is an unrealistic expectation that is guaranteed to lead to a bad day.

Believing You Are Indispensable

Whenever we think we are solely responsible for the success of our marriage, the growth of our business, the wise choices of our children, or—as in Elijah's case—the spiritual revival of our nation, we assume a responsibility God never intended for us to shoulder. If things go well, the result can be pride—*God can't pull this off without me*. But if things go wrong, the result can be despondency—*No one is as committed as I am*.

Elijah became the victim of both pride and despondency by assuming he alone was responsible for bringing revival to Israel. To lift His prophet out of the emotional doldrums,

God needed to have a revealing discussion with His servant. After running from Jezreel to Beersheba, Elijah walked further into the wilderness, to Mount Horeb.

Once Elijah reached Horeb, he found "a cave and lodged there" (1 Kings 19:9). We do not know how long Elijah lived in the cave, but he probably spent his time brooding over his fate. There, in the cave, "the word of the LORD came to him" with a question: "What are you doing here, Elijah?" (v. 9).

God was not asking because He had lost track of His servant and was surprised to find him in a cave. This was a soul-searching question meant as a wake-up call for Elijah. In fact, God asked the question twice for emphasis. It is as if God were saying, "I called you to be a mighty prophet. What are you doing hiding in a mountainside hole?"

I can look back on several key moments in my life when I was in places I had no business being. I am not talking about bars or casinos, but I was involved in secondary pursuits that were not in keeping with my primary calling from God. At those moments, I could hear God saying to me, "Robert, what are you doing in this place? This is not part of My plan for you."

But Elijah missed the point of God's probing question. So he responded twice with the same answer: "I have been very zealous for the LORD, the God of hosts; for the sons of Israel have forsaken Your covenant, torn down Your altars and killed Your prophets with the sword. And I alone am left; and they seek my life, to take it away" (vv. 10, 14).

Elijah's answer was true. Elijah had been zealous in carrying out his call, and the people of Israel had faithlessly forsaken God's covenant, torn down God's altars, and killed God's prophets. It was equally true that Jezebel was attempting to take Elijah's life. But how did Elijah know that he was the only faithful one left in Israel? Earlier, Obadiah had told Elijah that one hundred of the Lord's prophets were being sheltered in caves under his care (1 Kings 18:13).

And why did Elijah sound surprised that Jezebel was seeking his life? After humiliating her god and killing her prophets, did he really believe she would roll out a red carpet, fall on her knees, and confess the Lord as the true God? Such a hope was unrealistic. But it also reveals an attitude of pride. Elijah believed he was indispensable because he thought he was the last faithful man in Israel.

Remember, believing you are indispensable not only results in pride but also results in despondency. In effect, Elijah was really saying to God, "Lord, I'm the only one out there fighting Your battles for You. All the other Israelites have forgotten You. And now this out-of-control woman is trying to kill me. Is this how You reward Your only faithful servant? I guess I'll have to take care of myself and hide in this cave."

God has a way of sending us reminders that we are not as indispensable as we think so that we don't become despondent when we fail to meet unrealistic expectations. A pastor was feeling especially good after his Sunday sermon. On the way home from church, he said to his wife, "Honey, how many truly great preachers do you think there are in America?" His wife replied, "One less than you think!"

God essentially jolted his servant Elijah with the same message. Here is my translation of 1 Kings 19:18: "You think you are the only one left, do you? Well, I will have you know I will leave seven thousand in Israel who will never bow their knees to Baal and who, with their lips, will never kiss Baal's lips."

Besides these, the Lord told Elijah He had other servants to do His bidding—some more pagan than pious. God is not limited in the instruments He uses. God instructed Elijah to anoint Hazael, who came to the throne through assassination, as king over Aram, or modern Syria (1 Kings 19:15). Hazael would later become the rod God used to punish Israel. The Lord also told Elijah to anoint Jehu, who was not obedient to the Lord, as king over Israel (v. 16).[5] Jehu would later become a scourge to the house of Ahab.

In addition to Hazael and Jehu, God also instructed Elijah to anoint a man named Elisha, who would serve as his successor. In 1 Kings 19:16, the Lord told Elijah, "Elisha the son of Shaphat of Abel-meholah you shall anoint as prophet in your place." In verses 19–21 we read that Elijah found Elisha plowing the fields and called him to be his successor. In response to this call, Elisha "arose and followed Elijah and ministered to him" (v. 21).

The bottom-line truth is that God does not need any of us to accomplish His purposes. Jesus told the Pharisees that even if His disciples were silent, "the stones [would] cry out" in praise to Him (Luke 19:40). While God does not need us, He graciously allows us to partner with Him in fulfilling His plan. Maintaining a healthy perspective regarding our responsibility and God's responsibility will keep us from feeling indispensable and will help us not fall into despair.

What to Do When Bad Days Come

It would be wonderful if we could avoid bad days and live permanently on the sunny side of life, eluding those moments

182

when gray clouds hang over our heads. But the title of this chapter is not "Learn How to Avoid Bad Days." It is "Learn How to Handle Bad Days." Just as sparks always fly upward, so "Man is born for trouble" (Job 5:7).

Jesus said, "Here on earth you will have many trials and sorrows" (John 16:33 NLT). And though Jesus has "overcome the world," we who are still residents of earth must learn how to manage challenging seasons if we want to enjoy an extraordinary life. Elijah's experience after Mount Carmel illustrates four practical ways to handle bad days.

Expect Bad Days

Just because Elijah got blindsided by a difficult season of life does not mean you have to be. There are some events in your life that almost always will trigger bad days.

First, *the death or desertion of a loved one.* After the death of each of my parents, while I was in my late twenties and early thirties, I sank into a pit of despair that I could not climb out of for about six months. Even though I was a pastor who had ministered to others in similar situations, I did not realize I was suffering from depression. I now counsel people who have experienced the death of someone close that they should not expect to feel normal again for six months to a year. For many people, divorce produces the same sensation of loss as death.

Second, *a devastating loss.* Termination from a job, an unexpected financial setback, the destruction of one's home, or a criminal assault can cause people to question whether God is really watching over them or if they are simply victims of random forces in nature. Such questioning can often result in despair, just as it did for the patriarch Job. Although Job initially worshiped God after losing his possessions, his children, and his health, he eventually questioned God's sovereignty and wisdom.

Third, *an exhilarating success*. As I mentioned earlier, I recently returned home after an out-of-town trip during which I delivered a high-profile speech and was interviewed on several national television programs. Returning to my world of everyday responsibilities, I could barely function for the next few days. My lethargy was not the result of some deep spiritual problem that needed to be addressed. I was simply physically and emotionally spent.

Understanding that certain events will trigger bad days can help us not only expect them but even schedule them. For example, I know that after coming home from an overseas trip that involves time zone changes, I am going to experience a few bad days of shaking off the jet lag. While I cannot afford to stay in bed, I can schedule less challenging tasks such as correspondence or meetings instead of sermon preparation or writing—activities that require a great deal of concentration.

Refresh Yourself Physically

I already mentioned the observation that on occasion the most spiritual thing we can do is take a nap. After collapsing in a heap of despair following his long trek from Jezreel to Beersheba and then into the wilderness, Elijah prayed, "LORD, take my life" (1 Kings 19:4). The physical and emotional exhaustion that Elijah experienced distorted his perspective. It can do the same to us as well.

- If you have been terminated from your job, you may fear you will never be employed again.
- If you have lost your mate, you may fear you will be lonely the rest of your life.
- If you have suffered a financial setback, you may fear you will never recover.

God knew what Elijah needed more than anything to regain his emotional and spiritual equilibrium: rest. So the prophet "lay down and slept under a juniper tree" (1 Kings 19:5). The ability to experience deep, restoring sleep is a gift from God. The psalmist declared, "[God] grants sleep to those he loves" (Ps. 127:2 NIV).

Often sleep is the sure cure for a bad day. Conversely, the lack of sleep can be the sure cause of a bad day. Experts say the average adult needs between seven and eight hours of sleep a night. If you are getting too little or too much sleep, what adjustments do you need to make to your daily schedule?

We do not know how long Elijah slept under the juniper tree, but I assume he had sufficient rest because God sent an angelic wake-up call: "And behold, there was an angel touching him, and he said to him, 'Arise, eat.' Then he looked and behold, there was at his head a bread cake baked on hot stones, and a jar of water. So he ate and drank" (1 Kings 19:5–6).

Depression suppresses our desire to eat. Nothing looks enticing, and frankly, most things look nauseating. But eating a simple, light, and healthy meal—and staying properly hydrated—is one of the most important things we can do during bad days.

It always makes me smile when I come to passages like Acts 27:33–36, because we tend to think of the apostle Paul as a theological giant. And he was. But he was also a very practical man. After his arrest in Jerusalem, he was placed on a ship to Rome to stand trial before Nero. Caught in a violent storm, passengers and crew had not eaten in fourteen days. So Paul encouraged everyone to eat. "He took bread and gave thanks to God in the presence of all [two hundred and seventy-six people], and he broke it and began to eat. *All of them were encouraged* and they themselves also took food" (Acts 27:35–36).

Did you catch that? "All of them were encouraged." There is a reason we take food to those who are sick or bereaved. Food not only provides for their physical needs but it also encourages them that life goes on—that God and others care for them and that the darkness of the moment will not last forever.

When you are depressed, some of the most helpful things you can do are the simplest things—like getting some sleep and a good meal. When you do not get enough rest or take in enough nutrition, bad days turn into horrible days. That is one extreme.

The other extreme is sleeping and eating too much. Moving from the sofa to the refrigerator to the bed in an endless cycle will only cause your depression to deepen. That cycle must be broken. And with the help of the Holy Spirit, loved ones, and perhaps professional Christian counseling, you can find a balance to manage your sleeping and eating patterns until God turns your bad days into good days.

Strengthen Yourself Spiritually

When the angel came to Elijah and encouraged him to eat, it was probably in the evening, since Elijah had traveled a day's journey from Beersheba to the juniper tree. The next morning, the angel stirred Elijah again and fed him breakfast. "So he arose and ate and drank, and went in the strength of that food forty days and forty nights to Horeb, the mountain of God" (1 Kings 19:8).

We have already looked at God's question and Elijah's answer on Mount Horeb, but I want you to notice something unusual that occurs between the two exchanges. After the first conversation, the Lord commanded Elijah to come out of the cave.

> [God] said, Go forth, and stand upon the mount before the Lord. And, behold, the Lord passed by, and a great and strong wind rent the mountains, and brake in pieces the rocks before the Lord; but the Lord was not in the wind: and after the wind an earthquake; but the Lord was not in the earthquake:
> And after the earthquake a fire; but the Lord was not in the fire: and after the fire a still small voice. (vv. 11–12 KJV)

When bad days come, most of us want God to show up and do big things: miraculous healings, the sudden and unexpected return of a prodigal, addictions broken overnight, or a mountain of financial debt magically erased. But God usually answers in less dramatic ways. He offers us courage to face our illnesses, wisdom to handle our finances, and grace in our struggle with sin.

It is with a "still small voice" that God calls us out of our caves in which we have hidden. And with a gentle whisper,

God urges us to cry for help during the storm. But to hear and heed Him, especially when the wind is howling and the waves are crashing, we must learn how to discern and listen to God's voice.

David was an extraordinary leader and the textbook definition of *significance*. But David was not exempt from experiencing bad days. Perhaps his worst day (other than when the prophet Nathan exposed his sin with Bathsheba) is recorded in 1 Samuel 30. After one of their missions, David and his men returned to the town of Ziklag only to discover that the Amalekites had destroyed their homes and taken their wives and children. Incredibly discouraged, David's men talked openly about stoning him. Talk about a bad day! But notice how David responded:

> David was greatly distressed because the people spoke of stoning him, for all the people were embittered, each one because of his sons and his daughters. But *David strengthened himself in the LORD his God*. (1 Sam. 30:6)

You may never experience a devastating house fire, the kidnapping of a family member, or a mutiny by your most trusted allies—all on the same day—but you will inevitably face your own bad days. Everyone who wants to experience an extraordinary life must learn how to strengthen themselves in the Lord by listening to the voice of God.

Here are some practical things you can do to strengthen yourself in the Lord when you experience a bad day.

First, *dedicate a time and place where you get alone with God*. It doesn't matter whether it's the morning or evening, there needs to be a time when you have a regular appointment to meet with God. Some like to do this over a cup of coffee or sitting at the dining room table. I told you in the chapter dealing with prayer that I do this by kneeling beside the couch in my office. If you are unaccustomed to doing this, do not try and overdo it. Ten or fifteen minutes a day is a great way to start! If you are going through a particularly difficult season in your life that is the result of a major loss, a painful circumstance, or a wrong choice, you might consider setting aside a full day or half a day to meet with God.

Second, *select a portion of the Bible to read and meditate on.* Remember, God's primary means of communication to us is through His Word. When you read Scripture, you know you are listening to the voice of God. You might consider Psalm 34, which extols the faithfulness of God, or Psalm 51, which describes the forgiveness of God. For a longer passage, try reading Romans 8—my favorite chapter in the Bible— which reminds us of the love of God. Or you might want to read through an entire book of the Bible. Paul's brief letter to the Philippians is a great place to start, since it instructs us on how to be joyful despite difficult circumstances.

Third, *choose one or two verses to memorize.* Any verse or two that grabs your attention or brings comfort in your trial is fine. When bad days come your way in the future, the Lord loves to bring those verses back to your memory—to encourage you again.

Fourth, *after reading, spend time in prayer.* Your prayers do not have to be eloquent or lengthy. God does not pay more attention to long, drawn-out prayers laced with "Thees" and "Thous" than those offered in more common language. God does not weigh your words; He weighs your heart. This is a time to be honest with God, telling Him what is in your heart rather than what you think should be in your heart. Transparency with God in prayer begins with confessing any sin in your life. Remember, when you acknowledge your wrong actions or wrong attitudes, you are not giving God any new information!

Finally, *read a few pages in a good Christian book that is centered on the attributes of God.* Some I recommend are A. W. Tozer's *The Knowledge of the Holy*, J. Oswald Sanders's *The Pursuit of the Holy*, and J. I. Packer's *Knowing God*. Reading a chapter or two a day about the character qualities of God will remind you that you are not following a philosophy but a Person—the Creator of the universe, who cares about you and wants to help you overcome your bad days.

Encourage Yourself Emotionally

When we become discouraged, the first thing we want to do is find a place to hide, to be alone. What we should do, however, is find a place for encouragement.

Elijah "left his servant" at Beersheba, and "he himself went a day's journey into the wilderness" (1 Kings 19:3–4). There, all alone, he threw himself under a juniper tree. And then he went farther into the desolate desert and hid in a cave.

One of the most common reactions I see in those who are experiencing bad days is physical and emotional withdrawal from other people. The more we isolate ourselves from others, the more vulnerable we become to despair. Our very real adversary, Satan, has a three-pronged, effective strategy: isolate, attack, and destroy. If the enemy can pry us away from the emotional support and perspective other Christians can offer us, then he is free to relentlessly pummel and eventually destroy us.

But God did not design us to live as hermits in caves. He designed us to live in community with other people. And, of course, the most nurturing community of people we can surround ourselves with during a difficult season of life is the church. Yet, as my friend David Jeremiah observes, many Christians isolate themselves from the church during a bad season—just at the time they most need the support of other believers.

> Our faith isn't a luxury intended for periods of smooth sailing— neither is our fellowship. When trouble comes along, that's when it's wonderful to be part of a faithful, Bible-believing body of people who will rally around you. They'll pray for you, support you with their resources, encourage you, and counsel you in tough decisions. The devil is the only one whose opinion is that you should take a sabbatical from church in the hard times.[6]

The essential encouragement that a local fellowship of believers provides inspired the author of Hebrews to write, "Let us consider how to stimulate one another to love and good deeds, not forsaking our own assembling together . . . but encouraging one another" (Heb. 10:24–25).

That is what Elijah needed—what everyone needs during bad days—the encouragement that comes from other people, especially other believers. As we have seen, God told Elijah, "Go, return on your way . . . and Elisha the son of Shaphat of Abel-meholah you shall anoint as prophet in your place" (1 Kings 19:15–16). Refreshed and restored, Elijah left his cave and connected with other people, including the person who would eventually succeed him in ministry.

Bad days are inevitable, but they do not have to last forever. Those who experience an extraordinary life have learned how to navigate through times of discouragement by strengthening themselves physically, emotionally, and spiritually. Experiencing a bad season of life is like traveling through a dark tunnel. The bad news is that while you are in the tunnel, you cannot see anything in front of you. The good news is that once you have entered the tunnel, you are already on your way out of it.

SECRET #7

Live Life with the End in View

My parents died within a few years of one another. Strangely, the scenario was the same for each. After several weeks of feeling ill, each went to the doctor, who decided to perform exploratory surgery. Terminal cancer was discovered in both my mother and father. Both were given only four or five months to live, and both died within that period.

At some point during their final months—knowing they would soon be departing for their home in heaven—both my father and mother asked me to drive them to places that were important to them: a favorite hamburger joint where they enjoyed a final meal, their childhood homes, and even our family cemetery plot where they would be buried. But at the top of their lists were the places where they felt they had made a lasting impact. For my mother, it was the high school where she had spent three decades investing in students. For my dad, it was his church (the church I now pastor), which had been the center of our family's life.

I often wonder how I would respond if, like my parents, I was told I only had a few months to live. What places would I want to visit where I had made an eternal difference? Who would I want to see and talk with one last time? And after I was gone, what places and which people would my wife and children take others to visit to show where my legacy continued?

What if it was you? How would you respond to those questions?

Those who want to live an extraordinary life realize that the best use of their finite time on earth is to spend it on those things that are infinite—that will outlast life on earth. Significant people spend their days with one eye on the clock, counting down to the day of their departure, and the other eye on the calculator, determining how to multiply their influence for the glory of God and the good of others. Significant people live their lives with the end in view.

Death: Certain . . . and Soon

The one constant in human history is death. The writer of the book of Hebrews declared, "It is appointed for men to die once and after this comes judgment" (Heb. 9:27). The Greek word for "appointed" means, "to be laid away" or "reserved." In the context of Hebrews 9, we could think of it like this: our lives are on layaway until death comes to claim them. And your time *is* coming.

Like my parents, you may get advance notice about the timing of your departure, or it may sneak up on you without warning. But make no mistake about it: God has already written on His calendar in indelible ink the date of your death. David declared, "In Your book were all written the days that were ordained for me, when as yet there was not one of them" (Ps. 139:16).

Think about that! Before you were even born, God predetermined the day of your birth and the day of your death—and all the days represented by the tiny dash between those two milestone events. Every second that ticks away moves you closer and closer to the fixed time of your departure.

What will you leave behind when the inevitable departure day arrives?

Lasting legacies are not made by squandering time on worthless pursuits—watching mindless television or scrolling through social media. From God's perspective, significant lives are not even built on the foundation of material wealth or vocational success, which in the end will be nothing more than "wood, hay, [and] straw" (1 Cor. 3:12).

Elijah left a solid legacy that continued long after he departed this world. In previous chapters, we looked at his experiences in Cherith, Zarephath, and Mount Carmel and learned where he lived and ministered. We have explored his life and have discovered the secrets of significance. But to ensure we leave a legacy that endures long after we have departed this earth, Elijah has one more lesson to teach us: to live with the end in view.

Most of us tend to live in the present tense. But if we want a lasting legacy like Elijah's, then we must learn how to think in the future tense. Doing that requires embracing the right perspective, the right principle, and the right priority.

The Right Perspective: Take the Long View of Your Life

Most of us are addicted to instantaneous results. This is true whether we are building a house, a business, or a family. We want things to be done right the first time, every time. And we want it done *right now*!

The problem with this mind-set is that speedy often leads to sloppy. And sloppy does not make the kind of impact we want to make in life. Significance is not microwaveable. It is simmered and slow-cooked over a generation. It takes a lifetime to build a legacy. If you have read this far, you obviously want to leave a positive legacy that outlasts you. To see how well your legacy is coming along, you need to look into your past—to see where you have traveled in life and determine if you need to make any course corrections while you still have time. And then you need to look into your future—to see if you have established a solid foundation others can build on.

Remembering Your Past Will Prepare You for the Future

Every person is the lengthening shadow of his or her past. We all come from somewhere and from someone. And the people and places of our past help shape our present and our future.

The Lord knew this and often told the children of Israel to remember their past—that they were once slaves whom God had emancipated. He instructed them to build memorials as reminders of His faithfulness in the past so they might have confidence of His faithfulness in the future.

While the Israelites were in bondage to the Babylonians, the prophet Isaiah encouraged them to recall God's promise to bless Abraham and his descendants: "Look to the rock from which you were hewn and to the quarry from which you were dug" (Isa. 51:1).

Later, after the Israelites were back in the promised land, they began to rebel against the Lord—again. However, a group of Jews who feared the Lord determined to maintain a righteous life in the midst of unrighteousness. One way they did this was to create a "book of remembrance," a journal recounting God's faithfulness, mercy, and grace in their past (Mal. 3:16). Reflecting on their history and writing down God's past favors would give them confidence for the future.

I have created my own book of remembrance, though I do not call it that. As I mentioned earlier, it is a journal that records my prayer requests and how the Lord has answered each one. My journal also contains some honest moments of confession when I needed to make course corrections in my life. My journal is part of my legacy. I hope when I am gone my children and grandchildren will read it and find confidence in the faithfulness of God.

Have you created your own book of remembrance? If not, you should. Get a journal and begin writing down what God is showing you and doing in your life, as well as in the lives of your family and friends. When the day comes for you to depart this earth, it will be a treasured heirloom for generations to come. You and your legacy will live on. As a friend of mine says, "Those who keep a journal outlive the lives they've lived."

When we come to the final day of Elijah's earthly life—a day Elijah knew was coming—we watch as Elijah takes his protégé Elisha on a tour of spiritually significant places in the prophet's life and in the history of Israel. Elijah was leaving Elisha with a verbal book of remembrance—a map of where God showed Himself faithful to Elijah and to the nation. There was nothing random about these locations.[1] As Chuck Swindoll notes, each represented a significant event in Israel's history and reminded Elijah of key moments in his relationship with God.

Gilgal—the Place of Beginning

The first location Elijah and Elisha visited was the city of Gilgal (2 Kings 2:1), the place of beginning. According to Joshua 4:19, Gilgal was the place where the children of Israel first camped in the promised land after crossing the Jordan River. It was the place where Israel celebrated the first Passover in the land, eating the fruit of their homeland instead of the food of the wilderness—manna (Josh. 5:10–12). For Elijah, Gilgal marked the beginning of his final journey, the one that would take him to heaven.

My own Gilgal is the church I pastor, First Baptist Church in Dallas. Although a few years ago we completely re-created our downtown campus and built a new state-of-the-art worship center, we kept the original 120-year-old sanctuary. Occasionally on a Friday afternoon, when few other people are around, I go into that old sanctuary and look at the center aisle I walked down as a five-year-old boy when I trusted in Christ. I look at the altar where I knelt as the leaders of the church laid hands on me during my ordination to the ministry almost forty years ago. I stand behind the pulpit and remember the sermons I preached there.

Where is your Gilgal? Where is the place where you first came to understand your own sinfulness and the truth of Christ's death and resurrection as the only remedy for sin?

What events and people led you to faith in Jesus Christ? Recording those events in your book of remembrance will be a great encouragement to those you leave behind.

Bethel—the Place of Prayer

Next, the Lord sent Elijah and Elisha to Bethel (2 Kings 2:2)—the place of prayer. "Beth-el" means "house of God." It was the place where Abraham built an altar after God's promise to bless him (Gen. 12:8). Perhaps by walking the ancient streets of Bethel, Elijah remembered the altars in his own life: the campsite at Cherith, where the ravens brought him breakfast and dinner; the household at Zarephath, where the widow fed him from the endless supply of flour and oil and God raised the widow's son from the dead; and the mountain of Carmel, where Elijah stood against evil and the Lord answered his prayer for rain.

When I was in high school, my Bethel was a park near my school. I would go there early in the morning before classes and talk with and listen to God. Later, after Amy and I married, my Bethel changed to a baseball field near our first home. Today it is the couch in my office, which I kneel beside every morning.

You probably have a Bethel—a place where you poured out your heart to the Lord. It is the place you surrendered something precious: the death of a child, the fatal sickness of a spouse, the loss of a job or a business, the death of a dream. It is the place where you "crouched down on the earth and put [your] face between [your] knees" in prayer (1 Kings 18:42). Make a note of this place in your book of remembrance.

Jericho—the Place of Battle

Then the Lord sent Elijah and Elisha to Jericho (2 Kings 2:4)—the place of battle. As Chuck Swindoll notes, Jericho, where the walls came crashing down, was to the ancient Hebrews what Normandy was to the Allied Forces in World War II. This was a place of conquest, of reclaiming territory that had been temporarily lost to the enemy.

Replaying the battle in his mind—the blast of trumpets, the shouts of warriors, the rumble of walls, the swish of arrows, the clang of swords—Elijah must have recalled the battles in his own life: his verbal fencing with Ahab, his titanic struggle against the prophets of Baal and Asherah, and his personal struggle with discouragement and disillusionment under the juniper tree and in the cave on Mount Horeb.

Survey your past. Where was your Jericho—the place where you did battle against rebellion, addictions, lusts, anger, laziness, selfishness, or doubt? You do not need to write a tell-all account, but jot down in your book of remembrance some of the struggles you had in life and how God forgave you. It will not only encourage you but also build confidence in the lives of those who come after you.

The Jordan River—the Place of Departure

Then the Lord sent Elijah and Elisha to the Jordan River (v. 6)—the place of departure. The Jordan was the place of Elijah's translation from earth to heaven. Since Adam and Eve's rebellion in the Garden of Eden, every human being has experienced physical death—with two exceptions: Enoch (Gen. 5:22–24) and Elijah. Enoch and Elijah stepped over the threshold of heaven without ever tasting of death.

As [Elijah and Elisha] were going along and talking, behold, there appeared a chariot of fire and horses of fire which separated the two of them. And Elijah went up by a whirlwind to heaven. (2 Kings 2:11)

Instead of focusing on why God may have chosen to exempt Elijah from physical death, I want to center on how Elijah used his impending departure as an opportunity to build a godly legacy for the one he would leave behind: Elisha. Of all the words Elijah had spoken to his protégé, none would be more memorable than the prophecy made before Elijah was caught up into heaven, assuring Elisha that he, too, would experience the power of God's Spirit.

Part of leaving an enduring legacy is preparing those closest to you for your inevitable departure from this life. Our family cemetery plot is located in the town of Van Alstyne, Texas, about thirty miles north of Dallas. At the end of every visit to my grandparents, the whole family would pile into the car and drive the short distance to the cemetery. As we stood in a circle around the graves of family members, my grandfather would say, "When I'm gone, don't grieve for me. I'll be in a better place." He would then lead us in prayer, thanking God for those who had gone before us.

Later, when my parents were facing their own deaths, I drove them to that same cemetery where their bodies would be placed. "Robert, be faithful in the ministry God has given you," they charged me. While they were alive, my parents taught me many important lessons about life. But their most memorable words were their final ones—words that remind me of what truly matters in life.

Today, when Amy, the kids, and I visit the graves of my parents and grandparents, I take the opportunity to remind them that my greatest desire when I am gone is that they live God-centered lives. They sometimes roll their eyes and tease me about "Dad's Death Talk," but I know after I have departed from their sight, they will remember just as I remember.

If conducting a "death talk" with your family members on your cemetery plot seems a little morbid, do not miss the important principle: foundational to leaving a legacy of significance is preparing those closest to you for your inevitable death. Talk openly about the brevity of life on earth. Assure them that you do not fear your departure for, as the Scripture says, "to be absent from the body [is] to be at home with the Lord" (2 Cor. 5:8). Verbally, and perhaps in your book of remembrance, emphasize the essential truths you want them to remember.

Never Forget: The Work Goes On

After God scooped up Elijah, Elisha returned to the Jordan River with Elijah's mantle—the cloak that signified his prophetic office. As Elijah had done, Elisha touched the water of the river with the cloak and it divided so he could cross over on dry ground (2 Kings 2:8, 14). Then Elisha asked, "Where is the LORD, the God of Elijah?" (v. 14).

Elisha was not doubting God's presence or power, as if God had retracted into heaven in the same whirlwind that transported Elijah heavenward. Rather, Elisha was expressing confidence that the same God who was with Elijah was now with him. In fact, Elisha's question points to two encouraging truths.

God's Power Is Not Limited to a Particular Time or Place

Jesus, the Son of God, "is the same yesterday and today and forever" (Heb. 13:8). God does not change. From the very beginning, God has been active in the affairs of humanity. The God of 850 BC —the time of Elijah and Elisha—is just as powerful and active in whatever year you happen to be reading this book!

The passing of time does not cause God's arm to atrophy. Jesus is still leading men and women to salvation. God the Father is still protecting His people from evil. And the Holy Spirit is still empowering believers to experience supernatural lives.

God's Power Is Not Limited to a Particular Person

God's leaders may change, but God's power remains constant. Elijah had been taken, but Elisha remained—and the people observed, "The spirit of Elijah rests on Elisha" (2 Kings 2:15).

We easily get caught up in the cult of personality, believing that only so-and-so can carry on the work of God. As I said in the previous chapter, no one is indispensable! God always has seven thousand waiting in the wings; He always has a backup plan—and a backup to the backup plan.

God worked powerfully through Moses and then through Joshua, through David and then through Solomon, through Elijah and then through Elisha. And God can work powerfully through you, right where you are. Nothing you do will be more significant than living for Christ and helping others live for Christ. That is a legacy worth handing down to generations. And all it takes is an obedient heart, a humble spirit, and a little bit of faith. This is the perspective that significant legacies are built upon. But leaving a significant legacy requires more than the right perspective. We must also utilize the right principle.

The Right Principle: Valuing Faithfulness

Former British politician Tony Benn was brought up on the Bible. In fact, his mother was a biblical scholar, reading the Old Testament in Hebrew and the New Testament in Greek. In an interview, Tony recalled his mother telling him that the Old Testament could be summarized as the struggle between kings and prophets. "There are kings and there are prophets," he said. "The kings have the power, and the prophets have the principles."[2]

What principles will transform your ordinary life into an extraordinary life—into a life of true significance? One principle foundational to all others is this: God measures significance by faithfulness, not by success.

Faithfulness versus Success

Most people have concluded that to have an extraordinary life—to be a significant person—they must be world-shakers and world-changers. In other words, they measure significance in terms of visible results. Truly successful—and therefore significant—people are those with microphones wowing crowds of thousands with brilliant, life-altering ideas or those who have the political muscle to change the status quo.

By these measures, we have to conclude that Elijah was *not* successful. Sure, he did a lot of miraculous things, but his dream of seeing his wayward countrymen return to God never materialized. He did have a modicum of success after Mount Carmel, but in the end even that success evaporated. Within a few generations, the Assyrian army swept through the northern kingdom of Israel, decimated the capital city, and dragged the people into exile. The few who remained intermarried with foreigners and became the mixed-race Samaritans so hated by the Jews of Jesus's day.

If Elijah had defined significance as immediate and visible results, then it seems odd that his protégé Elisha would desire to be just like his mentor. After they crossed the Jordan, Elijah said, "Ask what I shall do for you before I am taken from you." Elisha responded, "Please, let a double portion of your spirit be upon me" (1 Kings 2:9).

If significance equaled success in the eyes of Elisha, then his request is strange indeed, given that he wanted to be like a man who had very few tangible results to show from a lifetime of ministry. Imagine a father who died bankrupt after teaching his son that money was the best way to keep score in life. Would the son say, "I want to be just like my dad—only twice as much"? I doubt it. But Elijah had faithfully taught Elisha by word and by example that God's measure of success is calculated not by dollars and cents or conversions but by continued faithfulness.

Faithfulness is one of those Christian words we throw around without precisely defining it. Because faithfulness is God's measure of significance, it is important to understand what the word means.

Faithfulness means consistently following God's calling for your life and leaving the results to Him. Practically speaking, faithfulness looks like this:

- A faithful worker continues to give her best for a boss who shows little appreciation.
- A faithful husband continues to love his mate even when that love is unreturned.
- A faithful parent continues to pray for her rebellious child who continues to harden his heart toward God.
- A faithful pastor continues to preach God's Word and minister in a church with declining attendance and critical leaders.

Except for that brief time he spent hiding in the cave, Elijah was Exhibit A of faithfulness. His life illustrated what Eugene Peterson calls "a long obedience in the same direction."[3] When Elisha asked for a double portion of Elijah's spirit, he was asking for the same quality that made his mentor a truly significant person in God's eyes: the ability to follow God against the headwinds of opposition and discouragement—and a lack of visible results.

In the spiritual realm—where Elijah made his lasting impact—success is out of our control. We are called to be faithful servants of God and stewards of God's truth and to leave the results to Him. This is not reserved for preachers and "professional" Christians but is for all who follow Jesus.

Learn to Sweat the Small Stuff

"One of the dangers in our world is wanting to do big things, heroic things," philosopher and theologian Jean Vanier once wrote. But the truth is, few of us will do heroic things. However, all of us "are called to do little things lovingly"—faithfully.[4]

206

Jesus said virtually the same thing:

> He who is faithful in a very little thing is faithful also in much;
> and he who is unrighteous in a very little thing is unrighteous
> also in much. Therefore if you have not been faithful in the
> use of unrighteous wealth, who will entrust the true riches
> to you? (Luke 16:10–11)

Significant people understand there are two reasons to
faithfully fulfill small, seemingly mundane tasks with excellence. First, small things—when added together—become big
things. For example, a twenty-year-old who invests only one
hundred dollars a month at a reasonable rate of return over a
long period of time will have millions of dollars by the time
he or she is seventy-two. Similarly, investing ten minutes a
day reading, praying, listening to your mate, or encouraging
your family over several years can yield tremendous dividends.

However, there is another reason for striving for excellence
in the seemingly small things in life: God uses small assignments as tests to see if we are capable of handling bigger assignments. I experienced that truth firsthand many years ago.

As I wrote earlier, my first assignment as a senior pastor
was in a small town in West Texas. Amy and I went to the
church filled with anticipation about our new ministry, but
while God certainly blessed our church with growth, life in
a small town was different than the life in the big city I had
been accustomed to. In Eastland, ministry became monoto-
nous for me, especially Sunday night services.

Back then, many churches held Sunday evening services.
These services mostly attracted only a remnant of the faithful, who returned for a second dose of music and preaching.

Because of the diminished crowds—and the exhaustion of both the people and the pastor—Sunday evening services were often anticlimactic.

Frankly, I hated going back to church on Sunday night and preaching to a group of about 120 people, sparsely scattered throughout the sanctuary. I rationalized, *If the congregation isn't going to bother to show up, then why should I put much effort into this?* And so, for a while I gave up careful preparation for my Sunday evening messages. I preached a warmed-over morning sermon. I was so unenthused about preaching that I would spend the hour before the service watching *60 Minutes* on television, waiting until the last possible moment before walking to the church from our parsonage.

Then God convicted me of my slothfulness. *If one hundred people are willing to come and listen to My Word, shouldn't you give them your very best effort?* the Lord seemed to say to me. So I began preparing for my Sunday evening messages with as much fervor as I did for Sunday morning. I announced a series on the book of Daniel, which I had never preached before. The crowd for those services began to grow, and people started attending from other churches in the community that did not have an evening service.

One Monday morning, I received a call from a pastoral search committee from one of the most influential churches in our denomination. Eventually, they called me to be the pastor of their church—and I served there for fifteen years. What made them want to call me as their pastor? They told me that one Sunday evening they had planned to visit a well-known church to listen to their pastor. They called that morning and found out he was gone that day. Then they called a second church on their list and discovered that church had no

Sunday evening service. Finally, as a last resort, they came to my little church because we had an evening service and I was preaching. The committee later said to me, "After we listened to your sermon from Daniel we thought, 'We want a pastor who gives his best—even for a Sunday evening sermon.'" Sometimes, faithfulness in small things leads to bigger things.

Whether our assignment is large or seemingly insignificant, God is glorified when we faithfully do the job He has given us. My sister asked me an interesting question the other day. She said, "Robert, if, like our parents, you got the news you had only a few months to live, how would you spend your time?"

How about you? What would you do if you only had a few months to live?

Would you quit your job?

Would you pull your money out of the bank, liquidate your assets, and buy a ticket to some exotic location?

Would you fall into a depression and drink yourself into oblivion?

As Elijah's last hours approached, he did not spend them on his knees, making peace with God. Nor did he spend them in quiet contemplation, cloistered away from daily activities. Rather, Elijah spent his last day faithfully fulfilling the assignments God had given him—going to Gilgal, Bethel, Jericho, and the Jordan River to encourage the prophets in training and to prepare his protégé Elisha to take over his ministry.

Your office or your home is just as good of a departure point for heaven as the Jordan River was for Elijah. Those who want to experience a life of significance value faithfulness in the small things of life until the moment they are caught up into heaven. To help test whether you are faithful in everyday activities, let me ask you some penetrating questions—questions you ought to ask yourself at the end of every day:

- Did I tell and show my spouse and kids that I love them?
- Did I do my job honestly and to the best of my ability, giving my employer a full day's work?
- Did I demonstrate care and concern for my neighbors and my coworkers?
- Did I express gratitude for the blessings in my life?
- Did I take my anxieties to God and leave them with Him?
- Did I keep my heart, mind, and body pure, confessing my sins when I failed?
- Did I obey the Word of God?
- Did I put others before myself?
- Did I do to others what I would want them to do to me?
- Did I try to glorify God in my thoughts, words, and actions?

These questions can be applied to any walk of life—whether you are the president of the United States, a homemaker, a salesperson, or a student.

The Right Priority: People

Living a life marked by significance requires the *right perspective*: taking the long view of life. Significant people also embrace the *right principle*: long-term faithfulness is more valuable than immediate, visible success. Finally, Elijah's life illustrates the importance of focusing on the *right priority* in life.

When Amy and I were in high school, we had an assistant principal named Ernest Kelly, who often stopped and asked students probing questions in hopes of providing guidance for our futures. Amy and I still laugh about one of Mr. Kelly's favorite questions: "Do you like working with people or things?" There have been times—like after a lackluster Sunday service or a challenging deacons' meeting—when I would have answered, "Things!" As one pastor said, "Ministry would be great if it weren't for the people."

However, Elijah would have answered without equivocation, "People!" God's prophet understood that the way to influence the world is by influencing people. Those who want to live significant lives grasp the futility of building their lives around things like money, homes, positions, or achievements, because they are ultimately lost, stolen, destroyed, or diminished in value.

However, people—both Christians and non-Christians— have a shelf life of "forever." Those who have trusted in Christ will exist forever in heaven, while those who have rejected God's offer of forgiveness will exist forever in hell. People who live life with the end in view understand that their best chance for making an impact on the world is to invest in the lives of people—lives that will go on and on and on.

Throughout this book, I have quoted one of my mentors, Dr. Howard Hendricks, not only because he was a careful student and great communicator of Scripture but because he made a significant difference in the lives of people. "Prof," as his students called him, tried pastoring a small church for a while but soon resigned. I once asked him why, and with his usual sharp wit he replied, "I got tired of deciding who could and could not have a key to the church kitchen!" But beyond not wanting to referee the petty squabbles of small-church politics, Prof felt he could make a greater impact for God's kingdom by training pastors than by being a pastor. And impact the kingdom he did! People such as David Jeremiah, Tony Evans, Bruce Wilkinson, and a host of others—including me—sat at the feet of Prof Hendricks and were privileged to call him mentor and friend. There is no telling how many millions of lives have been impacted for God's kingdom through this influencer of influencers.

I do not know whether Prof ever read this piece of advice Theodore Roosevelt received from his father, but I know he would wholeheartedly agree with it: "All that gives me most pleasure in the retrospect is connected with others, an evidence that we are not placed here to live exclusively for ourselves."[5]

I do not think it is an accident that Elijah spent his final day on earth with the people who would carry on his legacy—Elisha and the sons of the prophets. But Elijah did more than just hang out with these men. He used his limited time intentionally: encouraging them and mentoring them.

Spend Your Life Encouraging Others

When Billy Graham was asked whether one person's courageous acts could inspire others to be courageous, he said, "Courage is contagious. When a brave man takes a stand, the spines of others are often stiffened."[6]

This was certainly true during the days of Elijah. Even though Obadiah hid one hundred prophets in caves and the Lord preserved seven thousand who did not bow to Baal, Elijah often described himself as a lone prophet. But no prophet who is bold and uncompromising remains alone for long. In time, Elijah's courage encouraged others—especially on the last day of his life.

Among the seven thousand Israelites who did not worship Baal was a group of future leaders known as the "sons of the prophets" (2 Kings 2:3, 5, 7). At least two seminaries were formed to train these would-be prophets: one at Bethel and one at Jericho. The curriculum must have been outstanding, since these students knew that Elijah's final day had come. At both campuses, the sons of the prophets asked Elisha, "Do you know that the LORD will take away your master from over you today?" (vv. 3, 5). "Yes, I know," was Elisha's reply.

We have already seen that God commanded Elijah to cross over the Jordan River, where the whirlwind whooshed him away. So why did the Lord command Elijah to visit Bethel and Jericho? Why not send Elijah immediately to the Jordan, either to preach a great sermon to the Israelites or to take an early departure to heaven? God knew that, like Prof Hendricks, the best way for Elijah to spend his limited time on earth was to influence the influencers—in this case the up-and-coming prophets of Israel.

I wish God had recorded Elijah's final words to these students. But since He didn't, I imagine Elijah might have

- related how God protected him when he confronted Ahab with the news that the Lord was sending a severe drought because of Ahab's idolatry,

- recounted how God preserved his life at Cherith and Zarephath, just as creeks and cisterns were drying up and containers of food were empty,
- regaled them with the story of his dramatic contest on Mount Carmel when God answered his prayer with fire,
- spoken honestly about his battle with fear and depression over Jezebel's threat,
- exhorted them to choose an extraordinary life and to learn the secrets of significance, and
- above all, encouraged them with his own life message: the Lord is the only true God and can be trusted to do what He has promised.

Elijah's time with the sons of the prophets—especially on the last day of his life—tells me that people are the best investment of my time. Frankly, I did not always believe that. In my younger days of ministry, I confess, I saw other people only as means to an end: workers to staff a new ministry, donors to fund a new initiative, or advocates to push through my agenda. Any time I spent with other people was a necessary investment to get the job done. The goal is what mattered—or so I thought.

But the longer I live, the more I realize that goals, projects, and accomplishments are quickly forgotten or superseded by the accomplishments of others. People—not projects—are what really matter. And more than anything, the people God has placed in our lives need encouragement. When I think about the people who have made an indelible impression on my life, it is those who have visualized a great future for me by helping me to identify and maximize my God-given gifts.

I told you about my ninth-grade teacher Miss Fry, who encouraged me to pursue a career as a preacher. She had a profound impact on the direction of my life. The first time I saw the movie *The King's Speech*, I thought of her and how one person could influence the destiny of a single life—or the destiny of a nation.

If you saw the movie, you may recall that King George VI had such a severe stutter that, when called upon to speak in public, he was unintelligible. He hired Lionel Logue, a speech therapist, to help him with his speech impediment. Working together, doing breathing exercises and tongue twisters, Logue discovered that the king's stammer was not due to a physical defect but a psychological one. As a boy, the young prince had been sickly. As a result, he was bullied by his older brother, treated harshly by his nannies, and dismissed by his father, King Edward V.

But with perseverance, hard work, and the encouragement of Logue, King George VI became a confident and calming voice for the British people at the outset of World War II. At one point, Logue wrote the king these encouraging words:

> When a fresh patient comes to me his usual query is: "Will I be able to speak like the King?" and my reply is: "Yes, if you will work like he does." I will cure anyone of intelligence if they will only work like you did—for you are now reaping the benefit of this tremendously hard work you did at the beginning.[7]

Flattered by this and other notes of encouragement, the king expressed his gratitude for what Logue had done in his life. "I wonder if you realise how grateful I am to you for having made it possible for me to carry out this vital part of my job," the king wrote. "I cannot thank you enough."[8]

Time spent encouraging others is never time wasted. Who knows? After you are long gone, someone might write about you as they did about Lionel Logue: "There must be thousands of people who, like myself, are living to bless the name of Lionel Logue."[9] Changing the life of a king—and a nation—is not a bad legacy!

Spend Your Life Mentoring Others

Elijah knew that if the good work he had done in Israel was to endure, he needed a protégé into whom he could pour his life. For Elijah, that someone was Elisha. In your life, that someone may be your child or another younger person you believe has the potential to make a significant difference in the world, especially after you are gone.

God blessed me with two faithful mentors: Dr. Howard Hendricks, whom I have said much about, and Dr. W. A. Criswell, my predecessor at the church I now pastor. When I was fifteen years old I went to Dr. Criswell's office to tell him of my call to the ministry. He said, "Robert, that is tremendous. Now, here is what I want you to do. I want you to spend the entire summer working here at the church—in the missions department, the children's area, the music ministry, and every place else. I want you to learn every square inch of this church—because one day it will all be yours!" And then he had me kneel beside him as he prayed for me, asking God to prepare me for the day when I would become the pastor of First Baptist Church, Dallas. Until the day Dr. Criswell died, he invested his life in me, believing that one day I would be the undershepherd of the church I now serve.

Any impact I have made in this world is a direct result of the investment these men made in my life. Both of these men—along with Elijah—illustrate three key characteristics of effective mentoring.[10]

The Mentor Must Take the Initiative

In obedience to the Lord's instructions, Elijah proactively found Elisha and threw his cloak around Elisha's shoulders (1 Kings 19:19). Those who want to mentor others cannot simply sit back and wait for people to knock on their door. You must actively seek out younger men and women who are eager to learn.

The Mentor Must Be Available

Elisha "went with Elijah as his assistant" (v. 21 NLT). That speaks of a relationship where these two men spent considerable time together. Mentoring takes time.

Many people think they do not have the time to mentor someone. Their calendars are overflowing with appointments and endless responsibilities. Believe me, I understand—you should take a look at my calendar! But mentoring another person does not have to take extra time. You have to eat lunch, don't you? Spend time with someone over lunch—share your life, your victories, your defeats, how the Lord has been faithful to you, and what the Lord is teaching you.

If you are running an errand or taking a short trip, then it might be appropriate to invite your protégé to join you. I will never forget Prof Hendricks taking me with him to several conferences where he was speaking when I was in my twenties. On one occasion, after we had settled into our seats on the plane, he asked, "Robert, what are you dreaming about these days?" For the next three hours, we talked about my goals and dreams for the future. Prof not only affirmed my dreams but offered invaluable counsel from his own life that helped me ultimately realize those dreams.

The Mentor Must Serve As a Model of Godliness

People tend to forget what they hear, but they rarely forget what they see. Mentors become a kind of spiritual and ethical mold their protégés are poured into.

We do not know how much time elapsed from Elisha's call to follow Elijah and Elijah's departure, but enough time must have passed for Elisha to note how Elijah handled some very difficult and delicate situations. Those lessons proved invaluable to Elisha when he began his own ministry.

I will never forget a lesson I learned from Prof Hendricks— a lesson he had no idea he was teaching me. On one of our trips together, having retired to our rooms for the night, I could not sleep. I got up and went down to the conference hall where Prof had spoken earlier in the evening. I noticed his Bible was still on the podium. I hesitantly opened it, thinking I would find a few favorite passages underlined. Instead, I found just about every page of his Bible marked with his insights scribbled in the margins in a variety of colored pens.

It was at that moment I grasped the secret of Howard Hendricks's remarkable ministry. He was truly a man of the Book. He did not just talk about the Bible. He breathed the Bible. God's Word was the foundation of his life and ministry.

What would someone learn if they hung around you long enough—or opened your Bible while you were asleep?

- Would they learn how important God's Word is in living a significant life?
- Would they learn how to pray when a crisis came crashing down?
- Would they learn what it means to be a faithful spouse and a loving parent?
- Would they learn how to share the gospel with an unbeliever?

The possibilities of what someone could learn from you are endless, if you make yourself available and are willing to share your life with another person.

In the business world, mentoring is about success—about helping another person reach his or her career goals. But in the spiritual world, mentoring is about significance—about making a spiritual difference in another person's life, so that person in turn might make a difference in another person's life. The apostle Paul put it like this: "The things which you have heard from me in the presence of many witnesses, entrust these to faithful men [and women] who will be able to teach others also" (2 Tim. 2:2). Paul was outlining for his protégé Timothy the multiplying impact of mentoring: one life poured into another life, who in turn pours his or her life into another life, and on and on it goes.

While writing this chapter, I often wondered what went through Elijah's mind as he felt that mighty gust of wind lift him off his feet and carry him skyward. I am sure the anticipation of what heaven was like flashed through his mind. But I wonder if Elijah looked down—even for a moment—and saw Elisha looking up and thought, *By God's grace I have lived an extraordinary life. Not only that but I am also leaving a legacy of faith—and there he is, standing along the banks of the Jordan!*

If you come to the end of your life and look back, while looking ahead to the glories of heaven, and come to a similar conclusion, then I would say you have lived an extraordinary life—a life of true significance.

A Final Thought

Each of my two daughters is like me in certain ways. My younger daughter, Dorothy, and I share a love for movies and a wicked sense of humor. But Dorothy is more like her mom—creative, highly intelligent, and empathetic. However, my older daughter, Julia, looks like my clone and has inherited many of my hopes and a few of my fears.

Over a recent holiday weekend, I took some time to spend with Julia, talking with her about her dreams for the future. She runs a successful girls' ministry at our church, is a licensed professional counselor, and is just about to publish her first book—and she's not even thirty! Yet she expressed apprehension that she was not progressing quickly enough in her goals and was afraid that many of her dreams might go unfulfilled.

It was like listening to myself thirty years ago. After our talk, Julia and her husband left, and I looked over my personal journals from three decades ago and was reminded of the anxiety I felt when I was Julia's age: the fear that I would be sentenced to an ordinary life. But looking back over the last three decades, I can say that my life has been truly extraordinary.

And your life can be extraordinary, as well. Not because the plans for our lives are the same, but because the extraordinary God who develops our unique life plans is the same "yesterday and today and forever" (Heb. 13:8).

As I conclude this book, I want to ask you the all-important question: Have you made the choice to live an extraordinary life? When the time comes for you to leave this earth, either through death or in the whirlwind like Elijah, are you determined to depart this life with a short list of regrets and long list of lives you have impacted for the kingdom of God? If so, consider offering this prayer to the God of Abraham, Isaac, Jacob, Elijah . . . and you:

Father, thank You for the breath of life and for creating me for a truly unique purpose. Right now, I am committing to myself and to You that I will discover and live out that purpose for which You have gifted me. Keep me from settling for an ordinary life. Today, I'm asking You to give me a laserlike focus as I pursue the truly extraordinary life You have planned for me. I pray my life would glorify You and Your Son, the Lord Jesus Christ, in whose name I pray, Amen.

Notes

An Ordinary Person in Extraordinary Times

1. James C. Dobson, as quoted in Charles R. Swindoll, *Living on the Ragged Edge: Coming to Terms with Reality* (Waco, TX: Word Books, 1985), 19.

2. Dwight L. Moody, as quoted in David Jeremiah, *Life Wide Open: Unleashing the Power of a Passionate Life* (Nashville: Integrity Publishers, 2003), 103.

3. A. W. Tozer, *The Pursuit of God: The Human Thirst for the Divine* (Camp Hill, PA: WingSpread Publishers, 1993), 96.

4. Peggy Noonan, "Remembering a Hero, 15 Years after 9/11," *The Wall Street Journal*, September 9, 2016, peggynoonan.com/remembering-a-hero-15-years-after-911.

Secret #1: Discover Your Unique Purpose

1. Carl Sandburg, *The People, Yes* (New York: Harcourt Brace, 1990), 103.

2. *The Shorter Catechism* (Atlanta: John Knox Press, 1965), 3.

3. John Piper, "God Is Most Glorified in Us When We Are Most Satisfied in Him," sermon, Bethlehem Baptist Church, Minneapolis, Minnesota, October 13, 2012, http://www.desiringgod.org/messages/god-is-most-glorified-in-us-when-we-are-most-satisfied-in-him.

4. Myles Udland, "Bank of America: There's a 20%–50% Chance We're Inside the Matrix and Reality Is Just a Simulation," September 8, 2016, *Business Insider*, http://www.businessinsider.com/bank-of-america-wonders-about-the-matrix-2016-9.

5. Os Guinness, *The Call: Finding and Fulfilling the Central Purpose of Your Life* (Nashville: Word Publishing, 1998), 3–4.

6. Bruce K. Waltke, *Finding the Will of God: A Pagan Notion?* (Grand Rapids: Eerdmans, 1995), 118.

7. Frederick Buechner, *Wishful Thinking: A Theological ABC* (New York: Harper & Row, 1973), 95.

8. Os Guinness, *Rising to the Call: Discovering the Ultimate Purpose of Your Life* (Nashville: W Publishing Group, 2003), 45.

9. Max Lucado, *Cure for the Common Life: Living in Your Sweet Spot* (Nashville: W Publishing Group, 2005), 7.

Secret #2: Determine to Influence Your Culture

1. Billy Graham, *World Aflame* (Garden City, NY: Doubleday, 1965), 16–17.

2. Andy Crouch, *Culture Making: Recovering Our Creative Calling* (Downers Grove, IL: InterVarsity, 2008), 37.

3. J. Budziszewski, *The Revenge of Conscience: Politics and the Fall of Man* (Dallas, TX: Spence Publishing, 1999), 20.

4. Howard G. Hendricks, *Take a Stand: What God Can Do through Ordinary You* (Portland: Multnomah Press, 1983), 9.

5. Robert Jeffress, *Not All Roads Lead to Heaven: Sharing an Exclusive Jesus in an Inclusive World* (Grand Rapids: Baker Books, 2016), 24.

Secret #3: Wait On God's Timing

1. Steve Farrar, "Can I Trust God with My Future?" sermon, Stonebriar Community Church, Frisco, Texas, March 13, 2016.

2. Rick Warren, *The Purpose Driven Life: What on Earth Am I Here For?* (Grand Rapids: Zondervan, 2002), 222.

3. Malik Jefferson, as quoted in Wescott Eberts, "Texas LB Malik Jefferson on Pre-benching Attitude: 'I Wasn't Trying to Get Better,'" *SB Nation*, November 7, 2016, www.burntorangenation.com/2016/11/7/13 556222/malik-jefferson-benching-texas-longhorns-charlie-strong.

4. The metaphor of the boot camp and the crucible is adapted from Charles R. Swindoll, *Elijah: A Man of Heroism and Humility* (Nashville: Thomas Nelson, 2000), 21–22, 45.

5. The Hebrew word for "hide" in 1 Kings 17:3 is not the same word used in Joshua 6:17, 25 when Rahab hid the spies in Jericho or in 1 Kings 18:4, 13 when Obadiah hid the one hundred prophets of the Lord. Both Rahab and Obadiah were attempting to protect God's people from harm. The word in 1 Kings 17:3 is akin to the use in Genesis 31:49: "May the

LORD watch between you and me when we are *absent* one from the other," meaning separated from each other.

6. A. W. Pink, *The Life of Elijah* (Edinburgh: The Banner of Truth Trust, 2011), 31–32.

7. Hendricks, *Take a Stand*, 25.

8. Jezebel had issued "wanted posters" for God's prophets and had already "destroyed [some] prophets of the LORD" (1 Kings 18:4).

9. At least eight times Scripture declares that nothing is impossible for God (Gen. 18:14; Job 42:2; Jer. 32:27; Zech. 8:6; Matt. 19:26; Mark 10:27; Luke 1:37; 18:27).

10. Adapted from Peggy Noonan, "Ronald Reagan," *Character Above All: Ten Presidents from FDR to George Bush*, ed. Robert A. Wilson (New York: Simon & Schuster, 1995), 219–21.

Secret #4: Burn the Ships

1. It is very unlikely Cortés actually ordered the burning of the ships. According to later testimony, Cortés ordered the ships be grounded and stripped of their riggings, sails, anchors, guns, and other tackle. Cortés claimed the ships had been rendered unseaworthy because of a wood beetle. Instead of destroying the wood, however, Cortés planned to use the timbers to build houses. See Hugh Thomas, *Conquest: Montezuma, Cortés, and the Fall of Old Mexico* (New York: Simon & Schuster, 1993), 222–23, for a detailed account of Cortés's order and the legend of "burning the ships."

2. Thomas, *Conquest*, 223.

3. See Swindoll, *Elijah*, 75.

4. Dale Ralph Davis, *1 Kings: The Wisdom and the Folly* (Scotland: Christian Focus Publications, 2013), 233.

5. Kirsten Powers, "Fox News' Highly Reluctant Jesus Follower," *Christianity Today*, October 22, 2013, www.christianitytoday.com/ct/2013/november/fox-news-highly-reluctant-jesus-follower-kirsten-powers.html?start=1.

6. Author unknown, as quoted in R. Kent Hughes, *1001 Great Stories and Quotes* (Wheaton, IL: Tyndale, 1998), 61–62.

Secret #5: Unleash the Power of Prayer

1. Davis, *1 Kings*, 234.

2. The authorization is important since Elijah was establishing a place of worship outside of the temple in Jerusalem, the place where God had determined to establish His name (1 Kings 9:3; 2 Chron. 7:16).

3. "Two measures of seed" is literally two *seahs* of seed. One *seah* equals approximately eleven quarts.

4. Some critics question where Elijah got twelve large jugs of water since there was a severe drought. Though several springs surround Mount Carmel, these were probably dried up. However, the Mediterranean Sea, which was unaffected by the drought, was just down the hill.

5. George Müller, *A Narrative of Some of the Lord's Dealings with George Müller*, part 3 (London: J. Nisbet & Co., 1855), 476.

6. A. J. Gordon, as quoted in Ben Patterson, *Deepening Your Conversation with God: Learning to Love to Pray* (Bloomington, MN: Bethany House, 2001), 20.

Secret #6: Learn How to Handle Bad Days

1. *Lone Survivor*, directed by Peter Berg (Universal City, CA: Universal Pictures Home Entertainment, 2004), Blu-ray.

2. Bertrand Russell, *The Autobiography of Bertrand Russell, 1872–1914*, vol. 1 (Boston: Little, Brown & Co., 1967), 287.

3. Theodore Roosevelt, as quoted in Edmund Morris, *The Rise of Theodore Roosevelt* (New York: Coward, McCann & Geoghegan, 1979), 241.

4. Theodore Roosevelt, *Ranch Life and the Hunting-Trail* (New York: The Century Co., 1899), 59.

5. See 1 Kings 19:15–16, as well as 10:31 and 2 Kings 5:12; 8:15; 10:32; 12:3, 17. On the anointing of Jehu to be king over Israel we are told that "one of the sons of the prophets" was commissioned by Elisha to anoint Jehu (2 Kings 9:1–6). So in what sense did Elijah anoint Jehu? Jehu may have been anointed twice, as David was (see 1 Sam. 16:13; 2 Sam. 2:4). Or, in the same way Jesus was said to have baptized more disciples than John, though Jesus never baptized anyone, Jesus's baptisms were carried out by His disciples (John 4:1–2). So Jehu may have been anointed by one of Elijah's disciples.

6. David Jeremiah, *A Bend in the Road: Experiencing God When Your World Caves In* (Nashville: W Publishing Group, 2000), 97.

Secret #7: Live Life with the End in View

1. I am indebted to Chuck Swindoll for the historic importance of Gilgal, Bethel, and Jericho, and the possible significance of these places in the life of Elijah. See Swindoll, *Elijah*, 165–67.

2. Tony Benn, as quoted in Howard G. Hendricks, *Standing Together: Impacting Your Generation* (Gresham, OR: Vision House Publishing, 1995), 200.

3. Eugene H. Peterson, *A Long Obedience in the Same Direction: Discipleship in an Instant Society* (Downers Grove, IL: InterVarsity, 2000).

4. Jean Vanier, as quoted in Jean Bethke Elshtain, *Sovereignty: God, State, and Self* (New York: Basic Books, 2008), 248.

5. Theodore Roosevelt Sr., as quoted in David McCullough, *Mornings on Horseback: The Story of an Extraordinary Family, a Vanished Way of Life, and the Unique Child Who Became Theodore Roosevelt* (New York: Simon & Schuster, 1981), 137.

6. Billy Graham, as quoted in Bill Adler, *Ask Billy Graham: The World's Best-Loved Preacher Answers Your Most Important Questions* (Nashville: Thomas Nelson, 2007), 224.

7. Lionel Logue, as quoted in Mark Logue and Peter Conradi, *The King's Speech* (New York: Sterling, 2010), 202.

8. King George VI, as quoted in Logue and Conradi, *King's Speech*, 202.

9. J. C. Wimbusch, as quoted in Logue and Conradi, *King's Speech*, 227.

10. I am indebted to Howard Hendricks for many of the ideas and much of the structure of this material. See Hendricks, *Standing Together*, 98–105.

About the Author

Dr. Robert Jeffress is senior pastor of the thirteen-thousand-member First Baptist Church, Dallas, Texas, a Fox News contributor, and an adjunct professor at Dallas Theological Seminary.

Dr. Jeffress has made more than two thousand guest appearances on various radio and television programs and regularly appears on major mainstream media outlets such as Fox News channel's *Fox and Friends*, *Hannity*, *Lou Dobbs Tonight*, *Varney and Co.*, and *Judge Jeanine*; ABC's *Good Morning America*; and HBO's *Real Time with Bill Maher*.

Dr. Jeffress hosts a daily radio program, *Pathway to Victory*, that is heard nationwide on over 930 stations in major markets such as Dallas–Fort Worth, New York City, Chicago, Los Angeles, Houston, Washington, DC, San Francisco, Philadelphia, and Seattle. His weekly television program can be seen in 195 countries and on 11,295 cable and satellite systems throughout the world, including China, and on the Trinity Broadcasting Network and Daystar.

Dr. Jeffress is the author of over twenty books, including *When Forgiveness Doesn't Make Sense*, *Countdown to the*

Apocalypse, Not All Roads Lead to Heaven, and *A Place Called Heaven: 10 Surprising Truths about Your Eternal Home*.

Dr. Jeffress has a DMin from Southwestern Baptist Theological Seminary, a ThM from Dallas Theological Seminary, and a BS from Baylor University. In May 2010 he was awarded a Doctor of Divinity degree from Dallas Baptist University, and in June 2011 he received the Distinguished Alumnus of the Year award from Southwestern Baptist Theological Seminary.

Dr. Jeffress and his wife, Amy, have two daughters and three grandchildren.

"My friend Robert Jeffress has done an excellent job of highlighting and illustrating the seven timeless principles from Elijah's life for spiritual significance and success that anyone can utilize today. I highly recommend this insightful and practical book for everyone who truly desires an extraordinary life. This may well be Jeffress's best book yet!"

Greg Laurie, senior pastor, Harvest Christian Fellowship, Riverside, California

"Using riveting illustrations from Elijah and modern-day believers, Robert Jeffress will inspire you to aim for the extraordinary life God has planned for you too."

James Robison, founder and president, LIFE Outreach International, Fort Worth, Texas

"I believe God has uniquely gifted Dr. Robert Jeffress to be a voice to our nation at this time. In his newest book, *Choosing the Extraordinary Life*, he leads us on a path to discover the truth to fulfilling God's plans and purposes for our lives. With engaging and biblically sound insight, he reveals seven secrets for living the extraordinary life God designed for us."

Robert Morris, founding senior pastor, Gateway Church; bestselling author, *The Blessed Life*, *The God I Never Knew*, and *Frequency*

"Biblical, relevant, and very straightforward. Dr. Jeffress has written a remarkable and on-time book about the seven secrets to 'finding, keeping, and living' an extraordinary life. His unique approach and practical insights will guide you on a new and fresh journey, leading you away from any distractions that would keep you from intimacy and favor with your loving, heavenly Father."

Marcus D. Lamb, founder and president,
Daystar Television Network

"Dr. Jeffress brings Scripture alive with the truth God's Spirit put into it. If you like rich, useful Bible teaching, you'll appreciate this book. Jeffress wisely unpacks seven secrets from Elijah's life and ministry for leading the life we were meant to live. No formulas or pat answers here. Depend on this book to guide you on the narrow road that leads to life."

Dr. Larry Crabb, psychologist; Bible teacher;
author, *When God's Ways Make No Sense*

"We love this book! It's a must-read for every Christian. Thank you, Dr. Jeffress, for inspiring and challenging us to rise above the status quo of this world. *Choosing the Extraordinary Life* is one of those books that's honest, motivating, and life-changing. If you want to live a life that's truly worth living, the seven secrets inside this book will show you how. Your life will never be the same again."

Kristen Clark and Bethany Baird, cofounders, GirlDefined
Ministries; coauthors, *Girl Defined* and *Love Defined*

Steps to Peace With God

1. God's Purpose: Peace and Life

God loves you and wants you to experience peace and life—abundant and eternal.

The Bible says ...

"We have peace with God through our Lord Jesus Christ." *Romans 5:1, NKJV*

"For God so loved the world that He gave His only begotten Son, that whoever believes in Him should not perish but have everlasting life." *John 3:16, NKJV*

"I have come that they may have life, and that they may have it more abundantly." *John 10:10, NKJV*

Since God planned for us to have peace and the abundant life right now, why are most people not having this experience?

2. Our Problem: Separation From God

God created us in His own image to have an abundant life. He did not make us as robots to automatically love and obey Him, but gave us a will and a freedom of choice.

We chose to disobey God and go our own willful way. We still make this choice today. This results in separation from God.

The Bible says ...

"For all have sinned and fall short of the glory of God." *Romans 3:23, NKJV*

"For the wages of sin is death, but the gift of God is eternal life in Christ Jesus our Lord." *Romans 6:23, NKJV*

Our choice results in separation from God.

People (Sinful) God (Holy)

Our Attempts

Through the ages, individuals have tried in many ways to bridge this gap ... without success ...

The Bible says ...

"There is a way that seems right to a man, but its end is the way of death."
Proverbs 14:12, NKJV

"But your iniquities have separated you from your God; and your sins have hidden His face from you, so that He will not hear."
Isaiah 59:2, NKJV

There is only one remedy for this problem of separation.

3. God's Remedy: The Cross

Jesus Christ is the only answer to this problem. He died on the cross and rose from the grave, paying the penalty for our sin and bridging the gap between God and people.

The Bible says ...

"For there is one God and one Mediator between God and men, the Man Christ Jesus."
1 Timothy 2:5, NKJV

"For Christ also suffered once for sins, the just for the unjust, that He might bring us to God."
1 Peter 3:18, NKJV

"But God shows his love for us in that while we were still sinners, Christ died for us." *Romans 5:8, ESV*

God has provided the only way ... we must make the choice ...

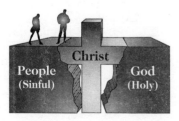

4. OUR RESPONSE: RECEIVE CHRIST

We must trust Jesus Christ and receive Him by personal invitation.

THE BIBLE SAYS ...

"Behold, I stand at the door and knock. If anyone hears My voice and opens the door, I will come in to him and dine with him, and he with Me." *Revelation 3:20, NKJV*

"But to all who did receive him, who believed in his name, he gave the right to become children of God." *John 1:12, ESV*

"If you confess with your mouth that Jesus is Lord and believe in your heart that God raised him from the dead, you will be saved." *Romans 10:9, ESV*

Are you here ... or here?

People
Sin
Rebellion
Separation

Christ

God
Peace
Forgiveness
Abundant Life
Eternal Life

Is there any good reason why you cannot receive Jesus Christ right now?

HOW TO RECEIVE CHRIST:

1. Admit your need (say, "I am a sinner").
2. Be willing to turn from your sins (repent) and ask for God's forgiveness.
3. Believe that Jesus Christ died for you on the cross and rose from the grave.
4. Through prayer, invite Jesus Christ to come in and control your life through the Holy Spirit (receive Jesus as Lord and Savior).

WHAT TO PRAY:

> Dear God,
>   I know that I am a sinner. I want to turn from my sins, and I ask for Your forgiveness. I believe that Jesus Christ is Your Son. I believe He died for my sins and that You raised Him to life. I want Him to come into my heart and to take control of my life. I want to trust Jesus as my Savior and follow Him as my Lord from this day forward.
>
>   In Jesus' Name, amen.
>
> _____   _____
> Date   Signature

GOD'S ASSURANCE: HIS WORD

IF YOU PRAYED THIS PRAYER,

THE BIBLE SAYS ...

"For 'everyone who calls on the name of the Lord will be saved.'"
Romans 10:13, ESV

Did you sincerely ask Jesus Christ to come into your life?
Where is He right now? What has He given you?

"For by grace you have been saved through faith. And this is not your
own doing; it is the gift of God, not a result of works, so that no one may
boast." *Ephesians 2:8–9, ESV*

THE BIBLE SAYS ...

"He who has the Son has life; he who does not have the Son of God does
not have life. These things I have written to you who believe in the name of
the Son of God, that you may know that you have eternal life, and that you
may continue to believe in the name of the Son of God."
1 John 5:12–13, NKJV

Receiving Christ, we are born into God's family through the
supernatural work of the Holy Spirit, who indwells every believer.
This is called regeneration or the "new birth."

This is just the beginning of a wonderful new life in Christ. To deepen
this relationship you should:

1. Read your Bible every day to know Christ better.
2. Talk to God in prayer every day.
3. Tell others about Christ.
4. Worship, fellowship, and serve with other Christians in a church where
   Christ is preached.
5. As Christ's representative in a needy world, demonstrate your new life by
   your love and concern for others.

God bless you as you do.

Franklin Graham

If you want further help in the decision you have made, write to:
Billy Graham Evangelistic Association
1 Billy Graham Parkway, Charlotte, NC 28201-0001

1-877-2GRAHAM (1-877-247-2426)
BillyGraham.org/commitment

The Elements of the Bahá'í Faith

Joseph Sheppherd has been a Bahá'í since the age of fifteen. He was born in the United States in 1949 into a family of Californian cattlemen and fruit farmers. His membership of the Bahá'í Faith at an early age sparked his interest in the diversity of culture and language in the world. As an anthropologist he has travelled extensively through more than fifty countries and carried out research in Guatemala, Colombia, Cameroon and Equatorial Guinea, where he worked for two years as the Anthropological Advisor to the Government, and Curator of National Ethnological and Archaeological Museum in Malabo. He received his Bachelor's Degree with Honours in Anthropology from the University of California, and his Master's Degree in Archaeology from the University of Cambridge. He presently lectures at the American College in London and writes from his home in Oxford, where he is finishing his Doctorate.

Joseph Sheppherd is the author of: *Mama Buzurg is Coming*, *Guebe and the Toy Truck*, and *A Leaf of Honey and the Proverbs of the Rainforest*.

The *Elements Of* is a series designed to present high quality introductions to a broad range of essential subjects.

The books are commissioned specifically from experts in their fields. They provide readable and often unique views of the various topics covered, and are therefore of interest both to those who have some knowledge of the subject, as well as those who are approaching it for the first time.

Many of these concise yet comprehensive books have practical suggestions and exercises which allow personal experience as well as theoretical understanding, and offer a valuable source of information on many important themes.

In the same series

THE ELEMENTS OF

THE
BAHÁ'Í
FAITH

Joseph Sheppherd

ELEMENT

Shaftesbury, Dorset • Rockport, Massachusetts
Brisbane, Australia

© Joseph Sheppherd 1992

Published in Great Britain in 1992 by
Element Books Limited
Longmead, Shaftesbury, Dorset

Published in the USA in 1992 by
Element, Inc.
42 Broadway, Rockport, MA 01966

Published in Australia in 1992 by
Element Books Ltd for
Jacaranda Wiley Ltd
33 Park Road, Milton, Brisbane, 4064

Reprinted 1993

Cover and textual illustration by Joseph Sheppherd
Cover design by Max Fairbrother
Typeset by Falcon Typographic Art Ltd, Fife, Scotland
Printed and bound in Great Britain by
Biddles Ltd, Guildford and King's Lynn

British Library Cataloguing in Publication
data available

Library of Congress Cataloging in Publication
data available

ISBN 1–85230–372–7

This book is dedicated
to my mother
Greta
with much love
and to the memory of
Lucile Jordan
of Bell Mountain

It is not for him to pride himself who loveth his own country, but rather for him who loveth the whole world. The earth is but one country, and mankind its citizens. GWB:CXVII

Bahá'u'lláh

CONTENTS

Part 4: The Bahá'í Way of Life

PREFACE

Although this survey of the Bahá'í Faith endeavours to present a clear and succinct introduction to the origins, basic teachings and way of life of the religion, it is offered with the humble knowledge that it is far from complete in its description of the life and mission of Bahá'u'lláh, the Founder of the Bahá'í Faith. I have tried to write especially for the reader who may know nothing more than the name 'Bahá'í' and who is interested to find out a little about the religion. At the same time, I have attempted to construct my explanations in such a way that those who perhaps have a Bahá'í friend or relative and therefore know something of the religion, but who lack an overall picture, may gain a more coherent understanding of the subject. Many learned scholars have written biographies of the life of Bahá'u'lláh and I could have quoted from these. I have, however, declined to do this because I wanted to tell the story of Bahá'u'lláh as it was told to me, and to explain as simply as possible His teachings.

Bahá'u'lláh wrote in two languages, Persian and Arabic, and of the hundred or so volumes He wrote during His lifetime, a substantial number have been translated into English. Because this year marks the 100th anniversary of His passing, it seemed appropriate to draw passages from some of these translations and include them in the text.

No book is ever written alone, and I would like to acknowledge the assistance of my friends Johanna O'Connor, Tak Sum Ho, Thelma Batchelor and Andy Scott. I am also grateful to Phillip Hall-Patch, Gandhimohan Viswanathan, Richard Goodson, and Tiffani Betts of the Oxford University Bahá'í Society for reading the text and offering suggestions.

Oxford, England
16 February 1992 AD
10 Mulk 148 BE

PART 1
INTRODUCTION

1 · WHO ARE THE BAHÁ'ÍS?

About thirty years ago, a friend by the name of Lucile Jordan lent a couple of books to my mother and me. At the time it was not possible to see how this simple act would change the course of my life, but looking back this was the event which led me to discover the Bahá'í Faith. Now, three decades later, I know that many Bahá'ís would tell how their first introduction to the Faith came through the loan of a book.

Lucile was a kind-hearted old lady who was employed by the same hospital where my mother worked as a nurse. Even though she lived some distance from us in the sparsely populated area around Bell Mountain, we visited each other regularly. Distances between neighbours and friends are greater in the Mojave Desert than other places in California. Even in the arid and optimistically named Apple Valley where we lived, there were few houses nearby. Bell Mountain was even worse; it was more a community of tumbleweeds and sagebrush than people. Knowing that my mother and I were interested in religion, Lucile lent us the books.

Like many people living in the desert, we were interested in God but not very impressed with churches. Over the years we had attended, on one occasion or another, every church in the surrounding towns to hear what they had to say, but we were not members of any particular faith. They all seemed to be vying with one another for the exclusive rights on God,

3

each one insisting that their church was the only true religion. Competition was fierce to attract membership among
the scant inhabitants of the desert, and preachers went to
extreme lengths. For example, in desperation one preacher
erected a small white picket fence around a well-watered
square metre of grass in front of his church. He informed
his congregation that when Jesus returned to earth, this tiny
grassy square was the precise spot where His foot would first
touch the ground as He descended from heaven. I think it
was at this point we stopped going there!

The best information about God and religion was to be
found not in the pulpit but in books; and so with no further
churches to attend in the area, we contented ourselves with
reading. Books were a part of our household and lifestyle,
and my mother taught me that books were not mere decora-
tions or units of good intentions. Bookshelves were designed
to hold books you had already read and wished to read again.
As I grew up, I inherited my mother's voracious appetite for
knowledge, and her belief that people are what they read.
From looking at our bookshelves anyone could tell that we
were seekers.

Knowing this, Lucile lent us some books about a religion
we had never heard of: the Bahá'í Faith. In the evening of
the day she received them, my mother sat down in a chair
and began to read, and when I went to bed she was still
reading. In the morning when I woke up, she was still
awake, sitting there with a book in her hands. By now
the table beside her was covered with other books laid
open and stacked on top of each other. My mother had
not only read both of Lucile's books in one night, she had
been comparing what they said with other books we had in
the house.

That morning when she got to work, she asked Lucile if
she were a member of this religion, if she were a *Bahá'í*.
The word was new and she did not know exactly how
to pronounce it, or for that matter what it meant. She
discovered that Lucile did not know either. Lucile was
not a Bahá'í – the books had been given to her by someone
else whose name and phone number were written inside the

cover. She had not had a chance to read them before my mother borrowed them.

That evening my mother phoned the number. I remember how the conversation began. My mother introduced herself and said: 'I have a houseful of books on religion. How is it I have never heard of the Bahá'í Faith before?' My mother could be very direct, and I could only imagine the other side of the conversation. She continued: 'You people must be the best kept secret in the universe. I've been looking for you for twenty years. I knew that there must be a religion like this out there somewhere, I just didn't know what it was called.'

After a lifetime of searching for the truth it had, in a sense, found her. It was amazing that it had taken so long to discover the Bahá'í Faith, because once we knew what it was, it was easy to find. There were Bahá'ís everywhere – we kept running into them. There were books about the Bahá'í Faith in the public library, and entries in the dictionary and encyclopedia. It was even listed in the phone book. It had been there all along; we just hadn't seen it.

My mother went through a remarkable transformation. Within a few weeks she had gone to visit the lady she had spoken to on the telephone, read half a dozen other books on the religion, and become a Bahá'í. Soon afterwards, when Lucile was able to get the books back and read them for herself, she decided that she was a Bahá'í also.

I had to wait my turn to read the books. In the meantime my mother explained what she had found in her reading, and for days we talked about nothing else. The Bahá'í Faith was a real discovery. I found the story fascinating: I learned that a new Messenger of God had lived in the middle of the last century in a place called Persia. His name was *Bahá'u'lláh* which translated into English meant 'Glory of God'; and the people who followed His teachings were *Bahá'ís*, literally 'followers of Bahá'u'lláh'.

Bahá'u'lláh had brought a new set of teachings which held the answers to the modern world's problems. Eventually, when I could get hold of some books and read them for myself, I found Bahá'u'lláh's explanations were extraordinarily profound and insightful concerning the spiritual and

5

social needs of humanity. My favourite book of His was entitled *Hidden Words*. It was a compilation of moral aphorisms full of ethical wisdom – a distillation of the spiritual guidance of all the Revelations of the past. I read and re-read the passages. Now things seemed to make sense.

When I started using in school what I was learning at home, my teachers must have thought that I had had a brain transplant. I remember the stunned expression on one English teacher's face when she asked me to use the word 'justice' in a sentence. 'Beyond a sort of vague ideal,' I replied, 'it is difficult to know what justice looks like in an age so burdened with tyranny. Justice can only be possible among people who are free from the prejudices of race, nationality and gender. In a way, injustice blinds us to the reality of justice. In its absence, we are forced to guess what it looks like. I feel people are mistaken to think of it as some kind of product. Justice itself is not an end, it is the means to greater things, it is the means to seeing and understanding things for ourselves.'

The teacher was not used to hearing such answers from the mouth of such a bored, lacklustre and apparently clueless student. In the silence which ensued in the wake of my answer, I forgot to tell them that the reason I had these thoughts was because I had been reading books by Bahá'u'lláh. Fortunately, the class bell rang about then!

School was never the same after that, and teachers were no longer boring. I was interested in their ideas. In fact, the entire educational process now had meaning, and I was beginning to understand that education was not exclusively found in schools. Ultimately, teachers do not teach students, they get students to teach themselves. I was twelve years old at the time. I suddenly realized one day, in the middle of my science class, that my education was my own responsibility and there were no limits in the world except the ones I imposed upon myself through neglect of my studies. This also applied to my spiritual education. This realization led to many others about myself and the lifetime that lay ahead; being twelve became an age of wonder and discovery.

At that time, I did not know what I wanted to be, what

profession or career to follow. One day I wanted to be an artist, the next a scientist, and the day after something else. This diversity of interest did not really concern me – it was normal for twelve-year-olds to vacillate between future professions from one minute to the next. (Even at forty-two, I still sometimes wonder what I want to be when I grow up.)

However, back then I did worry about being inconsistent with my religious interests, for I had begun to take religion seriously. I realized that religions are not like professions; people should not change them just because they want a change. I knew that I believed in the teachings of Bahá'u'lláh, and I knew that I wanted to be a Bahá'í more than anything else. But I was young and I wondered if I would change my mind later. I decided to wait and look at other religions again before I became a Bahá'í. If, after more investigation and comparison, I still believed in Bahá'u'lláh, I would know that I could become a sincere Bahá'í.

Looking back, I can now see that this was a mature decision. But at the time I think it was influenced by something my mother pointed out to me. She informed me that in the Bahá'í Faith children were not automatically born into the religion or expected to follow blindly the religious choices of their parents. Children decided for themselves if and when they wanted to become Bahá'ís. This meant that even though my mother had become a Bahá'í, I could still choose my own religion. I considered this and decided to wait until I was older before I registered as a Bahá'í, so that I would be sure that I was adopting a religion because I believed in it myself, independently of my mother. I had read in the writings of Bahá'u'lláh that the age of maturity began at fifteen. I chose to wait until then to make my decision.

2·WHERE DO BAHÁ'ÍS WORSHIP AND MEET?

By the time I was fifteen, my mother and I had moved to Germany and were living in a little village named Sembach near the city of Kaiserslautern. The shady strolls along the leaf-strewn paths through dark forests and grassy meadows were quite a contrast to the sandstorm-swept treks we had previously made across expanses of desert randomly dotted by the occasional cactus and Joshua tree.

In the past three years, we had not only travelled to Europe, but to many places within the United States meeting Bahá'ís from other cultures. The Navajo Bahá'ís invited Indians and non-Indians alike from all over America to join them in a week-long conference and cultural festival. My mother and I went. Looking back, I think that it was that week of listening to the ancient legends of the Indians who attended the festival that sparked my interest in anthropology.

Two weeks after my fifteenth birthday, Bahá'ís from around the world began to arrive in a small town called Langenhain on a hill overlooking Frankfurt, just a few hours' drive from our home in Sembach near the French border. Langenhain had been chosen some years before as the site of the first Bahá'í House of Worship in Europe. An elegantly beautiful nine-sided temple had been constructed symbolizing the unity of all the world's religions. It was to be dedicated on the 4th of July 1964, and I chose that day to declare my faith in Bahá'u'lláh and register as a Bahá'í.

When my mother and I arrived, there were already more than a thousand people present. I had never seen such a diverse gathering. Every continent and scores of countries were represented by Bahá'ís from every race and of every colour. They greeted each other as friends and associated without reticence or prejudice. It was then that I began to understand Bahá'u'lláh's teaching of 'unity in diversity'. It is one thing to read about a principle which says that unity in the world is only achievable if the individual races and cultures are appreciated, but quite another to see it in practice. The dedication ceremony was uplifting and simple. Bahá'í prayers were read in German, Persian, English, Swedish, French and Spanish; as were passages from the holy scriptures of various religions – the Old and New Testaments, the Bhagavad Gita, and the Qur'án.

In the afternoon, when the dedication ceremony was complete, and people began their journeys home, I found a quiet spot beside the House of Worship and wrote a note to the Bahá'í Centre in Frankfurt-on-Main that I wished to be registered as a member. Since that day twenty-eight years ago, I have been a Bahá'í. As a story about finding the truth and embracing a new religion, this is perhaps less dramatic than many I have heard. However, the process of personal transformation which resulted from studying the teachings of Bahá'u'lláh was just as profound for me as for those whose lives were salvaged from destruction by becoming Bahá'ís.

Soon after the dedication of the Bahá'í House of Worship, my mother and I moved back to California. In the three years in which we had been away, the Bahá'í Faith had grown substantially. Many people were doing what my mother and I had done: investigating the Bahá'í Faith.

By now, there were many more people of my own age who had somehow met a Bahá'í or had read a book by Bahá'u'lláh and had become Bahá'ís themselves. Because we were young, we automatically gravitated together. In the midst of the hedonism of the hippy movement and

Bahá'í House of Worship, Langenhain, Germany

the demonstrations against the war in Vietnam, our group of Bahá'í youth were doing what we could to solve some of the social ills of the times by telling others about what we had learned from the teachings of Bahá'u'lláh. Some people listened. Every weekend we hosted meetings to which we invited our classmates and friends to discuss how to overcome the obstacles which stood in the way of achieving peace and unity in the world. Some towns had Bahá'í Centres where we could meet but, where the Bahá'í community was still small in numbers, we met in each other's homes.

It is much the same today, although there are many more Bahá'í Centres and many more Bahá'í homes where people gather, pray, read from the writings of Bahá'u'lláh, discuss the issues at hand, and enjoy the fellowship of each other. The place where Bahá'ís meet is not important. Bahá'u'lláh reminds us that:

> Blessed is the spot, and the house, and the place, and the city, and the heart, and the mountain, and the refuge, and the cave, and the valley, and the land, and the sea, and the island, and meadow where mention of God has been made, and His praise glorified. BP:iii

I have good memories of those times. The friends I made when I was young are now grown up and scattered all over the globe. It is the same for me as I now live in Oxford, in England. Except for Bahá'í conferences, I rarely see them now. Just as I have decided to be an anthropologist, so they have all chosen professions in which they can find ways to use their talents to serve mankind. They are farmers, ecologists, teachers, biologists, physicists, social workers, doctors, journalists, and above all, parents. They are bringing up their children to love mankind, and by example teaching them to treat each other with equality and justice. They are putting into practice the Bahá'í way of life.

Now, wherever my anthropological work takes me in the world, I meet a new generation of Bahá'ís who are carrying on the responsibility of promoting an ever-advancing

Bahá'í House of Worship, Wilmette, Illinois, USA

civilization. Whenever I am close enough I try to visit a Bahá'í House of Worship. There are now many more in the world. To date there are seven, one for each continent. They are located in: Wilmette, Illinois, USA; Kampala, Uganda; Langenhain near Frankfurt, Germany; Sydney, Australia; Apia, Western Samoa; Panama City, Panama; and New Delhi, India.

Lucile Jordan passed away a few years ago, a Bahá'í who truly loved Bahá'u'lláh and who served humanity in her day-to-day work among the poor and needy. I am very grateful for the rôle she and my mother played in my becoming a Bahá'í. Although Lucile was not a relative, she was a kind of spiritual ancestor in a continuum of people who discovered the teachings of Bahá'u'lláh and passed the knowledge on to others like me. After all these years, it is ironic to be asked to write a book about the Bahá'í Faith, which may itself be lent to others like the books she lent to me.

PART 2
BAHÁ'U'LLÁH

3·The Origins of the Bahá'í Faith

At the origin and centre of any religion is the Founder; He, not His followers, is the One who defines the religion. The Messenger of God, not the interpretations or limited ideas of those who come after, is the standard by which we should evaluate a religion. In every respect, Bahá'u'lláh is the foundation of the Bahá'í Faith, and the pivot around which revolve all the teachings and principles of His religion. To know Bahá'u'lláh is to read His writings; therein lies the essence of the Messenger of God.

I find my words to be inadequate in describing Him; no description or characterization seems to be satisfactory. How can I describe Bahá'u'lláh's majesty, His essential holiness and radiance of being, in a way in which you can share the esteem and reverence I feel when I read passages of His writings? Only reading them for yourself will achieve this. Even the contemporary historians who witnessed and recorded the unparalleled events of His life were often left wordless in their attempt to describe Bahá'u'lláh Himself.

The best attempt occurred just two years before His death when Bahá'u'lláh received one of the few Westerners ever to meet Him. The visitor was Edward Granville Browne, a rising young orientalist and future professor from Cambridge

University in England. Years later, describing his meeting with Bahá'u'lláh, Browne wrote:

> Though I dimly suspected whither I was going and whom I was to behold (for no distinct intimation had been given me), a second or two elapsed ere, with a throb of wonder and awe, I became definitely conscious that the room was not untenanted. In the corner where the divan met the wall sat a wondrous and venerable figure . . . The face of Him on whom I gazed I can never forget, though I cannot describe it. Those piercing eyes seemed to read one's very soul; power and authority sat on that ample brow . . . No need to ask in whose presence I stood, as I bowed myself before one who is the object of a devotion and love which kings might envy and emperors sigh for in vain! A mild dignified voice bade me be seated.

Bahá'u'lláh spoke these words to Browne:

> Praise be to God that thou hast attained! . . . Thou hast come to see a prisoner and exile . . . We desire but the good of the world and the happiness of the nations; yet they deem Us a stirrer up of strife and sedition worthy of bondage and banishment . . . That all nations should become one in faith and all men as brothers; that the bonds of affection and unity between the sons of men should be strengthened; that diversity of religion should cease, and the differences of race be annulled – what harm is there in this? . . . Yet so shall it be; these fruitless strifes, these ruinous wars shall pass away, and the 'Most Great Peace' shall come . . . Yet do We see your kings and rulers lavishing their treasures more freely on means of destruction of the human race than on that which would conduce to the happiness of mankind . . . These strifes and this bloodshed and discord must cease, and all men be as one kindred and one family . . . Let not a man glory in this, that he loves his country; let him rather glory in this, that he loves his kind . . . PB:v

There are no satisfactory words to portray the character or personality of Bahá'u'lláh, or for that matter the nature of Messengerhood itself. In the past, people have tried to describe in retrospect Moses, Jesus, or Muhammad, but have failed to capture the spirit of adoration with which the earliest apostles and disciples held the Messenger of God. Over the years, little by little, people finally settled on a handful of designations for the Messenger of God for their age: words like Prophet, Seer, Revelator, Mouthpiece, Saviour, Messiah, Redeemer, Enlightened One. These are our impoverished efforts to describe something which has come from God and is beyond our vocabulary.

It is the same for Bahá'u'lláh. In a sense, describing the Messenger of God is like describing the sun. I can describe the sun's light and warmth, but in the end words fail to convey its reality. Perhaps the best portrayal of both the sun and the Messenger of God requires the analogy of the mirror: like a perfect mirror placed in the sunlight, Bahá'u'lláh, in common with all the past Messengers, reflects the Glory of God. Bahá'u'lláh and these Messengers are not God, just as the reflection in the mirror is not the sun. Although the bright reflection and the sun itself appear equal, both shedding their light and warmth upon us, they are separate. It is impossible for us to approach the sun without being consumed in a mighty force beyond our comprehension, but we can draw near to the reflection in the mirror and understand something of the light and power of the sun. In the same sense, the Messenger is the intermediary between God and man, the mirror in whose reflection we can see the attributes of God.

The concept of an intermediary is expressed in one of the symbols of the Bahá'í Faith. Bahá'ís wishing to wear a symbol of their religion sometimes use this as an emblem on a ring. The symbol has two basic elements: the design itself and the calligraphic Arabic letters it contains. Firstly, as a design, the horizonal strokes represent, from top to bottom, the world of God, the Creator; the world of the Messenger and His Cause; and the world of man, the creation. The vertical line is a repeat of the middle horizontal line: the world of

A symbol of the Bahá'í faith

the Messenger, thus joining the world of the Creator with that of His creation. The two five-pointed stars to either side of the middle line represent the human body, as well as symbolizing the two Messengers for this age – Bahá'u'lláh and His fororunnor, tho Báb. Tho dooign io compooed of the Arabic letters 'b' and 'h' which stand for the consonants in the words Bahá and Báb, the titles of the two most recent Messengers of God. Often, in classical Arabic the vowels are not written or included in calligraphy.

During the first years of being a Bahá'í, I wondered what Bahá'u'lláh looked like and what it would have been like to travel to visit Him in prison as so many early Bahá'ís did during His lifetime. I am sure these kinds of thoughts are common not just to Bahá'ís but to anyone who loves the Founder of their Faith. People cannot help but wonder what it was like to live during the times of the Messenger of God, to have been able to meet Moses or Jesus or Muhammad.

As a child, I grew up seeing paintings of Jesus on the walls of churches and in the homes of my schoolmates. Jesus lived long before the invention of the camera and photography, so these were of course artists' conceptions. Looking at them, I always wondered if Jesus was being portrayed in the race of the artist. He was usually painted in the centre foreground as a tall, blue-eyed, blond-haired man against a background of darker people. Jesus appeared as if He were a

Scandinavian or northern European like my ancestors. This was unrealistic. Jesus was born into a Jewish family in a remote eastern outpost of the Roman Empire. In Palestine, in that part of the Levant where He was born, the people were and are racially dark, both in the colour of their eyes and hair. Later I discovered that artists from different races and countries tended to produce portraits of a Jesus with which they could identify. White artists painted Jesus white, black artists painted Him black. I began to understand how misleading these portraits were. In many ways, they made racism religiously justifiable in the minds of some people.

It would be better to have no imaginary portraits of Jesus at all, either on the walls of rooms or within the minds of people. It would be better to replace these exterior and interior pictures with the words and actions of Jesus. It would be better to concentrate on His teachings than to attach false significance to the imagination of an artist.

Nevertheless, I wondered what Bahá'u'lláh looked like. He lived during a time in which photography had been invented, and I discovered that one photograph did exist, but I would have to visit the Holy Land to see it. Copies were not made and I would have to wait until I could go on pilgrimage to the Bahá'í World Centre. Having been born in 1949, a photograph was the nearest I could get to meeting Bahá'u'lláh Himself.

By the time I was born, I had missed living during Bahá'u'lláh's lifetime by fifty-seven years. As a very young Bahá'í, part of me regretted having been born too late. But then I began to realize that even if I had been born a hundred years sooner, there would have been no guarantee that I would have known about Bahá'u'lláh, much less have met Him. Only a few of the people alive during His lifetime heard about Bahá'u'lláh, and only a few of those recognized him as a Messenger of God. In my native country of the United States, the first mention of the Bahá'í Faith was not until 1892 at a presentation at the World's Columbian Exposition in Chicago. This was the same year in which Bahá'u'lláh died. It was two years before the first American, Thornton Chase, became a Bahá'í.

It takes time for the news of the existence of the Messenger of God to spread. It was the same during the lifetime of Jesus – few people outside Judaea, Galilee and Samaria were aware of His existence, and relatively few people within those three regions actually arose to follow Him. Christianity took centuries to reach America – depending on whether you read Irish, Viking or Spanish history, it was either 554, 1,121, or 1,497 years before the first Christian reached the shores of North America. And it was not until 1,500 years after the death of Jesus that the first anonymous native American became a Christian.

Reading biographies about Bahá'u'lláh's life answered many questions about what it was like to be alive during His lifetime, but in 1967 I had the privilege of meeting someone who had actually met Bahá'u'lláh personally. This was living history.

His name was Tarázu'lláh Samandarí and at that time he was probably one of the last people alive to have been in the presence of Bahá'u'lláh. Mr Samandarí's father had been one of the nineteen Apostles of Bahá'u'lláh, and as a young man his son had journeyed overland from his native Persia to 'Akká to meet Him. When I heard that Mr Samandarí was staying for a few days in Los Angeles, I hitch-hiked down from Apple Valley to meet him. I was not surprised to find the room full of fellow Bahá'ís when I arrived. It seemed that many of us had had the same idea. We had all recognized that this was an opportunity which would not come again. Tarázu'lláh Samandarí was a very old man of ninety-two, and his son Mihdí, who was himself quite old, translated for his father.

I sat on the floor in the crowded living-room and listened as Mr Samandarí told the story of the occasions on which he had been in the presence of Bahá'u'lláh. He was seventeen when he first made the long trip from Persia to the Turkish penal colony of 'Akká where Bahá'u'lláh had been incarcerated for more than twenty years. The trip had taken many weeks, but had been worth it. For a period of six months he had been in the company of Bahá'u'lláh's family, and on several occasions had heard

Him reveal the words of God as He dictated tablets and prayers.

Every scene was there like a photograph in his mind. As he described the events that he had witnessed, even the smallest detail was included. He told how on one occasion he was asked by Bahá'u'lláh to distribute roses to all the people present; he cherished the honour of having provided even this small and simple service. His stories were like small windows on a different time and place which we could see through his eyes. He had seen the early Bahá'ís coming on foot as pilgrims from far away in an effort to witness for themselves the author of the teachings they had read and adopted as their religion. During the first years of Bahá'u'lláh's imprisonment, pilgrims would arrive at the prison gate and beg to be admitted. This would leave the prison guards bewildered. They could not understand why anyone would want to try to get into prison.

Those who were allowed to enter would stay for weeks or months in the foulest and most squalid of conditions just to be near the Messenger of God. Disease at that time was rampant in the prison city, and the pilgrims ran the very real risk of contracting something fatal, and dying before they could leave. Sometimes the pilgrims were turned away and not allowed entrance. They would have to content themselves with standing on the far side of the double moat which surrounded the city, and seeing only Bahá'u'lláh's hand as He waved to them through the barred window of His cell. Broken-hearted, they would return on foot the hundreds of miles back to their homelands having seen only His hand.

As Mr Samandarí described what he had seen, we sat enwrapped in the images of his words. He had been fortunate to arrive during a time in which people were more freely allowed to visit Bahá'u'lláh. The personality of Bahá'u'lláh finally won over the guards and the governor of the prison city himself. They recognized His guiltlessness, and without the authority of their governmental superiors, permitted Him to live outside the walls of 'Akká.

Via his translator, Mr Samandarí humbly described Bahá'u'lláh's majesty and kindness; the memories of a time when he was a youth of my age of seventeen. When he was finished, some of us asked questions about what it was like to have been a Bahá'í during the time of the Messenger of God Himself. He told of the honour he had in serving Bahá'u'lláh both during His life and afterwards, and that it is the duty of everyone to respond to the needs of the times in which they live and to do what they can as Bahá'ís.

I realized then that in a sense I had not missed meeting Bahá'u'lláh. I had not missed knowing about Him – I had read His books and recognized the divine origin of His teachings. I had even met someone who had met Him. Above all, I had become a Bahá'í. It was not important that I had not seen Bahá'u'lláh with my own eyes or heard the tones of His voice with my own ears; His words and teachings were what mattered. The Message was still here even if the Messenger of God had gone away.

Someone in the room then asked about the passing of Bahá'u'lláh. Mr Samandarí's voice was suddenly sorrowful as he reluctantly recounted how he had been amongst the visiting pilgrims and resident Bahá'ís from around 'Akká who were summoned to the presence of Bahá'u'lláh while He was lying ill in bed, being tended by His family. As he stood there as a young man so many years ago, Mr Samandarí realized that Bahá'u'lláh was dying.

He paused for a while and then repeated what Bahá'u'lláh had told the grief-stricken assembly of devoted Bahá'ís. His voice was clear, but softer because of the fever He had contracted. He spoke about the importance of unity. From the way Mr Samandarí spoke and his humble gestures, even before the words were translated from Persian, it was obvious with what love he regarded Bahá'u'lláh. Before excusing himself and retiring for the night, Mr Samandarí gave us the same message Bahá'u'lláh had given him: that we should be united and seek to promote unity in the world.

In 1978, as a pilgrim myself, I travelled to Israel, and the former prison city of 'Akká, and visited nearby Bahjí, the resting place of Bahá'u'lláh. For the Bahá'ís, Bahjí is the holiest place on earth, the Qiblih of the Bahá'í Faith; the place towards which Bahá'ís turn in prayer. The simple

Entrance to the Shrine of Bahá'u'lláh

and dignified shrine which encloses His tomb beneath it, is adjacent to where young Samandarí had met Bahá'u'lláh and where He had passed away. After I had bowed and humbly placed my forehead at the threshold of the room over Bahá'u'lláh's tomb, I prayed for the enlightenment of my own soul and for the peace and unity of the nations of the earth.

Later that day, I crossed the Bay of 'Akká to the slopes of Mount Carmel, the mountain spoken of by Isaiah as the 'mountain of the Lord'. Part of every pilgrimage is a visit to the Shrine of the Báb, the resting place of the Herald-Prophet who announced the coming of Bahá'u'lláh. Set among the gardens, monuments and buildings of the Bahá'í World Centre above Haifa on Mount Carmel is the International Bahá'í Archives in which the only photograph of Bahá'u'lláh is kept. Every Bahá'í pilgrim has an opportunity to view it, and as I stood before it I finally knew what Bahá'u'lláh looked like. Like Professor Browne, I cannot describe the face I saw in that small photograph.

The picture showed Bahá'u'lláh seated in a chair with one arm resting on a table. He was wearing an abba which flowed from His shoulders down to the ground. He was bearded, and His head was covered with a turban, the kind worn by people from this part of the world in the latter half of the nineteenth century. I knew the historical circumstances of the photograph. Bahá'u'lláh was being exiled yet again and this was an official photograph of a prisoner. There was seriousness and profound resolve in His tired yet radiant face. This was the countenance of the Messenger of God, the Lord of the Age Who had borne the torture, imprisonment and banishment of His enemies from the birth of His religion. Looking at the photograph, I suddenly realized that it really did not matter whether or not I knew what Bahá'u'lláh looked like. The love I felt for him transcended any mental image. It was His teachings which were important.

As I stood there with the other pilgrims, I remembered what I had read of the life of the man in the photograph. It was a story which began many years before His exiles and imprisonment. The actual birth of the Bahá'í Faith

The Shrine of the Báb

began in the city of Shíráz, Persia, on the night of the 22nd of May 1844. The middle of the nineteenth century was a time of great messianic expectation in the world. Throughout Europe and America millennialist Christian groups like the Templers and Millerites believed they had found in the Christian scriptures evidence supporting their conviction that history had ended and the return of Jesus Christ was at hand. In the Middle East, a markedly similar ferment developed around the belief that the fulfilment of various prophecies in the Qur'án and Islamic Traditions was imminent.

It was against this backdrop of expectations that a young descendent of the Prophet Muhammad, by the name of Siyyid 'Alí Muhammad, declared Himself to be a Messenger of God. He assumed the title of *Báb* or Gate. Like John the Baptist, He claimed to be the Herald of One greater than Himself. In preparation for the One Whom He called 'Him Whom God shall manifest', the Báb initiated new religious practices which replaced the old, outdated ones. He revealed prayers and laws providing His followers with insights into the spiritual and social requirements of a new age.

The story of the Báb is fascinating in its own right but too long to tell here. After eighteen people had spontaneously recognized the validity of His claim through dreams and visions, and had become His disciples, the Báb wrote a letter and instructed the first of His followers to deliver it to Bahá'u'lláh. The letter informed Him of the new Revelation. Upon receiving this missive from the Báb, Bahá'u'lláh immediately championed His Cause.

The years following the Báb's Declaration were filled with turmoil. In a single year the ferociously fanatical and ignorant Persian Muslims murdered four thousand adherents to His Cause. After only six years, the Báb's mission was complete and it was for His love of Bahá'u'lláh that He sacrificed His own life. At the time of the dramatic martyrdom of the Báb in the northern city of Tabríz in 1850, His followers were unaware that Bahá'u'lláh had been chosen to be 'Him Whom God shall manifest', the Messenger of God foretold by the Báb.

4·THE BIRTH OF THE BAHÁ'Í REVELATION

Bahá'u'lláh's given name was Mírzá Husayn 'Alí, and the title of Bahá was adopted by Him during the time when He was a follower of the Báb. To break with the traditions of Islam, many of the followers of the Báb adopted non-Muslim names. In Arabic, *Bahá* means 'Glory', and later he was known to His followers as *Bahá'u'lláh*, 'The Glory of God'.

Bahá'u'lláh was born in Teheran, Persia on the 12th of November 1817 into a noble, respected and wealthy family. A career in government was open to Him as His father was a minister of state in the court of the King. However, Bahá'u'lláh was not interested in politics, His kingdom was not of this world.

Bahá'u'lláh's mission began in August 1852 in a subterranean dungeon in Teheran's notorious *Siyáh-Chál*, the 'Black Pit', where he was confined during the height of the persecution of the followers of the Báb. It was in this dungeon that Bahá'u'lláh received His revelation. Every Messenger of God receives His revelation in a distinctive way: Moses was given the Commandments of God from a Burning Bush on the slopes of Mount Sinai; Jesus received the Holy Spirit in the form of a dove which descended upon Him while He was being baptized in the River Jordan; Muhammad was visited by the archangel Gabriel and given the *súrihs* of the Qur'án.

Bahá'u'lláh described the moment of His revelation in an Epistle to the Persian King, Násiri'd-Dín Sháh, who had confined Him in the Black Pit of Teheran and then exiled Him from His native land:

> O King! I was but a man like others, asleep upon my couch, when lo, the breezes of the All-Glorious were wafted over Me, and taught Me the knowledge of all that hath been. This thing is not of Me, but from the One Who is Almighty and All-Knowing. He bade Me lift up My voice between earth and heaven, and for this there befell Me what hath caused the tears of every man of understanding to flow ... This is but a leaf which the winds of the will of Thy Lord, the Almighty, the All-Praised, have stirred ... His all-compelling summons hath reached Me, and caused Me to speak His praise amidst all people. I was indeed as one dead when His behest was uttered. The hand of the will of Thy Lord, the Compassionate, the Merciful, transformed Me. GPB:102

Bahá'u'lláh is being very generous and forgiving here in describing the floor of the dungeon into which the King had thrown Him as a 'couch'. Towards the end of His life, Bahá'u'lláh, writing about His early experiences, included a brief description of the conditions in the Black Pit:

> We were consigned for four months to a place foul beyond comparison. The dungeon was wrapped in thick darkness, and our fellow-prisoners numbered nearly a hundred and fifty souls: thieves, assassins and highwaymen. Though crowded, it had no other outlet than the passage by which We entered. Most of these men had neither clothes nor bedding to lie on. God alone knoweth what befell Us in that most foul-smelling and gloomy place. ESW:20–21

It was a cruel time for the followers of the Báb. Each day the guards would descend the three flights of stairs to the

Pit (the only way in or out of the dungeon), seize one or more of the prisoners and drag them out to be executed. In the streets of Teheran, Western observers were appalled by the scenes of the followers of the Báb being blown out of the mouths of cannons, hacked to death with axes and swords, and led to their deaths with burning candles inserted into wounds cut into their bodies. It was in these circumstances and faced with the prospect of His own imminent death that Bahá'u'lláh received the first intimation of His mission:

> During the days I lay in the prison of Teheran, though the galling weight of the chains and the stench-filled air allowed Me but little sleep, still in those infrequent moments of slumber I felt as if something flowed from the crown of My head over My breast, even as a mighty torrent that precipitateth itself upon the earth from the summit of a lofty mountain. ESW:22

> One night, in a dream, these exalted words were heard on every side: 'Verily, We shall render Thee victorious by Thyself and by Thy Pen. Grieve Thou not for that which hath befallen Thee, neither be Thou afraid, for Thou art in safety. Erelong will God raise up the treasures of the earth – men who will aid Thee through Thyself and through Thy name, wherewith God hath revived the hearts of such as have recognised Him.' ESW:21

5·THE EXILE

When people ask me about Bahá'u'lláh and I tell them that
He spent nearly forty years of His life as a prisoner and an
exile, they invariably ask me what He was imprisoned for.
'He must have done *something*,' they say. It is difficult if
you live in a society where there are religious freedoms
and civil rights to imagine what it is like to live in a time
or place where a social standard of religious tolerance does
not exist.

Whenever a Messenger of God comes and begins teaching
new ideas, the people rise up against Him. This opposition
usually originates from two sectors. Firstly the religious
leaders see the birth of a new religion as a threat to their
own. They are more concerned with their own power than
considering the spiritual truths the Messenger is teaching.
They oppose the Messenger because they cannot maintain
control over the population if they begin to doubt their
right to control their spiritual lives. The second source of
opposition comes from the secular powers of the day, the
kings and rulers who do their utmost to squash the birth of
religions. Consider for a moment the histories of the other
Messengers and recall what they had to withstand from the
likes of Pharaoh and Herod Antipas during Their age.

Bahá'u'lláh was initially persecuted for being a supporter
of the Báb and then when He received and revealed His own

revelation, he was persecuted again. The religious leaders and the rulers of Persia tried to destroy the emerging religion in their midst. When they publicly executed the Báb, killed tens of thousands of His followers, and imprisoned most of the rest, they thought that they had succeeded.

Eventually, after four months, Bahá'u'lláh was released from the Black Pit, and still without trial or recourse He was immediately banished with His family from His native land. Although he could have gone north into Russia, Bahá'u'lláh instead chose banishment to neighbouring 'Iráq which was then under the rule of the Ottoman Empire. The Persian government confiscated His wealth and properties, and His family including His small children had to climb in the dead of winter through the snow-swept mountain passes between Persia and 'Iráq. He was never to return to Persia again.

This expulsion was the beginning of forty years of exile, imprisonment and bitter persecution. Upon His arrival in Baghdad, Bahá'u'lláh gave priority to the needs of the community of the followers of the Báb who had fled the persecution in their homeland. With the execution of the Báb and decimation of the leadership among His followers, Bahá'u'lláh found the community in Baghdad despondent and disorganized. Over the next ten years Bahá'u'lláh shaped and unified the community without informing them of the revelation He had received in the Black Pit. Steadily the fame and prestige of Bahá'u'lláh grew, not only among the followers of the teachings of the Báb, but among the general population of 'Iráq. Persian followers of the Báb began to arrive in Baghdad to seek the advice of Bahá'u'lláh, and then carried back encouraging letters and messages. The Islamic religious leaders of Baghdad became alarmed at the influence which this Persian exile had, and incited the Ottoman officials to remove Bahá'u'lláh farther away from Persia. Until He was finally ordered to leave Baghdad, Bahá'u'lláh continued preparing the followers of the Báb for the realization that the One Whom the Báb had foretold, had indeed come.

Some already recognized in the character of Bahá'u'lláh the One of Whom the Báb had written, but they saw that

33

the time was not right to refer openly to Bahá'u'lláh as the Promised One. Bahá'u'lláh chose the occasion of His forced departure from Baghdad to declare that He was in fact 'Him Whom God shall manifest'.

Situated on the outskirts of Baghdad, across the River Tigris from the house where Bahá'u'lláh was held under house arrest, there was a garden where He assembled the band of followers who were going with him into exile in Constantinople, and also those who were to stay behind. Bahá'u'lláh named this garden Ridván, which means 'Paradise' in Arabic.

Over a period of twelve days Bahá'u'lláh made His public declaration of His mission, and informed the people present that the prophecies and promises of the Báb were fulfilled. Every year, this twelve-day period is commemorated during the Festival of Ridván, and the first, ninth and twelfth days of this festival are set aside as Holy Days. From this point forward the vast majority of the followers of the Báb turned to Bahá'u'lláh and became known as Bahá'ís. The exile which had begun when Bahá'u'lláh was forced to leave Teheran and which then led to Baghdad, was now set to continue to Constantinople, Adrianople, and finally to the prison city of 'Akká.

6 · THE WRITINGS OF BAHÁ'U'LLÁH

We are privileged to live in the age of the written word. In previous ages, the words of the Messengers of God were most often passed down from generation to generation by word of mouth, becoming the oral tradition of a people until they were finally written down. The words of Jesus were recorded in the Gospels of the Bible by His disciples long after He had died. Jesus spoke to people and they remembered what He said. There is no indication that Jesus could read or write, nor did he need to. He was a teacher of men's hearts, and the principle means of communication in His lifetime was verbal.

In the Bahá'í Faith, meticulous effort has been made to gather together the writings of Bahá'u'lláh and preserve the original text written in His own hand. Bahá'ís are fortunate to have such authoritative texts to which to refer. This in itself will avoid the confusion which other religions have had to face in the past concerning what were or were not the actual words of the Messenger of God.

Bahá'u'lláh continued to write during His entire ministry while in prison and in exile. The sum total of His books, tablets, and epistles numbers more than a hundred volumes. He wrote most of them to specific individuals in response to questions asked of Him. Each missive was composed in the language and vocabulary the recipient understood and within the literary style he would recognize. To the Islamic theologian, Bahá'u'lláh wrote in terms of Qur'ánic law and the traditions of the *hadith*; to the Christian clergyman, He employed biblical concepts and symbols; to the Súfí, He spoke in the style of mystic symbolism; to the political ruler, He chose direct and didactic words.

Regardless of their intended recipient, Bahá'u'lláh's books are at once personal and universal. They not only answered the enquirers' questions and satisfied their particular needs, but at the same time each missive reveals knowledge appropriate to all mankind. Bahá'u'lláh wrote within a wide spectrum of subjects: the history of religion, practical and applied ethics, morality, spirituality, economics, social organization, human rights, jurisprudence, the arts, metaphysics, science, mysticism, and prophecy.

Some of the better known works of Bahá'u'lláh include the following: the *Kalimát-i-Maknúnih (Hidden Words)* is unlike any other religious book, itself a new genre of literature. It is composed of 153 proverb-like utterances which beautifully present the depths of religious understanding in general, the spiritual truths at the heart of all religions. It is wisdom wrapped in brevity. It was revealed in two parts, the first in Arabic and the second in Persian, each language reflecting a style of literature and having a flavour all its own.

The *Haft-Vádí (Seven Valleys)* has been described as the summit of achievement in the realm of mystical composition. In this timeless and placeless description of the inner verities of religion, Bahá'u'lláh employs the terminology of the twelfth-century Súfí, Farídu'd-Dín 'Attár to describe the stages on the mystic path along which the seeker must travel towards God. These seven stages or valleys as Bahá'u'lláh refers to them are: the Valley of Search, the Valley of Love, the Valley of Knowledge, the Valley of Unity, the Valley of Contentment, the Valley of Wonderment, and the Valley of True Poverty and Absolute Nothingness.

The *Chihár-Vádí (Four Valleys)* is an epistle written in Baghdad, and like the *Seven Valleys* is a mystical composition in which Bahá'u'lláh describes the four ways in which the traces of the unseen God can be perceived, the four stages of the human heart, and the four kinds of mystic seeker in the quest for God.

The *Kitáb-i-Iqán (Book of Certitude)* presents the continuum of Divine revelation across the ages. It describes and affirms the common thread running through all religions.

The central book of the Bahá'í Faith is the *Kitáb-i-Aqdas (Most Holy Book)*. It is in this book that Bahá'u'lláh has outlined the laws and ordinances of this age.

While in prison We have revealed a Book which We have entitled 'The Most Holy Book'. We have enacted laws therein and adorned it with the commandments of thy Lord Who exerciseth authority over all that are in the heavens and on the earth. Say: Take hold of it, O people, and observe that which hath been set down in it of the wondrous precepts of your Lord, the Forgiving, the Bountiful. It will truly prosper you both in this world and the next and will purge you of whatsoever ill beseemeth you. He is indeed the Ordainer, the Expounder, the Giver, the Generous, the Gracious, the All-Praised. TB:262

Some of Bahá'u'lláh's other books include: the *Bishárát (Glad Tidings)*, the *Kalimát-i-Fidawsíyyih (Words of Paradise)*, and the *Kitáb-i-'Ahd (Book of the Covenant)*. The *Lawh-i-Ibn-i-Dhi'b (Epistle to the Son of the Wolf)* was the last major volume revealed by Bahá'u'lláh. It was addressed to the son of the man who was instrumental in the execution of many Bahá'ís and whom Bahá'u'lláh had named 'The Wolf'. In it, Bahá'u'lláh summarizes the Bahá'í Revelation and quotes selected passages from His own writing.

7 · THE ANNOUNCEMENT TO THE KINGS

Bahá'u'lláh remained in the capital of the Ottoman Empire, Constantinople, now called Istanbul, for a period of four months before He was exiled again by the Turkish government to the city of Adrianople. Adrianople, known today as Edirne, was in the European part of Turkey on the border with Greece and Bulgaria. As a result of this latest exile, Bahá'u'lláh became the first Messenger of God in recorded history to have crossed from Asia into Europe.

It was during the next five years while He lived in Adrianople, that Bahá'u'lláh began to proclaim His message to the kings and rulers of the earth, and announced that He was the Promised One of all ages. One after the other, Bahá'u'lláh turned His attention to the crowned heads of Europe and Asia, inviting them to resolve their differences and work for the establishment of world peace. These included Napoleon III of France, Kaiser William I of Germany, Tzar Nicolaevitch Alexander II of Russia, Sultán 'Abdu'l - 'Azíz of the Ottoman Empire, Francis Joseph, Emperor of Austria and King of Hungary, Násiri'd-Dín Sháh of Persia, Pope Pius IX of the Roman Catholic Church, and Queen Victoria of the British Empire. Although He spoke to each one, discussing the specific strengths or weaknesses of their individual policies, He also proclaimed the appearance of a new Messenger of God and outlined the responsibilities of those in power to safeguard the well-being of all people and to use their resources for the establishment of international peace.

Bahá'u'lláh praised those who had promoted justice and human rights, and warned those who were heading towards disaster. He promised each one a glorious destiny if they listened to His counsel, and predicted the downfall of those who were heedless.

The fate of each one of these rulers is fascinating. Bahá'u'lláh first wrote to the most powerful monarch of the times, Napoleon III of France:

> O King of Paris! Tell the priest to ring the bells no longer. By God, the True One! The Most Mighty Bell hath appeared . . . We have desired for thee naught except that which is better for thee than what thou dost possess and all the treasures of the earth . . . Set your face towards Him [Bahá'u'lláh] on this Day which God hath exalted above all other days, and whereon the All-Merciful hath shed the splendour of His effulgent glory upon all who are in heaven and all who are on earth. Arise thou to serve God and help His Cause. He verily, will assist thee with the hosts of the seen and the unseen, and will set thee king over all that whereon the sun riseth . . . PB:17

Napoleon III is reported to have read Bahá'u'lláh's letter and thrown it over his shoulder, arrogantly declaring that 'If this is of God, I am two Gods.' Napoleon III was to receive two letters. Soon after the first, Bahá'u'lláh wrote again reminding him of the value of courtesy and compassion for the victims of oppression. Bahá'u'lláh offered him the opportunity of redeeming his past behaviour by heeding the advice of the Messenger of God, at the same time predicting the ruin of Napoleon III if he did not.

> O King! . . . Hadst thou been sincere in thy words, thou wouldst have not cast behind thy back the Book

of God . . . For what thou hast done, thy kingdom shall be thrown into confusion, and thine empire shall pass from thine hands, as a punishment for that which thou hast wrought. Then wilt thou know how thou hast plainly erred . . . Hath thy pomp made thee proud? By My Life! It shall not endure; nay, it shall soon pass away . . . We see abasement hastening after thee, whilst thou art of the heedless . . . PB:20

Napoleon III, who was the most illustrious Western monarch of his day, sustained a sudden and ignominious defeat at the battle of Sedan in 1870, an event which marked one of the greatest military surrenders in modern history. He lost his kingdom and spent the remaining years of his life in disgrace and exile. When the empire collapsed, his monarchy was replaced by the third French Republic. Napoleon III was the last king of France. Kaiser William I of Germany, the king who defeated him, was crowned Emperor of a united Germany in a ceremony which took place in the Palace of Versailles.

After the defeat of Napoleon III, Kaiser William I of Germany also received a tablet from Bahá'u'lláh:

Say: O King of Berlin! Give ear unto the Voice calling from this manifest Temple . . . Take heed lest pride debar thee from recognizing the Dayspring of Divine Revelation, lest earthly desires shut thee out, as by a veil, from the Lord of the Throne above and the earth below . . . Do thou remember the one whose power transcended thy power [Napoleon III], and whose station excelled thy station? Where is he? Whither are gone the things he possessed? Take warning, and be not of them that are fast asleep. He it was who cast the Tablet of God behind him, when we made known unto him what the host of tyranny had caused Us to suffer. Wherefore, disgrace assailed him from all sides, and he went down to dust in great loss. Think deeply, O King, concerning him, and concerning them who, like unto thee, have conquered cities and ruled over men. The All-Merciful brought them down from their palaces to their graves. Be warned, be of them who reflect . . . PB:39

Kaiser William I of Germany, the conqueror of Napoleon III, did not think deeply or reflect. He failed to heed the warning of the very specific consequences which lay ahead if Germany were not to begin the process of disarmament. Bahá'u'lláh concluded His tablet to William I with these prophecies:

O banks of the Rhine! We have seen you covered with gore, inasmuch as the swords of retribution were drawn against you; and you shall have another turn. And We hear the lamentations of Berlin, though she be today in conspicuous glory. PB:39

It was with these words that Bahá'u'lláh predicted the two great conflicts of the twentieth century, forty-four years before the First World War, and sixty-nine years before the Second. Kaiser William I himself sustained two attempts on his life, and his throne was bequeathed to his son. William II, through pride and short-sightedness, engulfed Europe in a war which, when Germany lost, precipitated a swift and sudden revolution in the German capital. There were indeed great 'lamentations' in Berlin. Communism appeared in several cities, the Kaiser and the princes of the German states abdicated, and the constitution of the Weimar Republic marked the extinction of the empire. In its turn the weakness of the republic and the social instability of the times soon facilitated the rise to power of Adolf Hitler and Nazism.

To the east, Tzar Nicolaevitch Alexander II of Russia, also received a letter from Bahá'u'lláh:

O Tzar of Russia! Incline thine ear unto the voice of God, the King, the Holy, and turn thou unto the Paradise . . . Arise thou amongst men in the name of this

all-compelling Cause, and summon, then, the nations
unto God ... Blessed be the king whose sovereignty
hath withheld him not from his Sovereign, and who
hath turned unto God with his heart. PB:27

Nicolaevitch Alexander II, Tzar of Russia, also failed to heed
the call of Bahá'u'lláh and, after suffering several attempts on
his life, finally died at the hand of an assassin. The harsh
policy of repression which he initiated against his own people in the latter part of his reign, and which his successors
maintained, led eventually to the Bolshevik Revolution. The
people whom he and his heirs had oppressed finally rose
up and swept away the empire of the Tzars forever. They
executed the Tzar with his consort and family, and in so
doing extinguished the dynasty of the Romanoffs. A time of
war, disease and famine led to the establishment of a militant
proletariat government which, until very recently with the
collapse of Communism, oppressed the population in much
the same way as the Tzars had done.

Although condemned to the penal colony of 'Akká by
Sultán 'Abdu'l-'Azíz of the Ottoman Empire, Bahá'u'lláh
wrote to His captor advising:

Hearken, O King, to the speech of Him that speaketh
the truth, Him that doth not ask thee to recompense
Him with the things God hath chosen to bestow upon
thee, Him Who unerringly treadeth the straight Path. He
it is Who summoneth thee unto God, thy Lord, Who
showeth thee the right course, the way that leadeth to
true felicity, that haply thou mayest be of them with
whom it shall be well ... Observe, O king, with thine
inmost heart and with thy whole being, the precepts of
God, and walk not in the paths of the oppressor ...
Shouldst thou cause rivers of justice to spread their
waters amongst thy subjects, God would surely aid
thee with the hosts of the unseen and of the seen, and
would strengthen thee in thine affairs ... Overstep not
the bounds of moderation, and deal justly with them
that serve thee. PB:47

Sultán 'Abdu'l-'Azíz was deposed after a palace revolution and assassinated in 1876. Forty-two years later, the First World War saw the final dissolution of the Ottoman Empire and the abolition of the sultanate which had endured for more than six centuries.

Bahá'u'lláh then turned his attention to Francis Joseph, the Emperor of Austria and King of Hungary, whom He counselled thus:

> O Emperor of Austria! . . . We have been with thee at all times, and found thee clinging unto the Branch and heedless of the Root . . . We grieve to see thee circle round Our Name, whilst unaware of Us, though We were before thy face. PB:43

Francis Joseph made no response and soon found himself engulfed by an ocean of misfortune and tragedy. After a brief and precarious existence the shrunken republic which had been built on the ruins of his vanished Holy Roman Empire was blotted out from the political map of Europe.

Bahá'u'lláh then wrote to Násiri'd-Dín Sháh of Persia, the very king who had imprisoned and exiled Him thirteen years earlier:

> O King! . . . Look upon this Youth, O King, with the eyes of justice; judge thou, then, with truth concerning what hath befallen Him . . . They that surround thee love thee for their own sakes, whereas this Youth loveth thee for thine own sake, and hath had no desire except to draw thee nigh unto the seat of grace, and to turn thee toward the right-hand of justice. PB:58

Even the forgiving nature of Bahá'u'lláh's words could not persuade Násiri'd-Dín Sháh to change his ways and be wary of those who surrounded him. The Persian King was dramatically assassinated while at prayer on the eve of a jubilee celebration designed to go down in history as the greatest day in the annals of the Persian nation. The fortunes of his dynastic house steadily declined with the scandalous and irresponsible misconduct of his successor, which rapidly led to the disappearance of Násiri'd-Dín Sháh's corrupt Qájár dynasty.

To the head of the Roman Catholic Church, Pope Pius IX, Bahá'u'lláh openly declared that the long-awaited return of Christ had taken place:

> O Pope! Rend the veils asunder. He Who is the Lord of Lords is come overshadowed with clouds . . . this is the day whereon the Rock [Peter] crieth out and shouteth . . . saying: 'Lo, the Father is come, and that which ye were promised in the Kingdom is fulfilled.' PB:83

Pope Pius IX paid no attention to this announcement of the event for which he and all the 290 Popes before him had fervently prayed for the last 1,870 years. He was too busy with the internal politics of the Church. He had called the cardinals to Rome for the First Vatican Council and was lobbying their support for his doctrine of Papal Infallibility. Just as the Judaic Patriarchs and the Jewish population failed to recognize their Messiah the first time Christ had appeared, so Pope Pius IX and the largest church in Christendom failed to notice His return. They had forgotten the prophecy of the thief in the night. During his long occupancy of the Holy See, Pope Pius IX experienced the virtual extinction of the Pope's temporal sovereignty and power. The Papacy was changed forever. He saw the dispossession of the Papal States and of Rome itself, over which the Papal flag had flown for a thousand years.

Bahá'u'lláh also addressed one of His tablets to Queen Victoria of the British Empire:

> O Queen in London! Incline thine ear unto the voice of thy Lord, the Lord of all mankind . . . God hath, truly, destined a reward for thee . . . He, verily, will pay the doer of good his due recompense . . . thou hast entrusted the reins of council into the hands of the representatives of the people. Thou, indeed, hast done well, for thereby the foundations of the edifice

of thine affairs will be strengthened, and the hearts of all that are beneath thy shadow, whether high or low, will be tranquillized. PB:33

Queen Victoria was the only monarch who responded without arrogance, conceit or silence. She is reported to have commented upon reading Bahá'u'lláh's letter: 'If this is of God, it will endure; if it is not, it can do no harm.' Queen Victoria was the longest reigning monarch in her country's history, and of all the kings and queens Bahá'u'lláh wrote to, it is perhaps more than a coincidence that her throne is the only one still occupied. One by one the others either refused or ignored His call. In their eyes, Bahá'u'lláh was a lowly and presumptuous prisoner of the Ottoman Empire who dared to give counsel to kings.

Bahá'u'lláh was offering them the opportunity to achieve what He called the 'Most Great Peace' – a condition of permanent peace and world unity to be founded on Bahá'u'lláh's principles and teachings. The Most Great Peace would signal the coming of age and maturity of mankind, but the kings and rulers failed to gather together to resolve their differences. Had they begun the process of disarmament then in the latter part of the nineteenth century, the world would have been spared all the death and destruction of the wars we have seen in the twentieth century.

After the kings and rulers had failed to respond to His call, Bahá'u'lláh, in place of the Most Great Peace, offered them instead a 'Lesser Peace':

O Kings of the earth! We see you increasing every year your expenditures, and laying the burden thereof on your subjects. This, verily, is wholly and grossly unjust. Fear the sighs and tears of this Wronged One, and lay not excessive burdens on your peoples. Do not rob them to rear palaces for yourselves; nay rather choose for them that which ye choose for yourselves. Thus We unfold to your eyes that which profiteth you, if ye but perceive. Your people are your treasures. Beware lest your rule violate the commandments of God, and ye deliver your wards to the hands of the robber. By them ye rule, by their means ye subsist, by their aid ye conquer. Yet, how disdainfully ye look upon them! How strange, how very strange!

Now that ye have refused the Most Great Peace, hold ye fast unto this, the Lesser Peace, that haply ye may in some degree better your own condition and that of your dependants.

O rulers of the earth! Be reconciled among yourselves, that ye may need no more armaments save in a measure to safeguard your territories and dominions. Beware lest ye disregard the counsel of the All-Knowing, the Faithful.

Be united, O kings of the earth, for thereby will the tempest of discord be stilled amongst you, and your people find rest, if ye be of them that comprehend. PB:12

We can now witness in the world around us the process towards a Lesser Peace. Although a step in the right direction, the Lesser Peace is still just a political truce, in which the nations of the world try to bring about an end to war and open conflict without substantially changing their basic self-serving mentality. Little by little the nuclear weapons will be destroyed and strategic armaments reduced, but this is not a solution. If the bombs are taken away but the people's hearts are not changed, they will still think in terms of weapons. Anything can be used as a weapon: finance, technology, international trade, natural resources, even food. Until the root causes of war are eradicated, we will always be potentially at war, even though we are not fighting.

Bahá'ís believe we must strive for the equality of gender and races, and work to reduce the disparate extremes between rich and poor. Only when we have eliminated the prejudice and avarice we hold within us, will the Lesser Peace evolve into the Most Great Peace.

In the following words, Bahá'u'lláh describes the station of any monarch who heeds His call:

> How great is the blessedness that awaiteth the king who will arise to aid My Cause in My Kingdom, who will detach himself from all else but Me! PB:6

Nearly seventy years after Queen Victoria received the letter from Bahá'u'lláh, one of her granddaughters, the Dowager Queen Marie of Rumania, accepted the Cause of Bahá'u'lláh in the latter part of her life and became a supporter of the Bahá'í Faith. And exactly one hundred years after Bahá'u'lláh's proclamation to the kings of the earth, the first reigning monarch embraced the Bahá'í Faith – in 1968, after many months of investigating the teachings of Bahá'u'lláh, His Highness Malietoa Tanumafili II of the Pacific nation of Western Samoa, became a Bahá'í.

8·Bahá'u'lláh's Arrival in the Holy Land

As had happened in Baghdad and Constantinople, the fame of Bahá'u'lláh grew wherever the government sent Him. People would flock around the house where He was confined, seeking to hear the voice or behold the face of the Messenger of God. Finally the Turkish government decided that even Adrianople was too close to the capital, and exiled Bahá'u'lláh to the most remote outpost of the Ottoman Empire.

The place they chose for his next banishment was the fortress-city of 'Akká. This penal colony was notorious for the foulness of its climate and its many diseases. It was a place reserved for the incarceration of the most dangerous of criminals, a prison in which people were not expected to live very long. So bad was the very air that it was said that if a bird flew over the city of 'Akká it would fall down dead from the stench. The members of Bahá'u'lláh's family, together with a company of His followers, were exiled with Him.

For the next two years and two months, Bahá'u'lláh would be held in the fortress citadel itself under the strictest of orders to isolate Him from visitors and from the general populace. Bahá'ís, nevertheless, continued to arrive from distant provinces and nations, seeking to be near Him. It

The Prison of 'Akká

was during this particularly difficult period of Bahá'u'lláh's imprisonment that all pilgrims were turned away heart-broken without seeing Him; but this condition changed in a remarkable way.

One extremely hot night, one of Bahá'u'lláh's sons, Mírzá Mihdí, fell through a skylight while pacing the roof of the prison rapt in prayer. He fell on to some crates which mortally wounded him. Bahá'u'lláh found His son conscious and offered to save his life but, instead of asking to be healed, Mírzá Mihdí's dying wish to his Father was for his life to be accepted as a ransom for those who were prevented from entering Bahá'u'lláh's presence. He asked his Father to accept the sacrifice of his life so that the pilgrims who had come from so far could meet, face to face, the Messenger of God. Bahá'u'lláh granted His dying son's request, and Mírzá Mihdí was buried just outside the prison walls. Bahá'u'lláh frequently praised His son's selflessness and spirituality in His writings.

Very soon after the death of His son, Bahá'u'lláh's restricted confinement was lessened and He was allowed to live under house arrest in a nearby building. Miraculously, the guards at the gates of the prison city began to allow Bahá'í visitors through.

For a long time the exiles were shunned by the superstitious local population who had been warned in public sermons against 'the God of the Persians'. Life was very difficult for the small band of exiles, several of whom died as the result of the privations and other conditions to which they were subjected.

9·THE PASSING OF BAHÁ'U'LLÁH

After many years within the walls of 'Akká, Bahá'u'lláh was permitted to leave the prison and live nearby in a place called Bahjí. Today Bahjí is surrounded by beautiful gardens through which Bahá'í pilgrims and visitors walk as they approach Bahá'u'lláh's resting place. Aside from the gardens, Bahjí has been kept as it was during Bahá'u'lláh's final years. Inside the house one can see where He and His family lived, the room where Bahá'u'lláh received numerous early Bahá'ís and visiting dignitaries, including Edward Granville Browne, and the room where He died.

Bahá'u'lláh died at Bahjí on the 29th of May 1892, in His seventy-fifth year. At the time of His passing, the Cause which had been entrusted to Him during His imprisonment in the Black Pit had begun to spread far beyond the Islamic lands where it had taken shape, and it was beginning to be established in America, Europe and the rest of the world.

Bahá'u'lláh had appointed his eldest son, 'Abdu'l-Bahá (1844–1921) as His successor and the authorized interpreter of His writings. 'Abdu'l-Bahá, who since the age of eight had accompanied his Father in his imprisonments and exiles, sent the news of Bahá'u'lláh's passing to the Sultán of the Ottoman Empire, in a telegram which began with the words: 'The sun of Bahá has set . . .'

On the day of His passing, many notable personages,

among them Shí'ah and Sunní Moslems, Christians, Jews, and Druzes, as well as poets, religious leaders and government officials, began to arrive, lamenting the loss of Bahá'u'lláh and magnifying His virtues and greatness. For several weeks tributes and eulogies continued to arrive, in both verse and prose, in Arabic and Turkish, in the form of telegrams and letters. Even though the kings of the earth had ignored Bahá'u'lláh during His lifetime, countless thousands in Persia, India, Russia, 'Iráq, Turkey, Sudan, Palestine, Egypt and Syria had recognized Him as a Messenger of God.

During this first century since Bahá'u'lláh's passing, His followers have spread to every country, territory and island of the world. They have constantly, year after year, grown in number and remained united. The year 1992 is the centenary of Bahá'u'lláh's passing and has been declared a Holy Year in which Bahá'ís will dedicate their time to studying His writings and finding ways to implement His teachings and principles for the solution of the world's problems.

Bahá'u'lláh's vision of humanity united as one people, and His promise of the earth becoming a peaceful and common homeland to all mankind is as timely now as it was a hundred years ago. Now more than ever Bahá'ís are focusing on Bahá'u'lláh's message as the sole hope for humanity.

PART 3
THE BASIC TEACHINGS

10·God and the Purpose of Human Life

God was, is, and always will be beyond the knowledge of mankind. Just as the created can never fathom the creator, so humans, although striving to understand more and more of creation, can never comprehend God.

> God ... is immeasurably above the understanding of all created things, and is exalted beyond the grasp of the minds of men. GWB:XXVI

In His writings, Bahá'u'lláh reaffirms the singularity of God, a truth which it has taken some cultures longer to acknowledge than others. With the diversity of languages and customs in the world, it is understandable how people in the past were unable to recognize their God in the forms of worship of others. The name of God has varied from language to language, from people to people, and from time to time, around the world. For some, their particular name for God became an exclusive possession marking themselves as elite and religiously superior, and this has led throughout history to many internecine conflicts.

Thankfully, we now live in more enlightened times. We can now see that the Hebrew *Yahweh* or *Jehovah*, the Arabic

Allah, the Korean *Shin*, the Spanish *Dios*, the English *God*, and even, in the African language of the Ntumu, *Zamba*, all refer to the same Supreme Being Whose reality transcends names. We are beginning to acknowledge that no one group of people is more spiritually blessed than any other. Despite our linguistic, cultural and historical differences, everyone is equal in the sight of God.

Bahá'u'lláh explains that the creation is separate from the Creator. However, throughout all of creation are the traces of God's work. The majestic swirl of the stars and planets of our galaxy and the very atoms of which they are composed reflect the awesome and awe-inspiring workmanship of the Creator. The existence of the universe and the dynamic processes which govern the appearance of life itself are sufficient proof of their having emanated from the Divine Will. God is the Creator not only of the complex physical interaction of forces seen at work in nature, but also of more subtle planes of existence, dimensions unseen by human eyes, whose existence lies beyond the perception of senses and mind, a non-physical cosmos which interacts with our spiritual nature. These dimensions constitute a greater reality than the physical universe.

> He is really a believer in the Unity of God who recognizes in each and every created thing the sign of the revelation of Him Who is the Eternal Truth, and not he who maintaineth that the creature is indistinguishable from the Creator. GWB:XCIII

For the individual, the purpose of our creation is to know and love God. Throughout the Bahá'í Holy Scriptures, God is spoken of in attributes rather than descriptions: the All-Knowing, the All-Wise, the Ever-Forgiving, the Most Generous, the Almighty, the All-Glorious, the Most-Bountiful. These Divine qualities are expressed in words whose basic meanings lie within the grasp of human understanding but which can only be alluded to within the limits of language. We can never evolve a spiritual vocabulary adequate to describe the attributes of God. The use of these attributive terms within the writings of Bahá'u'lláh clearly demonstrates that God is beyond the notions of shape and form, above the concepts of race and gender. This existence is without location or condition, an unknowable essence which cannot be made anthropomorphic. God is not created in our image; we are created in the likeness of God. That ethereal part of us, our spiritual reality, is this Divine image.

Humans are essentially spiritual beings with outward bodies which change shape and size throughout the course of our lives, but whose inner being remains unaffected and continues to progress regardless of the condition of the physical vehicle which contains it. Collectively as a species, human beings have always been endowed with souls and the potential to acknowledge the existence of our Creator, regardless of the particular form our bodies have assumed throughout the continuum of our material existence. We are soul-bearing entities whose *raison d'être* has always been to know and love God.

> The purpose of God in creating man hath been, and will ever be, to enable him to know his Creator and to attain His Presence. To this most excellent aim, this supreme objective, all the heavenly Books and the divinely-revealed and weighty Scriptures unequivocally bear witness. GWB:XXIX

The lifespan of our physical existence is infinitesimal when compared to the infinite expanse and duration of the universe around us. Our life here on earth is but a fleeting moment and only a small part of the reason why God created us. Knowing and loving God is an eternal process which continues after this life. Within each of us there exists a spiritual aspect which is suited to that eternal process; it is deathless and part of an unseen spiritual dimension. The entire physical universe is encompassed and pervaded by this spiritual dimension – an infinity within an infinity.

11·THE NATURE OF LIFE AFTER DEATH

Life after death has always been described by analogy. The soul and eternal life can neither be defined in absolute terms like the physical phenomena of this world, nor explained in conditional terms like abstract concepts. They are neither tangible realities nor intellectual abstractions, and because of the limitation of our experience their existence can only be alluded to. Intimation is perhaps the only way to describe things which are metaphysical in nature.

It is a descriptive problem common to all religions throughout the ages. The Messengers of God in each age have employed in Their Holy Scriptures analogies of things familiar to the people of Their times. As times changed, however, so did the analogies. The comparisons of Moses were simple and direct, while Christ chose to teach His followers using parables, a special form of narrative analogy with hidden spiritual meanings. In this age, Bahá'u'lláh has written:

Know, verily, that the soul is a sign of God, a heavenly gem whose reality the learned of men hath failed to grasp, and whose mystery no mind, however acute, can ever hope to unravel. It is the first among all created things to declare the excellence of its Creator, the first to recognize His glory, to cleave to His

truth, and to bow down in adoration before Him.
GWB:LXXXII

The soul is the ultimate reality of the individual; it is one's true identity. The body and mind are the instruments of our individual physical and intellectual existence, but the soul transcends their limitations and possesses abilities which the others do not. Among these is the potential to recognize the existence and glory of God. On this physical and ephemeral plane of existence, however, the body and mind are necessary to the process of our spiritual development. This life is a preparation for what is to come after death, just as our pre-natal existence within the womb was a preparation for this life:

The world beyond is as different from this world as this world is different from that of the child while still in the womb of its mother. GWB:LXXXI

The purpose of something is often best seen in retrospect. This is evident when the following two questions are compared: What was the purpose of the time spent in the womb of our mother? and: What is the purpose of this life? Hindsight makes the former question easier to answer than the latter. That 36- to 40-week period of gestation was a preparation for our survival in this world. By analogy, the time we spend in this world is the gestation period for our birth into the next.

The parallel is useful in understanding why preparation is necessary to progress. In the womb of our mother, we lived in a self-contained and personal universe. It was small but sufficient in size to provide everything we needed for our existence; we had the sustaining warmth from our mother's body, the nutrition and oxygen we acquired through the placenta and umbilical cord, but above all we had the constant love and attention of our mother. Now that we are here in this world, it is not difficult to see that the purpose of that existence was to grow. However, this understanding is only possible because we can now look back. While we were in the womb, it was not so clear. Most of the things we were growing were of no real use to us in the confined and limited world of the womb. We were developing legs in a place where there was nowhere to walk; lungs in an airless aquatic world of amniotic fluid; eyes and ears in a place less than ideal for sights and sounds. It was not until after we were born that these limbs and organs became useful. Aside from this, we were not even aware that we were growing these faculties. In fact, if we were conscious of their existence at all, they would have been mysterious and alien because there was no way we could even have guessed their function and future value. Had we been given the choice, we might have decided not to grow them because we could not understand their use. Imagine how handicapped we would later have been in this world.

Continuing the analogy, this world is the womb of the next, and its purpose is to provide us with an environment conducive to a different kind of growth. What we are growing, so to speak, are those spiritual senses and abilities which we will need in the next world. These faculties are spiritual in nature – attributes of the soul such as the ability to love, to show kindness, to be selfless – attributes which adorn our soul as our limbs adorn our bodies. These are the spiritual qualities we take with us into the next world when we die. Just because on this earthly plane of existence we cannot fully recognize their worth, we should not neglect those things which are conducive to their growth.

Spiritual neglect can cause the soul to be hindered in its development, just as insufficient nutrition can stunt the physical growth of the unborn child. Prayer, meditation, obedience to the laws of God, and service to humanity are some of the spiritual nutrients of the soul. The question arises as to what happens in the afterlife if the soul is neglected in this life. In this life the progress of the soul is dependent upon the will of the individual; in the life beyond, progress continues by the Will of God.

With this in mind, it is understandable that Bahá'ís see eternal life as having already begun. Eternal life is not something that begins at death. Conception, birth, life, and death are all stages along a spiritual continuum. Our true reality emanates from our eternal Creator and from the moment of our conception; humans are both physical and spiritual beings already on the pathway of eternity. Carried by our body in this world and then joyously set free, the soul passes from one state of existence to the next on its journey back to God. This immortal part of our being is the repository of unseen faculties. The soul is mysterious in nature; in this life we only have an inkling of its abilities. Bahá'u'lláh further explains:

> Verily I say, the human soul is exalted above all egress and regress. It is still, and yet it soareth; it moveth, and yet it is still. It is, in itself, a testimony that beareth witness to the existence of a world that is contingent, as well as to the reality of a world that hath neither beginning nor end. Behold how the dream thou hast dreamed is, after the lapse of many years, re-enacted before thine eyes. Consider how strange is the mystery of the world that appeareth to thee in thy dream. Ponder in thine heart upon the unsearchable wisdom of God, and meditate on its manifold revelations . . . GWB:LXXXII

The paradox of the dreaming state in which sequence and distance are not restricted as they are in the waking state and the interaction between the two, is given as an analogy of the limitless nature of the soul. The physical universe, at least on the level at which we function within it, is bounded by four dimensions: three spatial and one temporal. Physical things, including our material selves, exist with height, breadth and depth, and at a particular moment in time. As with the subconscious mind in the dreaming state, the soul, together with the spiritual eternity in which it exists, is not limited by these four dimensions of our contingent world.

Our realization of the nature of the soul must embrace a concept of both physical and spiritual paradox. Within the physical universe, perceptually we will always find ourselves at the midway point between the microcosm and the macrocosm. Within us is folded the universe of molecules, atoms and subatomic particles which are infinitely smaller than humans, and at the same time, we as humans are enwrapped within the universe of a stellar system, galaxies and things infinitely larger than ourselves. The soul exists within and beyond this physical cosmology, in spiritual dimensions we cannot perceive from the limited vantage point of this earthly life. The human soul is endowed with potentialities which will only later become manifest. Again by analogy, just as the double-helix structured DNA in our cells carries the genetic code of physical life, so the soul somehow carries the spiritual code of our eternal existence.

Because of the evanescent nature of physical life, we must not become attached to the material world or forget we have a soul. Referring to the soul, Bahá'u'lláh explains:

> If it be faithful to God, it will reflect His light, and will, eventually, return unto Him. If it fail, however, in its allegiance to its Creator, it will become a victim to self and passion, and will, in the end sink in their depths. GWB:LXXXII

This message of detachment is ancient to religious teachings. The writings of Bahá'u'lláh repeatedly remind us that the soul is our most precious possession, and Bahá'ís are exhorted to remain undistracted by the material world:

> He is not to be numbered with the people of Bahá who followeth his mundane desire, or fixeth his heart on things of the earth. He is My true follower who, if he come to a valley of pure gold, will pass straight through it aloof as a cloud, and will neither turn back, nor pause. GWB:LX

Our knowledge of the existence of God and our understanding of the nature of the soul and eternal life have grown over the ages, as mankind has progressed from one stage to another in the ongoing process of our collective spiritual evolution.

12 · THE CONCEPT OF PROGRESSIVE REVELATION

The process of mankind's spiritual evolution continues because God sends Messengers from time to time. These Messengers are the means of humanity's development and progress throughout the ages; it is they who are responsible for our periodic elevation from a lesser to a greater degree of understanding regarding the existence and purpose of God. In fact, the only way people can know of God's purpose for us is through the Messengers He sends. These Messengers, or Manifestations of God as Bahá'u'lláh calls them, are the spiritual teachers of mankind. They educate the souls and minds of humanity and provide us with both spiritual and social guidance. Every thousand years or so, they appear and supply mankind with the teachings required for that age. They come one after another as teachers belonging to the same long-term educational process. Bahá'u'lláh refers to this process as Progressive Revelation:

> Contemplate with thine inward eye the chain of successive Revelations . . . I testify before God that each one of these Manifestations hath been sent down through the operation of the Divine Will and Purpose, that each hath been the bearer of a specific Message, that

each hath been entrusted with a divinely-revealed Book and been commissioned to unravel the mysteries of a mighty Tablet. The measure of the Revelation with which every one of them hath been identified had been definitely fore-ordained. GWB:XXXI

These Messengers raise the level of our spiritual understanding by revealing God's words, and each time they appear they fill the world with fresh spiritual impetus and advance mankind another step forward. Progressive Revelation is more than an educative process, it is part of the eternal covenant of Abraham in which God promised never to abandon mankind. In fulfilment of that covenant God has sent Krishna, Moses, Zoroaster, Buddha, Christ, Muhammad, the Báb and, most recently, Bahá'u'lláh.

Each of these Messengers brought a message appropriate to the time and place in which He appeared. His Dispensation, the sum-total of the teachings the Messenger has dispensed to mankind, is perfectly suited to that stage of our spiritual development:

Know of a certainty that in every Dispensation the light of Divine Revelation hath been vouchsafed unto men in direct proportion to their spiritual capacity. Consider the sun. How feeble its rays the moment it appeareth above the horizon. How gradually its warmth and potency increase as it approacheth the zenith, enabling meanwhile all created things to adapt themselves to the growing intensity of its light. How steadily it declineth until it reacheth its setting point. Were it, all of a sudden, to manifest the energies latent within it, it would, no doubt, cause injury to all created things . . . In like manner, if the Sun of Truth were suddenly to reveal, at the earliest stages of its manifestation, the full measure of the potencies which the providence of the Almighty hath bestowed upon it, the earth of human understanding would waste away and be consumed; for men's hearts would neither sustain the intensity of its revelation, nor be able to mirror forth the radiance of its

Bahá'í House of Worship, Kampala, Uganda

light. Dismayed and overpowered, they would cease to exist. GWB:XXXVIII

Progressive Revelation is an eternal process extending backwards into times before there were written records; and because of the antiquity of some of these Revelations, the names of the Messengers Themselves have been lost. Within the period of time for which we do have historical records, there is evidence of this process. As with our understanding of the purpose of our physical existence, Progressive Revelation is easier to understand in retrospect. The process of sequential Divine messages is not new to religious understanding. However, which of the Messengers a particular religion chooses to acknowledge is a matter of geography and chronology.

Throughout recorded history, many of the Messengers of God have arisen in that part of the Asian continent which extends from the shores of the Red and Mediterranean Seas in the West to the mouth of the River Ganges in the East. This part of the planet has been the birthplace of most of the world's religions. The western part of this region has a great religious tradition which has witnessed a long succession of Messengers. However, because of the chronology, the followers of each religion only recognize the Ones Who came before their particular Messenger. For example, Judaism acknowledges both Abraham and Moses; Christianity recognizes Abraham, Moses and then Christ; Islam identifies the succession of Abraham, Moses, Christ and then Muhammad.

Each of these religions has understood something of the process of Progressive Revelation but failed to see that it extends forwards as well as backwards into time. The Bahá'í Faith sees within its spiritual heritage all the Messengers of the past and recognizes Bahá'u'lláh as the most recent; but it also acknowledges that He will not be the last. To ensure that the succession of Messengers continues and that mankind is able to recognize them each time They appear, each One fulfils the prophecies of the previous Messengers and in turn foretells the coming of the next. In like manner, Bahá'u'lláh promises that another Messenger will come after Him, but not for at least a thousand years. Progressive Revelation is an eternal process forward. As long as there are human beings, God will continue to send His Messengers to guide our progress.

Each individual has the twin responsibilities of accepting the Messenger of God for the age in which he or she lives, and to follow the teachings that the Messenger brings. These teachings are found in the Sacred Scripture of each of the Messengers. In the times in which we live, the writings of Bahá'u'lláh provide us with the guidance we need in this age. His teachings contain primarily two kinds of guidance – spiritual and social – and take the form of laws and basic principles.

13·THE BASIC PRINCIPLES OF THE BAHÁ'Í FAITH

Spiritual teachings are universal and eternal. The Golden Rule, that epigraph which states that we should do unto others as we would have them do unto us, is ancient and found among the sayings of all the Messengers of God. Bahá'u'lláh in this age reminds us:

> O Son of Being! Ascribe not to any soul that which thou wouldst not have ascribed to thee, and say not that which thou doest not. This is My command unto thee, do thou observe it. AHW:29

Each time a Messenger appears, He reminds us of the spiritual nature of our true existence and prescribes attitudes of mind which are conducive to our spiritual growth. As with the process of Progressive Revelation, the spiritual teachings are likewise progressive and our understanding of them expands with the appearance of each new Messenger. These spiritual teachings are the threads which connect all the world religions. Spiritual guidance is universal to all times and places. Like the Messengers of the past, Bahá'u'lláh reiterates and augments these eternal spiritual verities in His writings by reminding us that:

> Thine eye is My trust, suffer not the dust of vain desires
> to becloud its lustre. Thine ear is a sign of My Bounty,
> let not the tumult of unseemly motives turn it away
> from My Word that encompasseth all creation. Thine
> heart is My treasury, allow not the treacherous hand
> of self to rob thee of the pearls which I have treasured
> therein. Thine hand is a symbol of My loving-kindness,
> hinder it not from holding fast unto My guarded and
> hidden Tablets ... Unasked, I have showered upon
> thee My grace. Unpetitioned, I have fulfilled thy wish.
> In spite of thy undeserving, I have singled thee out for
> My richest, My incalculable favours ... GWB:CLII

The followers of Bahá'u'lláh have several obligations which
promote the individual's spiritual growth and development.
In addition to daily prayer and reading from the Sacred
Writings each morning and evening, Bahá'ís fast from sunrise to sunset, abstaining from both food and drink, each
year during the nineteen-day fasting period. This spiritual
obligation begins at the age of fifteen and continues until the
age of seventy.

Spiritual teachings provide insight into the inner realities
and help to educate the soul of the individual, but these
represent only half of the guidance given by each Messenger
of God. Their social teachings address the outer realities and
assist in the education of society. These social teachings
often change with the coming of each Messenger, some of the
previous laws being maintained while others are abrogated
and replaced by new ones which suit the developmental and
social needs of the time.

The style and form of these spiritual and social teachings
have varied from age to age, but the message remains the
same. At one time the people of the world responded with
compliant and unquestioning obedience to the teachings
given to them by Moses in the Ten Commandments, whereas
in this day and age we are given guidance in the form of
injunctions which are often accompanied by an authoritative explanation or exegesis provided by the Messenger
Himself.

It is a sign of our collective progress towards social maturity that blind faith and fearful obedience have now been replaced by the kind of perceptive faith and loving obedience which spring from insight and understanding. Mankind has matured from a time in which we were instructed primarily with prohibitions. There are very few 'thou shalt not's' in the Bahá'í Faith; there are far more affirmative exhortations. For example, Bahá'ís are exhorted to associate with the followers of all religions with fellowship; to honour their parents; to study such arts and sciences as will benefit mankind; to distinguish themselves through good deeds; to be truthful, trustworthy and faithful; to be just and fair; to be tactful and wise; to be courteous, hospitable, persevering, detached, and closely united.

However, Bahá'u'lláh does prohibit His followers from those things which are personally and socially destructive. Bahá'ís are admonished to abstain from alcohol and drugs, aside from their prescriptive use in remedies by a physician. These substances impede the process of clear thinking and, what is more, their abuse is at the root of many diseases of the body and mind, to say nothing of their social harms. Gambling is also forbidden, for it ignites an obsessive addiction to materialism within the heart of the temporary winner and ultimately brings ruin to the eventual loser. Premarital and extramarital sexual relationships are likewise prohibited, reserving the intimacy of sexual intercourse as the appropriate expression of one's love and commitment within marriage. However, the strongest prohibition which Bahá'u'lláh delivers in His writings is against backbiting and calumny:

> O Son of Being! How couldst thou forget thine own faults and busy thyself with the faults of others? Whoso doeth this is accursed of Me. O Son of Man! Breathe not the sins of others so long as thou art thyself a sinner. Shouldst thou transgress this command, accursed wouldst thou be, and to this I bear witness. AHW:27–28

Bahá'ís recognize these as among the major social ailments

70

of our times. Contemporary society has somehow legiti-
mized the practice of subtle misrepresentation, derision
and fault-finding behind someone's back in both the spoken
and written word. It has become such an insidious social
habit that it pervades our conversations and the pages of
our newspapers and magazines. Bahá'ís are admonished by
Bahá'u'lláh to avoid backbiting and slander, and to strive
to attain a mentality which promotes unity and which
genuinely seeks to find the good qualities in others.

Bahá'u'lláh's teachings which address many other issues
and provide a wide-ranging source of guidance for both
the spiritual and practical aspects of daily life, may be
summarized in the basic principles of the Bahá'í Faith
outlined below.

There is only one God, and all the Messengers of the past
have come from Him in a continuous process of Progressive
Revelation. In addition to this, as Bahá'u'lláh points out, we
are all members of one global family:

> It is not for him to pride himself who loveth his own
> country, but rather for him who loveth the whole world.
> The earth is but one country, and mankind its citizens.
> GWB:CXVII

People should strive to eliminate all forms of prejudice.
Equality should be extended to everyone regardless of gender, race, religion, culture, age, heritage, language, occupa-
tion, social status, or their group's numerical strength:

> Observe equity in your judgement, ye men of under-
> standing heart! He that is unjust in his judgement is
> destitute of the characteristics that distinguish man's
> station. He Who is the Eternal Truth knoweth well what
> the hearts of men conceal. GWB:C

An understanding of the importance of justice is fundamental to the progress of the individual's soul, and paramount
to the advancement of the society at large:

O Son of Spirit! The best beloved of all things in My sight is Justice; turn not away therefrom if thou desirest Me, and neglect it not in that I may confide in thee. By its aid thou shalt see with thine own eyes and not through the eyes of others, and thou shalt know of thine own knowledge and not through the knowledge of thy neighbour. Ponder this in thy heart; how it behooveth thee to be. Verily justice is My gift to thee and the sign of My loving-kindness. Set it then before thine eyes. AHW:2

The injustices of starvation and deprivation arise from a lack of conscience in the hearts of men and women. Poverty and the dire economic problems which face mankind must be solved on both a practical and spiritual level. To be effective, the solution must come from a sense of collective and personal responsibility. Bahá'u'lláh writes:

O Children of Dust! Tell the rich of the midnight sighing of the poor, lest heedlessness lead them into the path of destruction, and deprive them of the Tree of Wealth. To give and be generous are attributes of Mine; well is it with him that adorneth himself with My virtues . . . O Ye Rich Ones on Earth! The poor in your midst are My trust; guard ye My trust, and be not intent only on your own ease. PHW:49, 54

To achieve this, education must play a principal rôle. Education should be universal and appropriate, for it is the key which unlocks the doors to both individual and social progress. It is the duty of parents and the community to enable children to actualize that potential through education:

Man is the supreme Talisman. Lack of a proper education hath, however, deprived him of that which he doth inherently possess. Through a word proceeding out of the mouth of God he was called into being; by one word more he was guided to recognize the Source of his education; by yet another word his station and destiny were safeguarded. The Great Being saith: Regard man as a mine rich in gems of inestimable value. Education can, alone, cause it to reveal its treasures, and enable mankind to benefit therefrom. GWB:CXXII

It is time that educational institutions presented scientific and religious perspectives in such a way that they are not seen as conflicting. Science and religion should not be in opposition to each other, but rather recognized as different ways of describing the same phenomena. Teachers and parents should teach their children that there cannot logically be two conflicting explanations for the same thing. Both the analytic reasoning of scientific thought and the ethical morality of religious insight are needed in this age to promote an ever-advancing civilization.

The world has several basic needs to fulfil before it can move towards a global civilization. To secure the establishment and maintenance of world peace there should be created a commonwealth of nations with an effective international tribunal for settling disputes peacefully, a common world currency, a common system of weights and measures. Together these constitute the beginnings of the New World Order envisioned by Bahá'u'lláh over a hundred years ago:

The time must come when the imperative necessity for the holding of a vast, an all-embracing assemblage of men will be universally realized. The rulers and kings of the earth must needs attend it, and, participating in its deliberations, must consider such ways and means as will lay the foundation of the world's Great Peace amongst men. Such a peace demandeth that the great powers should resolve, for the sake of the tranquillity of the peoples of the earth, to be fully reconciled among themselves. Should any king take up arms against another, all should unitedly arise and prevent him. If this be done, the nations of the world will no longer require any armaments, except for the purpose of preserving the security of their realms and of maintaining internal order within their territories.

This will ensure the peace and composure of every people, government and nation. We fain would hope that the kings and rulers of the earth, the mirrors of the gracious and almighty name of God, may attain unto this station, and shield mankind from the onslaught of tyranny. GWB:CXVII

As a major feature of this New World Order, there needs to be selected either an existing or an artificial language to serve as an international auxiliary language, which would be taught in every school throughout the world alongside the native language and literature of that country:

The day is approaching when all the peoples of the world will have adopted one universal language and one common script. When this time is achieved, to whatsoever city a man may journey, it shall be as if he were entering his own home. GWB:CXVII

These basic principles have one common aspect: unity. This unity, however, does not mean uniformity. The sharing of things in common on a worldwide basis, such as a general system of weights and measures, one international unit of currency, and a universal auxiliary language, constitute elements of the planetization of mankind, but within this, the cultural identity and diversity of individuals must be protected, respected and valued as integral to the whole. This unity is the hub of Bahá'u'lláh's teachings. These principles are given to us by the Messenger of God to facilitate the coming together of all mankind. This is a stage in our development which will be recognized in the future as the beginning of the maturity of mankind.

14·THE PROCESS OF AN EVER-ADVANCING CIVILIZATION

Just as the individual purpose of life is to know and love God, so, for human society as a whole, the purpose of life is to promote an ever-advancing civilization. Each Messenger brings new teachings, and it is upon these teachings that a civilization is founded. The Messengers establish new beliefs and attitudes about what is possible, and create new values and norms of behaviour which are appropriate to the times. These raise the level of religious, scientific and cultural understanding from one age to the next:

> All men have been created to carry forward an ever-advancing civilization. The Almighty beareth Me witness: To act like the beast of the field is unworthy of man. Those virtues that befit his dignity are forbearance, mercy, compassion and loving-kindness towards all the peoples and kindreds of the earth. GWB:CIX

The age in which we live is witnessing a profound change in the attitudes it holds, the values it shares, and the way it does things. The closing years of the twentieth century are turbulent times, as the process of rolling up the old world order and laying out the new one proceeds. The times are turbulent because, whereas in the past change came about slowly, the current rate of change in our world is now visible within our own lifetime. The way we appraise civilization is also changing. We are now beginning to recognize that civilization is comprised of spiritual values and ethical standards as well as of material culture and technological achievement. For civilization to be progressive and sustaining, it must be self-renewing – its institutions must incorporate the ability to adapt to the changing challenges of the times. The institutions of the Bahá'í Faith reflect this facility and they are offered to the world as a possible model for social development.

15 · THE ADMINISTRATION OF THE BAHÁ'Í FAITH

In His writings, Bahá'u'lláh forbids the creation of any form of priesthood or clergy among His followers. For this reason, there are no priests, clerics, mullahs, monks, rabbis, gurus, pastors, preachers, reverends or ministers in the Bahá'í Faith. In bygone ages, when the general population was for the most part illiterate, this kind of religious leader served a very important social rôle in the spiritual education of mankind. He was responsible for teaching the religion and representing its interests. In his capacity as teacher, the religious leader made the words of the Messenger of God accessible to people and answered questions about the Messenger's teachings.

Much historical credit must be given to these people because there were times when, if it had not been for their work, the light of religion would have gone out. In this age, however, in which the level of education has risen to the point where individuals can learn to read for themselves the Words of God, there is no longer a need for this kind of religious rôle. To perpetuate a clergy now would only be to substitute the opinions of the individual for the authority of the written word of God.

Although there are no religious leaders in the Bahá'í Faith, however, the religion is highly organized. Bahá'u'lláh

Bahá'í House of Worship, Apia, Western Samoa

established a system of administration which entrusts the authority to administer, adjudicate and legislate the affairs of the religion into the hands of elected institutions which are consultative in nature and presently composed of nine people. There are three levels of these administrative bodies: local, national and international. For example, the Local Spiritual Assembly of the Bahá'ís of Oxford is composed of nine annually elected individuals; the National Spiritual Assembly of the Bahá'ís of the United Kingdom is also elected each year; and an international convention is held every five years for the election of the Universal House of Justice. This is the supreme administrative body of the Bahá'í Faith and has the responsibility for guiding its progress and development. The Universal House of Justice has its seat at the Bahá'í World Centre on Mount Carmel, in the Holy Land.

In addition to these elected bodies, Bahá'u'lláh made provision for appointed institutions whose function is to act as learned advisers to the elected institutions. The responsibility of informing others about the Message of Bahá'u'lláh, however, rests on the shoulders of every individual Bahá'í. It is their duty to study the writings of Bahá'u'lláh for themselves, and to the best of their ability incorporate His teaching into their daily lives, so that when they are asked about the principles of the Bahá'í Faith, they can both describe and demonstrate these principles. They are, in a sense, offering themselves as an example of their faith in action, and the Bahá'í Faith is thus a religion in which one's deeds speak louder than one's words.

PART 4
THE BAHÁ'Í WAY
OF LIFE

16·THE POWER OF PRAYER AND MEDITATION

The Bahá'í Faith is both a religion and a way of life. Bahá'u'lláh does not make a distinction between the two – what people believe should be reflected in what they do. In His writings, Bahá'u'lláh repeatedly reminds His followers that the teachings of God must be manifested in one's deeds and integrated into one's life:

Let deeds, not words, be your adorning. PHW:5

There are many distinctive aspects to the Bahá'í way of life, but I shall describe only a few of them here. Among these, perhaps the most fundamental is the rôle of prayer in daily life. In one form or another, prayer is an integral part of every religion, but in this age its definition has been expanded so that it now encompasses feelings, thoughts, words and actions.

First, however, it is important to look at the purpose of prayer itself. This is not something which has always been clear and evident to me. When I was a child I used to say my bedtime prayers kneeling beside my bed with my mother watching over me. I used to say: 'Now I lay me down to sleep, I pray the Lord my soul to keep, but if I should die before

I wake, I pray the Lord my soul to take . . .' This would be followed by a long list of people I should not forget in my prayers: 'Bless mommy and daddy and grandma and granddad and . . .'

After saying my prayers, being tucked in and kissed goodnight, I would lie awake in the darkness and ask myself, Why should people pray? If God was All-Knowing, then He already knew what we wanted and needed without our having to ask. What was the point in praying? Did God need me to worship Him? The more I thought about this, the less I understood about prayer. Finally, I stopped thinking about it because I stopped praying. I was getting too old to be tucked in or stood over. I still believed in God but I regarded prayer as useless. By the time I found the Bahá'í Faith, I was beginning to suspect that all along I had been asking the wrong questions about prayer. Day-to-day living had taught me that some questions can be so loaded with presuppositions that people do not know where to look for the answers.

In studying the Bahá'í Faith, I began to see that it was the individual, not God, who benefited from the experience of prayer. Prayer was for our sake, not His. With regard to who needed what, I had been looking in the wrong direction – upwards instead of inwards. Now I could understand the purpose of prayer and that the impulse to pray was a natural one. People pray because they love God. The created loves the Creator. The love of God is all around us, and prayer is a means of receiving it. In the *Hidden Words*, Bahá'u'lláh explains the nature of Divine love:

> O Son of Being! Love Me, that I may love thee. If thou lovest Me not, My love can in no wise reach thee. Know this, O servant. AHW:5

Understanding the purpose of prayer was only the beginning. I started praying again, but now they were not the bed time prayers of childhood. Now I chose a moment when no one was home and read the prayers. On my thirteenth birthday, my mother gave me a Bahá'í prayer book and I had soon

memorized many of them from constant use. I had my
favourites:

> O God! O God! This is a broken-winged bird and his
> flight is very slow – assist him so that he may fly
> towards the apex of prosperity and salvation, wing
> his way with the utmost joy and happiness through-
> out the illimitable space, raise his melody in Thy
> Supreme Name in all the regions, exhilarate the ears
> with this call, brighten the eyes by beholding the signs
> of guidance.
> O Lord! I am single, alone and lowly. For me there
> is no support save Thee, no helper except Thee and
> sustainer beside Thee. Confirm me in Thy service,
> assist me with the cohorts of Thy angels, make me
> victorious in the promotion of Thy Word and suffer to
> speak out Thy wisdom amongst Thy creatures. Verily,
> Thou art the helper of the weak and the defender of the
> little ones, and verily Thou art the Powerful, the Mighty
> and the Unconstrained. BP:189

As I continued to study the Bahá'í writings, prayer became
part of my way of life. A part of each day was reserved for
prayer and reading from the Holy Scriptures of Bahá'u'lláh. It
was like water to a thirsty soul. As Bahá'u'lláh has written:

> The prayerful condition is the best of all conditions, for
> man in such a state communeth with God, especially
> when prayer is offered in private and at times when
> one's mind is free ... Indeed, prayer imparteth life.
> TBV1:85

The more I prayed, the more I realized that prayer is a
spiritual language which is not bounded by the limitations of
the syllables and sounds of the spoken word, it is a language
of the heart rather than the tongue. Prayer emanates from
within in an effort to communicate with God, it is more than
words, it is a spiritual attitude. The sincere feeling of love
towards God in one's heart, the silent remembrance of His

bounty, and the thought of thanksgiving for His mercy are all aspects of prayer. Bahá'u'lláh reveals that all the different levels on which we endeavour to communicate with God are valid, whether the prayer is found on the lips of someone praising his Creator, in the spiritual and mental attitudes we develop in the course of our lives, or in the selfless service we render others. These are all forms of prayer.

In the Bahá'í Faith, prayer is seen as a fundamental obligation for one's spiritual progress and the well-being of the world in general. To instill within us the habit of remembering God, Bahá'u'lláh has given His followers certain prayers which are to be used daily. He has provided us with three different styles, and Bahá'ís are free to select from these the one which is the most convenient and culturally familiar. The first of these prayers is to be said at any time during the day and requires about fifteen minutes to complete. The second is shorter and designed to be recited three times a day at morning, noon and evening. The third and shortest one of the three is to be recited each day around noon:

> I bear witness, O my God, that Thou hast created me to know Thee and to worship Thee. I testify, at this moment, to my powerlessness and to Thy might, to my poverty and to Thy wealth.
> There is no other God but thee the Help in Peril, the Self-Subsisting. BP:4

Each of these daily prayers reminds us of the purpose of our existence and the greatness of our Creator. Like all Bahá'í prayers, they are to be spoken aloud in the privacy of one's room:

> The reason why privacy hath been enjoined in moments of devotion is this, that thou mayest give thy best attention to the remembrance of God . . . SWB:93

Among Persian or Arabic speakers, the prayers are often chanted, while in other languages they are often set to music. In whatever form they are offered, be it spoken, chanted or sung, Bahá'í prayers soon become a vital part of one's day.

Whereas meditation is communication with one's own inner being, prayer is communication between the individual and the Creator. Prayer is the transforming power which enkindles the fire of the heart and not only benefits the spiritual progress of the individual but the world around him or her. Prayer has a positive influence on the life and soul of the individual even if at first it cannot be perceived. Although personally worded prayers are sincere and heard by God, Bahá'ís understand that there is a special power in the revealed word of God. Bahá'u'lláh has provided us with many prayers of adoration, glorification, thanksgiving, and supplication.

A Bahá'í prayer book brings together a selection of prayers which are grouped by subject. The following are just a few examples. Concerning the acquisition of spiritual qualities, Bahá'u'lláh writes:

From the sweet-scented streams of Thine eternity give me to drink, O my God, and of the fruits of the tree of Thy being enable me to taste, O my Hope! From the crystal springs of Thy love suffer me to quaff, O my Glory, and beneath the shadow of Thine everlasting providence let me abide, O my Light! Within the meadows of Thy nearness, before Thy presence, make me able to roam, O my Beloved, and at the right hand of the throne of Thy mercy, seat me, O my Desire! From the fragrant breezes of Thy joy let a breath pass over me, O my Goal, and into the heights of the paradise of Thy reality let me gain admission, O my Adored One! To the melodies of the dove of Thy oneness suffer me to harken, O Resplendent One, and through the spirit of Thy power and Thy might quicken me, O my Provider! In the spirit of Thy love keep me steadfast, O my Succourer, and in the path of Thy good pleasure set firm my steps, O my Maker! Within the garden of Thine immortality, before Thy countenance, let me abide for ever, O thou Who art merciful unto me, and upon the seat of Thy glory stablish me, O Thou Who art my Possessor! To the heaven of Thy loving-kindness lift me up, O my Quickener, and unto the Daystar of Thy guidance lead me, O Thou my Attractor! Before the revelations of Thine invisible spirit summon me to be present, O Thou Who art my Origin and my Highest Wish, and unto the essence of the fragrance of Thy beauty, which Thou wilt manifest, cause me to return, O Thou Who art my God!

Potent art Thou to do what pleaseth Thee. Thou art, verily, the Most Exalted, the All-Glorious, the All-Highest.

Regarding healing:

Thy name is my healing, O my God, and remembrance of Thee is my remedy. Nearness to Thee is my hope, and love for Thee is my companion. Thy mercy to me is my healing and my succour in both this world and the world to come. Thou, verily, art the All-Bountiful, the All-Knowing, the All-Wise. PB:87

For the establishment of unity:

O my God! O my God! Unite the hearts of Thy servants and reveal to them Thy great purpose. May they follow Thy commandments and abide in Thy law. Help them, O God, in their endeavour, and grant them strength to serve Thee. O God! Leave them not to themselves, but guide their steps by the light of Thy knowledge, and cheer their hearts by Thy love. Verily, Thou art their Helper and their Lord. PB:204

In praise and gratitude of God:

All praise, O my God, be to Thee Who art the Source of all glory and majesty, of greatness and honour, of sovereignty and dominion, of loftiness and grace, of awe and power. Whomsoever Thou willest Thou causest to draw nigh unto the Most Great Ocean, and on whomsoever Thou desirest Thou conferrest the honour of recognizing Thy Most Ancient Name. Of all who are in heaven and on earth, none can withstand the operation of Thy sovereign Will. From all eternity Thou didst rule the entire creation, and Thou wilt continue for evermore to exercise Thy dominion over all created things. There is none other God but Thee, the Almighty, the Most Exalted, the All-powerful, the All-Wise.

Illumine, O Lord, the faces of Thy servants, that they may behold Thee; and cleanse their hearts that they may turn unto the court of Thy heavenly favours, and recognize Him Who is the Manifestation of Thy Self and the Dayspring of Thine Essence. Verily, Thou art the Lord of all worlds. There is no God but thee, the Unconstrained, the All-Subduing. BP:120

As can be perceived from the content of the above selection from the writings of Bahá'u'lláh, prayer is about the acquisition of spiritual qualities and attuning our wants with what God desires for us. Prayer should not merely be a wish-list of things like a child's letter to Santa Claus:

The true worshipper, while praying, should endeavour not so much to ask God to fulfil his wishes and desires, but rather to adjust these and make them conform to the Divine Will. Only through such an attitude can one derive that feeling of inner peace and contentment which the power of prayer alone can confer. CIB:26/10/38

These prayers impart a mental attitude which is conducive to spiritual growth, but like everything else in the Bahá'í way of life, moderation is important if the individual is going to get anything out of the experience:

Should a person recite but a single verse from the Holy Writings in a spirit of joy and radiance, this would be

89

better for him than reciting wearily all the Scriptures of God . . .

Prayer is part of the practical process of spiritual guidance which extends beyond worship. It is a process which assists decision-making, and helps in the selection of appropriate actions. Although there are no dogmas or precise formulas within the Bahá'í Faith, there are at least five practical stages in the process of prayer and meditation:

1. Prayer
2. Meditation
3. Inspiration
4. Volition and Faith
5. Action

The process always begins with prayer. The individual who seeks enlightenment will use prayer as a means of turning his or her heart towards God as the Source of all knowledge. As Bahá'u'lláh has written:

> Intone, O My servant, the verses of God that have been received by thee, as intoned by them who have drawn nigh unto Him, that the sweetness of thy melody may kindle thine own soul, and attract the hearts of all men. Whoso reciteth, in the privacy of his own chamber, the verses revealed by God, the scattering angels of the Almighty shall scatter abroad the fragrance of the words uttered by his mouth, and shall cause the heart of every righteous man to throb. Though he may, at first, remain unaware of its effect, yet the virtue of the grace vouchsafed unto him must needs sooner or later exercise its influence upon his soul. Thus have the mysteries of the Revelation of God been decreed by virtue of the Will of Him Who is the Source of power and wisdom.

Prayer is then followed by meditation. Meditation is not the emptying the mind of all thought. It is the focusing of the mind on to a subject without external distractions. It is an art

Bahá'í House of Worship, Panama City, Panama

which takes practice to perfect. The more people use meditation, the more they discover its power to restore a sense of tranquillity and purpose. It is during this meditative period that people wait for the inspiration which will come.

Inspiration comes both from within and without. As many artists have tried to describe, inspiration is received rather than found. In one place in the Bahá'í writings, inspiration is explained as follows:

> This faculty brings forth from the invisible plane the science and arts. Through the meditative faculty inventions are made possible, colossal undertakings are carried out; through it governments can run smoothly. Through this faculty man enters into the very Kingdom of God ... Through the faculty of meditation man attains to eternal life; through it he receives the breath of the Holy Spirit ... Meditation is the key for opening the doors of mysteries. In that state man abstracts himself; in that state man withdraws himself from all outside objects; in that subjective mood he is immersed in the ocean of spiritual life and can unfold the secrets of things-in-themselves ... It is an axiomatic fact that while you meditate you are speaking with your own spirit. In that state of mind you put certain questions to your spirit and the spirit answers; the light breaks forth and the reality is revealed ... The meditative faculty is akin to the mirror: if you put it before earthly objects it will reflect them. Therefore, if the spirit of man is contemplating earthly objects he will be informed of these. But if you turn the mirror of your spirits heavenwards, the heavenly constellations and the Sun of Reality will be reflected in your hearts, and the virtues of the Kingdom will be obtained ... May we indeed become mirrors reflecting the heavenly realities, and may we become so pure as to reflect the stars of heaven. PT:174

Volition is essential to the next stage. Volition is the willpower to put into action the ideas and inspiration which have been received. Personal volition is vital if the individual is to be successful. Faith is also required. The individual must acquire an attitude of mind which believes that the inspiration is possible. Faith here is akin to visualization. The individual should be able to see the idea implemented and behave as if it has already been achieved.

Finally, action. The purpose and product of the prayer and meditative process is the practical application of the inspiration the individual has received. This process is a problem-solving mechanism for the individual, and the source and avenue of inspiration to the artist and scientist, the writer and professional person:

> Prayer and meditation are very important in deepening the spiritual life of the individual, but with them must go also action and example, as these are the tangible results of the former. Both are essential. CIB:15/06/44

> It is not sufficient to pray diligently for guidance, but this prayer must be followed by meditation as to the best methods of action and then action itself.

17·CONSULTATION AND UNIVERSAL PARTICIPATION

Consultation and universal participation are fundamental and distinctive aspects of the Bahá'í way of life. They are the means of collective problem-solving and decision-making within the Bahá'í community. Consultation and universal participation are seen to be as inseparable as bricks and mortar, and together they support the edifice of the Bahá'í administrative institutions. Consultation and universal participation are part of the practical philosophy of the religion, and the union of these two concepts allows the Bahá'í Faith to progress and develop. Philosophically, they supersede the need for any form of clergy.

> Take ye counsel together in all matters, inasmuch as consultation is the lamp of guidance which leadeth the way, and is the bestower of understanding.

Bahá'í consultation is more than a religious council or conference called to consider a particular matter. It is an integral part of the formal and informal decision-making process among all Bahá'ís. It is defined by the full and frank participation of the entire community in which every individual has the right and responsibility to have and offer his or her opinion. Bahá'í consultation is democratic in nature. I know that democracy means different things to different people, but the process of consultation and the expectation of universal participation within the Bahá'í Faith allows people openly to discuss matters of common concern and ultimately to reach decisions by voting as individuals for ideas. Bahá'ís vote on the merit of the idea and not the personality of the one who proposes it. In this sense, Bahá'í consultation employs a very unpolitical form of democracy. The process tends to unite the participants rather than divide them, and in so doing Bahá'í consultation offers a real alternative to traditional political thinking. It replaces the mentality which sees as appropriate such devices as bilateral debate, personality attacks, flattery, manipulation, coercion, collusion, the exchange of political assistance, lobbying, or the development of special-interest groups, parties, or factions. In the Bahá'í Faith, these are seen as elements of an old world order, and ethically bankrupt.

There is no specific step-by-step guide to the process of Bahá'í consultation, but the following sequence will give the reader a fairly clear picture of the process:

1. Spiritual and emotional preparation;
2. Establishment of mutual trust;
3. Frank and non-aggressive participation;
4. Collective consideration of ideas;
5. Non-personalization of ideas;
6. Problem definition;
7. Gathering possible solutions;
8. Refinement of solution;
9. The process of reaching a consensus;
10. Humble submission to the will of the majority;
11. Collective and affirmative action.

The process of Bahá'í consultation requires both spiritual and emotional preparation. Before the community meets the individuals pray and meditate as described above to prepare themselves spiritually for consultation. This assures that they are spiritually and emotionally refreshed, and prepared to contribute to the decision-making process. This preparation is important:

> True consultation is spiritual conference in the attitude and atmosphere of love.

The process is dependent upon the establishment of a mutual trust based upon courtesy, respect and the good behaviour of the participants. This is important because if consultation is to be beneficial, participation must be universal; mutual trust assures universal participation. This is true whether there are two or twenty people involved. Mutual trust is essential because this kind of participation does not mean merely waiting for an opportunity to speak. When one person speaks, all the rest carefully attend, sincerely trying to understand the point of view of the speaker. During the consultative process, listening constitutes about ninety per cent of one's participation. Once the participants have experienced this process several times with the same people, a profound mutual trust and respect develop. This trust empowers people to solve the kind of problems which require co-operation.

The Bahá'í consultative process is one of truth-seeking, not opinion-forcing. Everyone's opinion is regarded as equally valid, and as truth is relative to the sum total of collective understanding, the only way to discover what action would be appropriate is to have the frank participation of everyone involved. Each participant offers his or her opinion as an approximation and not an absolute, with the humble understanding that the total result will be greater than the sum of the individual contributions. Bahá'í consultation is both frank and loving; it is held in a non-aggressive atmosphere in which all the participants tacitly acknowledge from the outset the willingness to change their mind if a better idea emerges. In this way, opinions will clash but not individuals:

> The shining spark of truth cometh only after the clash of differing opinions.

The ideas which do emerge are considered collectively on their own merit and do not reflect on the personalities of the participants. The egos of the individuals are eclipsed by the ideas themselves. With this in mind, participants will know that the ideas they propose will be heard and considered fairly without having to be repeated or insisted upon:

> They must in every matter search out the truth and not insist upon their own opinion, for stubbornness and persistence in one's views will lead ultimately to discord and wrangling and the truth will remain hidden.

For this to be achieved, the participants must adopt a new philosophical attitude which allows for the non-personalization of ideas. This means simply that during the consultative process, their individual ideas are not their personal property. When a participant gives his or her opinion or proposes a solution, it is offered to the entire group. Once it is said, it is no longer the individual's point of view, but rather one of the ideas which has emerged from the consultation. In a sense, all ideas belong to the entire group. There is great benefit in adopting this attitude. If the idea is adopted, modified, amended or rejected then the individual who suggested it feels no personal triumph or defeat. This helps to remove the possibility of politics within the Bahá'í consultative process – without egos, politics dies from neglect.

Defining the problem is crucial to finding a solution, and only by listening to the perceptions of others can a collective problem be described and assessed. People see the world differently and there is great value in having access to a different perspective. Bahá'í consultation provides that access. If people are unaccustomed or unable to listen with empathy to the insights of others, then they are doomed to living in a world where their social perspective is exclusively personal. The habit of personalizing everything is a seriously incapacitating form of social blindness. Bahá'ís try to get away from the habit of relating to any problem with the words 'What about me?' Collective insight is the key to solving collective problems.

The great advantage of this type of consultation is that it allows people to consider several possible solutions to a particular problem. It is only when several plausible ideas are laid side by side and compared, not for their absolute rightness or wrongness but for their relative appropriateness, that there emerges a spectrum of possible solutions.

There is a propensity in Western civilization to think in terms of monocausalism and monosolutionalism. Many people tend to think along the lines of THE problem and THE solution. (I concede that this is a sweeping generalization, and that there are many other groups which do not think along these lines, but the propensity is still there among a considerable portion of the population.) Bahá'í consultation overcomes this monocausal and monosolutional mentality. And by attaching the word *Bahá'í* to this type of consultation, I am not implying that Bahá'ís hold some kind of philosophical patent or copyright on the concepts they employ. Ideas are born, but they then belong to all of mankind. The adjective *Bahá'í* is descriptive, not possessive.

Once all the participants have offered their ideas, and a selection of possible solutions has emerged from the consultation, the process of refinement begins. Many of the suggestions will be similar and their good points can be amalgamated. Eventually by weighing the merits of each possible solution, the most appropriate ones will be voted upon by the group.

Voting is the process by which the group reaches a consensus. Each participant has an equal vote, and either endorses or rejects the proposed solution. Within the Bahá'í consultative process there are no abstentions – universal participation is required at all stages of the process. Certainly, selecting a solution by unanimous consensus would be ideal, but if this is not possible, then the majority will decide whether the proposal should be adopted or not.

Next comes what is probably the most important part of the process. All the individual participants must lend their unstinting and earnest support to the decision of the majority. This kind of humble and sincere submission to the will of consensus is often the hardest thing to learn within the Bahá'í consultative process. The concept of proponents and opponents is so deeply ingrained in the mentality of modern-day social rôle-models like governmental and corporate organizations, that people initially doubt there is any other way. It seems natural for people to withdraw their support and wait on the sidelines for their chance to say 'I told you so', if their idea has not been accepted, and when failure comes, to feel vindicated.

This is a very destructive attitude. The act of withholding support by a minority never allows people to realize the full potential of a good idea, or the true worthlessness of a bad one. This underlying opposition and lack of unity very often leads to the desolation of the entire group. There is, however, great wisdom in wholeheartedly supporting the decision of the majority. Not only can any hidden potential be readily seen, but it is also the quickest way of determining whether the solution the group has chosen is correct or not.

Submission to the will of the majority is part of the mutual trust which develops within Bahá'í consultation. Participants soon understand that not all decisions are correct, even the ones reached by unanimous consensus. If something is going to go wrong, universal participation will very quickly reveal it. A great deal of time is saved which would otherwise be wasted trying to do something halfheartedly. Once they have tried this type of consultation, those who initially doubted that a concept such as submission to the will of the majority could be beneficial to the assessment of collective decision-making, soon become its greatest champions and find it hard to believe that others have not yet discovered its worth. It truly empowers people to achieve success:

No power can exist except through unity. No welfare and no well-being can be attained except through consultation.

We now come to the final stage — the goal of the Bahá'í consultative process. While most people have at some time found themselves in a meeting which seemed to exist for the sole purpose of planning other meetings, the process of Bahá'í consultation avoids this altogether. The discussion and decision-making process must be followed by collective and affirmative *action*. The solutions must be implemented, as I have stated, with the support of all the participants. This is the reason why consultation exists — words must become actions.

Bahá'í House of Worship, New Delhi, India

18·SERVICE TO HUMANITY

The brief span of time we have here on earth is our most precious possession. Life is a wondrous time of discovery, progress and fulfilment. Life, however, is not just a personal experience; it is shared with the rest of humanity. Our time here is not merely an individualistic preparation for the next stage in our personal spiritual development, but a priceless opportunity to assist in the social development of the planet. It is our personal and collective responsibility to leave this planet in a better condition than that in which we found it.

There are so many problems to solve in the world today – poverty, disease, ignorance, hatred and oppression – that it requires the concerted effort of everyone to overcome them and replace them with abundance, health, education, love and unity. Bahá'ís work to achieve these goals. Both of the distinctive aspects of the Bahá'í way of life described above reflect this: as individuals, Bahá'ís pray and meditate on how best to serve mankind; and collectively they consult together towards this same end.

> Blessed and happy is he that ariseth to promote the best interests of the peoples and kindreds of the earth. TB:167

Service to mankind is an integral part of being a Bahá'í. It is reflected in the Bahá'í attitude towards concepts such as work, motives, and achievement: work done in the spirit of service is a form of worship; the purity of one's motives is more important than the result of one's actions; and in achievements, the process is just as important as the product. It is a philosophy of deeds which replaces the anarchic belief that the ends justify the means. In the Bahá'í Faith, the means *are* the ends.

Fundamental to the concept of service is the belief that personal morality and ethical social behaviour are of great benefit to the progress of mankind. No one is power-less to effect beneficial change. Each person should see themselves as a significant component of the world; we should never feel helpless or insignificant. Everyone has the ability to help the world on many different levels. We can be productive individuals, responsible consumers, loving husbands and wives, exemplary parents, honourable sons and daughters, considerate neighbours, and good citizens, all at the same time. Basically, we all have the responsibility to be environmentally friendly to the spiritual, social, emotional and physical well-being of the planet. All these elements of service help the condition of the world immensely.

Beyond one's personal morality and ethical social behaviour, everyone is endowed with skills and talents which are useful to mankind on a professional level. Personal capacity is often dependent upon health and opportunity, but fulfilling one's capacity is everyone's duty. The person who has employed all of his few talents to the betterment of the planet is of greater value to mankind than the person who has a multiplicity of talents but selfishly uses them solely for his own benefit:

O son of man! If thine eyes be turned towards mercy, forsake the things that profit thee and cleave unto that which will profit mankind. And if thine eyes be turned towards justice, choose thou for thy neighbour that which thou choosest for thyself. Humility exalteth man to the heaven of glory and power, whilst pride

103

abaseth him to the depths of wretchedness and deg-
radation. TB:64

The concept of service extends beyond the Bahá'ís themselves.
The Bahá'í Faith as a religion supports the non-governmental
activities of the United Nations and the European Community
in their efforts to overcome the political differences which
divide us, and organizations like the Worldwide Fund for
Nature which work toward understanding the planet's ecology
and improving the environment. Bahá'u'lláh exhorted His
followers to serve mankind in whatever way they could:

Address yourselves to the promotion of the well-being
and tranquillity of the children of men. Bend your
minds and wills to the education of the peoples and
kindreds of the earth, that haply the dissensions that
divide it may, through the power of the Most Great
Name, be blotted out from its face, and all mankind
become the upholders of one Order, and the inhabitants
of one City. GWB:CLVI

Ultimately, everyone who becomes a Bahá'í brings his or her
talents and experience to the religion, and contributes to the
range of services the Bahá'í Faith can offer the world.

19·THE BAHÁ'Í EXPERIENCE

Being a Bahá'í and part of the community is a very distinctive way of life. In addition to its basic teachings, the Bahá'í Faith also has its own Festivals, Holy Days and calendar. The Bahá'í year begins on 21st March, with the celebration of Naw-Rúz, the Bahá'í New Year. This is the first day of spring, the equinox.

There are nineteen months in the Bahá'í calendar, and each month contains nineteen days. This gives a total of 361 days. There are four additional intercalary days, or days between the months, during normal years and five during leap years, to complete the requisite number of annual days.

Each Bahá'í month is named in Arabic after an attribute of God. Either numbers or names denote the day of the month. If the name is used then the names of the days of the month follow the same sequence as the names of the months. For example, in the Bahá'í calendar the 4th of July 1963, the date I became a Bahá'í, is:

11 Rahmat 121 BE, or the day of Mashíyyat of the month Rahmat in the 121st year of the Bahá'í Era

The Bahá'í Era began with the Declaration of the Báb on the 23rd of May 1844 and will end at some future date with the appearance of the next Messenger of God. Bahá'u'lláh promised that the Bahá'í Era would last not less than a thousand years.

At the beginning of every Bahá'í month, the Bahá'ís gather and celebrate the Nineteen Day Feast. The following is a list of the first day of each Bahá'í month:

21 March	Bahá	Splendour
9 April	Jalál	Glory
28 April	Jamál	Beauty
17 May	'Azamat	Grandeur
5 June	Núr	Light
24 June	Rahmat	Mercy
13 July	Kalimát	Words
1 August	Kamál	Perfection
20 August	Asmá'	Names
8 September	'Izzat	Might
27 September	Mashíyyat	Will
16 October	'Ilm	Knowledge
4 November	Qudrat	Power
23 November	Qawl	Speech
12 December	Masá'il	Questions
31 December	Sharaf	Honour
19 January	Sultán	Sovereignty
7 February	Mulk	Dominion
2 March	'Alá'	Loftiness

The Nineteen Day Feast brings together members of the Bahá'í community for worship, consultation and fellowship. It is an occasion of hospitality and unity. The programme for each Nineteen Day Feast is divided into three parts to correspond to these purposes. The devotional portion consists of reading primarily from the writings of Bahá'u'lláh, the Báb and 'Abdu'l-Bahá, and occasionally from the sacred scriptures of other religions; the purpose of the consultative portion is to enable individual Bahá'ís to offer suggestions to the Local Spiritual Assembly of the town or city; and the social portion consists of serving refreshments and offering fellowship.

There is no set service. Whoever has offered to host the

Nineteen Day Feast is free to select which writings are read, and sometimes there may be music or singing, depending on the musical talents of the Bahá'ís in the community. The refreshments are either supplied by the host or contributed by the Bahá'ís who attend. The form the Nineteen Day Feast takes is not as important as the spirit it generates. As Bahá'u'lláh has written:

> It hath been enjoined upon you once a month to offer hospitality, even should ye serve no more than water; for God hath willed to bind your hearts together, though it be through heavenly and earthly means combined. NDF:1

During the year there are certain Bahá'í Holy Days on which work is suspended:

21 March	Naw-Rúz, the Bahá'í New Year
21 April	The First Day of Ridván
29 April	The Ninth Day of Ridván
2 May	The Twelfth Day of Ridván
23 May	The Declaration of the Báb
29 May	The Ascension of Bahá'u'lláh
9 July	The Martyrdom of the Báb
20 October	The Birth of the Báb
12 November	The Birth of Bahá'u'lláh

Two further days associated with the life of 'Abdu'l-Bahá, the son of Bahá'u'lláh, are also commemorated but on these days work is not prohibited:

26 November	The Day of the Covenant
28 November	The Ascension of 'Abdu'l-Bahá

The Intercalary Days, or Ayyám-i-Há, occur between the 26th of February and the 1st of March inclusive. These are set aside as days of preparation for the Fast – days of hospitality, charity and the giving of gifts. Bahá'u'lláh has given us the following prayer for these days:

My God, my Fire and my Light! The days which Thou hast named Ayyám-i-Há in Thy Book have begun, O Thou Who art the King of names, and the fast which Thy most exalted Pen hath enjoined unto all who are in the kingdom of Thy creation to observe is approaching. I entreat Thee, O my Lord, by these days and by all such as have during that period clung to the cord of Thy commandments, and laid hold on the handle of Thy precepts, to grant that unto every soul may be assigned a place within the precincts of Thy court, and a seat at the revelation of the splendours of the light of Thy countenance. PMB:49

The fasting period within the Bahá'í Faith lasts nineteen days, one Bahá'í month. The month of 'Alá' (Loftiness) is the last month of the Bahá'í year. It is a period of abstinence from food and drink, from sunrise to sunset. For those Bahá'ís who smoke, the Fast also applies to smoking during the same daylight hours. Bahá'u'lláh has granted exemption for those younger than fifteen and older than seventy, and for those who are ill or travelling. Exemption is further granted to women who are pregnant, breast-feeding or menstruating. The purpose of the Fast is renewal:

It is essentially a period of meditation and prayer, of spiritual recuperation, during which the believer must strive to make the necessary readjustments in his inner life, and to refresh and reinvigorate the spiritual forces latent in his soul. Its significance and purpose are, therefore, fundamentally spiritual in character. Fasting is symbolic, and a reminder of abstinence from selfish and carnal desires. LG:487

The fasting ends with Naw-Rúz Festival, the Bahá'í New Year. This is a joyous time in which the Bahá'í community gathers and celebrates not only the end of the Fast but the beginning of a new year. 'Abdu'l-Bahá, the son of Bahá'u'lláh, described Naw-Rúz in the following words:

This sacred day, when the sun illumines equally the whole earth, is called the equinox, and the equinox is the symbol of the Manifestation of God. The Sun of Truth rises on the horizon of Divine Mercy and sends forth its rays. This day is consecrated to commemorate it. It is the beginning of Spring. When the sun appears at the equinox, it causes a movement in all living things. The mineral world is set in motion, plants begin to shoot, the desert is changed into a prairie, trees bud and every living thing responds, including the bodies of animal and men.

The rising of the sun at the equinox is the symbol of life, and likewise it is the symbol of the Divine Manifestation of God, for the rising of the Sun of Truth in the heaven of Divine Bounty established the signal of life for the world. The human reality begins to live, our thoughts are transformed and our intelligence is quickened. The Sun of Truth bestows Eternal Life, just as the solar sun is the cause of terrestrial life. SWV5N1:4

In addition to these Nineteen Day Feasts and Holy Day observances, Bahá'ís organize other meetings throughout the year to which they invite friends who are interested in knowing more about Bahá'u'lláh and His teachings. These meetings – sometimes called 'Firesides' – are very informal and are held either in the homes of individual Bahá'ís or at a Bahá'í Centre. Personally, I do not know the origin of the expression Fireside, but it dates back at least to the beginning of this century. At a Fireside, people are free to ask any questions they wish about the Bahá'í Faith, and during the course of an evening, the conversation usually ranges far and wide. Discussions will often centre around a particular theme such as unity, women's rights, the environment, world peace, the rainforests, or life after death.

Being a Bahá'í is about belonging to an international community of people from diverse racial, cultural and religious heritages who are working together to bring about world peace.

Wherever people reside there is usually a well-established Bahá'í community nearby. Becoming a Bahá'í is a personal decision and experience. There are no initiation ceremonies in the Bahá'í Faith – in fact there are no ceremonies at all. Quite simply, the Bahá'ís are the people who recognize Bahá'u'lláh as the Messenger of God for this age. People will know from reading the writings of Bahá'u'lláh whether they are Bahá'ís. Informing the National Bahá'í Centre of their decision puts new Bahá'ís in contact with other Bahá'ís.

If you feel you would like to register as a Bahá'í or obtain more information on the Bahá'í Faith, look in the telephone book for the Bahá'í Community nearest you or write to one of the addresses at the back of this book. I have included only a few of the hundreds of addresses possible. If you live outside these countries, any of the Bahá'í Centres listed can put you into contact with Bahá'ís in your own country.

I do not know of any appropriate way to end a book about the Bahá'í Faith. There is a lifetime of wonder and inspiration to be derived from the Bahá'í writings, and it is my whole-hearted hope that you will take the time to investigate more fully the teachings of Bahá'u'lláh and decide for yourself whether the Bahá'í Faith is for you. Perhaps it is befitting to leave you with Bahá'u'lláh's own words:

> Strive, O people, that your eyes may be directed towards the mercy of God, that your hearts may be attuned to His wondrous remembrance, that your souls may rest confidently upon His grace and bounty, that your feet may tread the path of His good-pleasure. GWB:296

BIBLIOGRAPHY

Abdu'l-Bahá, *The Promulgation of Universal Peace: Talks Delivered by 'Abdu'l-Bahá during His Visit to the United States and Canada in 1912*, comp. H MacNutt, 2nd ed. (Wilmette, Il: Bahá'í Publishing Trust, 1982).

Abdu'l-Bahá, *Paris Talks: Addresses Given by 'Abdu'l-Bahá in Paris in 1911–1912*, 11th ed. (London: Bahá'í Publishing Trust, 1971).

Bahá'u'lláh, *Tablets of Bahá'u'lláh Revealed after the Kitáb-i-Aqdas*, comp. Research Department of the Universal House of Justice, trans. Habib Taherzadeh and others, rev. ed. (Haifa: Bahá'í World Centre, 1982).

Bahá'u'lláh, *Gleanings of the Writings of Bahá'u'lláh*, comp. and trans. Shoghi Effendi, 2nd rev. ed. (Wilmette, Il: Bahá'í Publishing Trust, 1976).

Bahá'u'lláh *Selections from the Writings of Bahá'u'lláh*, (Wilmette, Il: Bahá'í Publishing Committee, 1943).

Bahá'u'lláh, *Proclamation of Bahá'u'lláh to the Kings and Leaders of the World*, (Haifa: Bahá'í World Centre, 1978).

Bahá'u'lláh, *Prayers and Meditations of Bahá'u'lláh*, comp. and trans. Shoghi Effendi, rev. ed. (London: Bahá'í Publishing Trust, 1978).

Bahá'u'lláh, *The Hidden Words*, trans. Shoghi Effendi, 'with the assistance of some English friends' (London: Nightingale Books, 1992).

Bahá'u'lláh, *Epistle to the Son of the Wolf*, trans. Shoghi Effendi (Wilmette, Il: Bahá'í Publishing Trust, 1969).

Bahá'u'lláh, Báb, 'Abdu'l-Bahá, *Bahá'í Prayers* (Wilmette, Il: Bahá'í Publishing Trust, 1985).

Shoghi Effendi, *Principles of Bahá'í Administration*, 4th ed. (London: Bahá'í Publishing Trust, 1976).

Shoghi Effendi, *God Passes By*, (Wilmette, Il: Bahá'í Publishing Trust, 1970).

Star of the West, V. 1 no. 1 (Mar. 21, 1910) – V. 25 no. 12 (Mar. 1924) reprinted in eight bound volumes (Oxford: George Ronald, 1978).

Universal House of Justice, *Synopsis and codification of the Laws and Ordinances of the Kitab-í-Aqdas*, comp. Research Department of the Universal House of Justice, trans. Shoghi Effendi (Haifa: Bahá'í World Centre, 1973).

Universal House of Justice, *Lights of Guidance: A Bahá'í Reference File*, comp. Helen Hornby (New Delhi: Bahá'í Publishing Trust, 1983).

Universal House of Justice, *Nineteen Day Feast*, comp. Research Department of the Universal House of Justice (London: Bahá'í Publishing Trust, 1989).

Ann Vickers, *Prayer and Meditation*, (Southam: Spiritual Assembly of the Bahá'ís of Warwick, 1990).

ABBREVIATED TITLES USED FOR QUOTED MATERIAL

PHW: Persian Hidden Words
  AHW: Arabic Hidden Words
  BP: Bahá'í Prayers
  SWB: Selections from the Writings of Bahá'u'lláh
  CIB: Correspondence to an Individual Believer
  KA: Kitab-i-Aqdas
  PT: Paris Talks
  PMP: Prayer and Meditation pamphlet
  PBA: Principles of Bahá'í Administration
  PUP: The Promulgation of Universal Peace
  TB: Tablets of Bahá'u'lláh
  GWB: Gleanings of the Writings of Bahá'u'lláh
  NDF: Nineteen Day Feast
  PMB: Prayers and Meditations of Bahá'u'lláh

LG: Lights of Guidance
SW: Star of the West
PB: Proclamation of Bahá'u'lláh
GPB: God Passes By
ESW: Epistle to the Son of the Wolf

USEFUL ADDRESSES

National Bahá'í Centre
27 Rutland Gate
London SW7 1PD
United Kingdom

National Bahá'í Centre
536 Sheridan Road
Wilmette
Illinois 60091
United States of America

National Bahá'í Centre
7200 Leslie Street
Thornhill
Ontario L3T 6L8
Canada

National Bahá'í Centre
Post Box 19
New Delhi 110 001
India

National Bahá'í Centre
Post Office Box 21–551
Henderson
Auckland 8
New Zealand

National Bahá'í Centre
Post Office Box 285
Mona Vale
NSW 2103
Australia

INDEX